BRITISH LITERATURE LIFEPAC 2
THE SIXTEENTH CENTURY

CONTENTS

I. **THE RENAISSANCE AND REFORMATION** 1
   INTRODUCTION 1
   THE EARLY RENAISSANCE 11
   Sir Thomas More 11
   Roger Ascham 18
   John Foxe 23

II. **RENAISSANCE POETS** 41
   Sir Thomas Wyatt the Elder 41
   Sir Philip Sydney 43
   Edmund Spenser 51
   Mary (Sydney) Herbert, Countess of Pembroke ... 60

III. **RENAISSANCE PROSE AND DRAMA** 67
   Sir Walter Raleigh 67
   William Shakespeare 71
   The English Bible 110

Author: Krista L. White, B.S.
Editor: Alan Christopherson, M.S.
Graphic Design: Alpha Omega Graphics

804 N. 2nd Ave. E., Rock Rapids, IA 51246-1759
© MM by Alpha Omega Publications, Inc. All rights reserved.
LIFEPAC is a registered trademark of Alpha Omega Publications, Inc.

All trademarks and/or service marks referenced in this material are the property of their respective owners. Alpha Omega Publications, Inc. makes no claim of ownership to any trademarks and/or service marks other than their own and their affiliates', and makes no claim of affiliation to any companies whose trademarks may be listed in this material, other than their own.

BRITISH LITERATURE LIFEPAC 2
THE SIXTEENTH CENTURY

OBJECTIVES:

When you have completed this LIFEPAC®, you should be able to:
1. Recognize the Bible's central importance to the English Reformation.
2. Understand the important role of Renaissance scholarship in the Reformation.
3. Discern the differences between the ideals of the Renaissance and those of the Reformation.
4. Understand the relationship between the ideals of the Reformation and those of Elizabethan culture.
5. Appreciate the wisdom and eloquence of the authors of each period.

VOCABULARY:

comedy - a play that is primarily humorous.
conceit - an elaborate comparison used in poetry.
couplet - two consecutive rhyming lines of poetic verse.
evangelical - a person who believes in the doctrine of justification by faith alone.
heresy - any belief that is in opposition to the standard system of doctrine.
humanism - the study of the literature, history, and art of ancient Greece and Rome.
octave - an eight-line stanza.*
pastoral - a poem exalting the rural life of shepherds.
quatrain - a four-line stanza.
recant - formally to withdraw a belief.
secular - unconcerned with things spiritual or religious.
sestet - a six-line stanza.
sonnet - a poem that usually contains fourteen lines, that follow a definite rhyme scheme.
stanza - a grouping of verse lines based on the poem's rhyme scheme.
tragedy - a play that dramatizes the flawed nature of man.

I. THE RENAISSANCE AND REFORMATION
INTRODUCTION

The Tudors and the Reformation 1485–1603. At the close of the Middle Ages, Henry VII ruled England. The Tudor reign lasted for three generations, ending with the death of Queen Elizabeth I in 1603. It was a time of momentous change. The Renaissance and the Reformation ended the Dark Ages and ushered in the light of ancient, timeless truths. Flowing from the fountain of God's Word, the Reformation in England effected changes in not only religion but also government, science, economics, society, art, and literature. England was reborn.

The Renaissance. The reign of Henry VII inaugurated a line of strong monarchs. After the early death of Henry's first son, Arthur, the crown passed to his younger son, Henry. Henry is known to posterity as a lusty, witty man with a will strong enough to overturn the power of kingdoms and nations. Some scholars credit him with the Reformation of the church in England. But, "To say that Henry VIII was the father of the Reformation is to betray history," says historian J. H. Merle d'Aubigné. "God was the Father of the Reformation in England." The rebirth of religion, society, and politics neither began nor ended during Henry VIII's reign. God in His providence worked through two means to bring about the Reformation: the revival of learning and the resurrection of the Word of God.

The revival of learning came through the Renaissance, the "rebirth" of culture. Beginning in 1300 with a renewed interest in classical literature and art, the Renaissance emphasized human reason and the value and dignity of the individual.

Truth was studied for its own sake rather than for its relevance to Christianity; it was a man-centered rather than a God-centered movement. Scholars of the Renaissance were known as humanists.

The center of the Renaissance was Italy. Scholars and government officials from around Europe traveled to this fount of knowledge. Among the English scholars who traveled to Italy were John Colet, William Grocyn, and Thomas Linacre. These men were part of a group known as the Oxford Reformers, so called because they brought the ideals of the Renaissance back to Oxford, England. John Colet was greatly interested in the writings of Plato. His lectures on the epistles of Paul were original and attracted the attention of many world-renowned scholars. Colet stressed the proper interpretation of Scripture, which later inspired Desiderius Erasmus (c. 1466–1536) to study more closely the biblical text in its original languages. William Grocyn further encouraged the study of Greek among English scholars by lecturing in that language—the first scholar to do so. Thomas Linacre, of no small reputation and influence, was a professor of medicine and Greek at the University of Oxford.

Erasmus

Among those who were influenced by the Oxford Reformers were Sir Thomas More and Erasmus. During the reign of Henry VIII, these two men became the leading humanists in England. Erasmus was a Dutch scholar who had spent many years in England, both learning and teaching the ideals of the Renaissance. From 1509–14, he taught Greek at Cambridge and consequently developed a keen interest in the Scriptures. At first, he favored the Reformation of the Catholic Church. Correcting the Latin Vulgate—the official Roman Catholic version of the Bible—Erasmus published an edited version of the New Testament in Greek and good Latin. He hoped that a fuller understanding of the Word of God would correct some of the corruption plaguing the church. However, Erasmus was not willing to challenge the power of the papacy. He wished only to reform the church from within. Erasmus later returned to the Continent to become its leading humanist.

Sir Thomas More, for a time a close friend of Henry VIII, eventually rose to the position of Lord Chancellor. His masterpiece, *Utopia*, published in 1516 (the same year in which Erasmus' Greek New Testament was published), resounded the ideals of the Renaissance. More wrote in Latin, the language of the educated. He was a lawyer and a politician who wished to see England correct its political, social and religious corruption. His answer, though, was not founded solely upon Scripture but upon reason. Like many other Renaissance scholars, More believed that the intellect was not fallen. Human reason alone, he thought, could lead us to the truth. *Utopia* is a critique of European society written, as one critic observed, "from the vantage point of an imaginary society based on reason."

Like many other humanists, More emphasized the powers of human reason because he was concerned with the education of Christian gentlemen. From its introduction into England, **humanism*** was a tool to develop ideal rulers. Princes, and courtiers were taught the wisdom of the Greeks and the Romans so that they might demonstrate superior ability in matters of statecraft. The educational method that the humanists used borrowed from the medieval model. It consisted of two parts: the trivium and the quadrivium. The trivium, according to medieval standards, consisted of the study of grammar, logic, and rhetoric. The quadrivium included the study of arithmetic, geometry, astronomy, and music. Studies were done in Latin with special emphasis on the works of Virgil, Cicero, and Horace.

Later, as the Reformation swept across England, the focus on the cultivation of Christian gentlemen took on a more significant meaning. The Scriptures became the primary focus of education. Human reason was not the ultimate authority. Nevertheless, the classic Greek and Roman texts remained an integral part of the education process. This new breed of English humanist believed that all truth was God's truth.

Chief among the Protestant humanists was Roger Ascham (1515–1568). Ascham, tutor to Princess Elizabeth and lecturer at the University of Cambridge, stridently opposed the **secular*** version of humanism that came out of Italy. Ascham and many others like him saw the intellect as fallen; Therefore, reason alone could not reveal the ultimate answers to life. Scripture was needed as the only trustworthy rule for life and faith. This division between the Catholic and the Protestant understandings of the intellect was no small matter.

The Reformation. When Martin Luther posted his Ninety-five Theses on the church door in Wittenburg, Germany, he was not intending to start a religious revolution. He simply wished to discuss academically the church's practice of indulgences. (Indulgences were allegedly a means to forgiveness that usually came by paying a fee to Rome). As a doctor of theology, Luther had studied the Scriptures, but he could not find in them the justification for the use of indulgences. Forgiveness was not for sale. He wanted the ecclesiastical abuse to stop and the church to be purified.

Luther first began to question the doctrines of the church while preparing for a lecture on "the righteousness of God." Seeking some aid in the matter, Luther turned to Romans 1: 17 and read, "For therein is the righteousness of God, revealed from faith to faith; as it is written, The just shall live by faith." As a Catholic monk, Luther had always understood "the righteousness of God" to mean that goodness which one obtains by the keeping of the sacraments. The Romans passage contradicted everything he had known. A man was made righteous by his faith in Christ, not by his moral worth. Forgiveness was free. Luther described his reaction to this revelation thus:

"When I had realized this I felt myself absolutely born again. The gates of paradise had been flung open and I had entered. There and then the whole of scripture took on another look to me..."

Luther's new view of Scripture was soon shared by many other people across Europe. In Germany, France, and England, Scripture became the fountain of reform. The leaders of the Reformation developed the slogan *Sola Scriptura*— "Scripture alone." The Protestant Reformers in England held firmly to this view. Scripture, not the pope or a king, was the sole guide to faith and life. Consequently, this passion for the authority of the Scriptures created a movement in opposition to the authority of the church. Protestants were so called because they protested the church's doctrines and practices. They wanted to reform the church by bringing it back to a correct understanding of the gospel—sinners are saved by grace alone through faith alone in the work of Christ alone. The Reformation was, in essence, a God-centered movement based on the knowledge of Scripture.

In England, however, a love for the Scriptures had sprung up long before Luther penned his Ninety-five Theses. Beginning with the Lollard movement during Chaucer's time, people of little education had come to believe the gospel as it was preached to them from the Bible. John Wycliffe and other learned men sought to raise the Scriptures in importance within the church, but their efforts were largely suppressed by the church. Not until the publication of Erasmus's New Testament in Greek did the learned class in England begin to examine Scripture afresh.

William Tyndale was one of the scholars who at first regarded the New Testament in Greek as only a "work of learning, or at most as a manual of piety, whose beauties were calculated to excite religious feelings." But it was not long before God changed his heart and he cried out, "I have found it!" The Master for whom his heart had longed had lovingly revealed Himself in the Words of Scripture. Desirous that all of his countrymen should have the Scriptures to read in their own language, Tyndale set out to accomplish that task. He carried with him both Erasmus's New Testament in his sack and the support of many merchants in his pockets. Fraught with many trials, Tyndale nevertheless completed the work in 1526; two editions of Tyndale's English Bible were published that year in Germany. But by that time, Henry VIII had already been convinced that the English translation was the source of all heresies. Henry called for the destruction of Tyndale and his Bibles. To get the Bibles to the English people, merchants smuggled them in sacks of flour and dispersed them through secret booksellers. Thousands of copies were sold, ironically enough, to pauper, priest, and aristocrat alike.

Allegory of Good Government-1339

Along with the translations of Tyndale, the works of Martin Luther also had to be sold underground. Henry hated Luther's objections to the Catholic faith. He even wrote a tract against Lutheranism for which the pope bestowed upon him the title "Defender of the Faith." But not even the mighty Henry VIII could control the hearts of his people. That power was left to God alone. Lutheranism, with its emphasis on the authority of Scripture, spread rapidly across England. Neither pope nor priest nor king could put out its flame. More joined Henry in the attempt to fend off the ensuing wave of Protestantism by writing scathing tracts against Tyndale and Luther. But these works did nothing to dampen the belief of the elect. As time marched on, the interest of the people in the New Testament only increased among both the upper and the lower classes.

The growing interest in the Scriptures providentially coincided with King Henry's desperate need for an heir. Henry, desirous for a wife who could bare him a son, revived a controversy over the legitimacy of his union to Catherine of Aragon. Catherine had been married to Henry's older brother Arthur. But after Arthur's death, Catherine was betrothed to Henry in an attempt to maintain good relations with Spain. Despite some initial questions over the marriage, the pope gave his approval, and the two were married. Catherine's years of barrenness, however caused Henry to doubt the validity of the marriage. He wondered if God was cursing him for taking the wife of his brother, a practice that Scripture condemned.

Henry's doubt was further encouraged when the beautiful Anne Boleyn, one of Catherine's ladies of the court, enraptured him with her charm. Taking advantage of the king's questionable desires, Cardinal Wolsey sought to avenge himself on Catherine's kinsman, Charles V of Spain, and suggested an answer to both problems: annulment by the pope. Liking Wolsey's advice, the king immediately set up a commission to build evidence for the divorce. In the end, it was to the authority of Scripture that Henry appealed for his annulment from Catherine. It is not lawful for a man to marry his brother's wife, Henry's cardinal protested to the pope, for he shall be left childless. But the pope would not grant an annulment. His alliance with Spain was too important to the survival of the papacy. Besides, overturning the blessing of an earlier pope on the basis of Scripture would give credence to the Protestant cause and call into question the authority of the church.

Henry would not be refused. He called Parliament into session and began his separation with Rome. From 1529–1536, the so-called Reformation Parliament implemented changes that slowly removed the pope's control over affairs of the English church and state. In 1531, Henry put Catherine away, continuing proceedings among his own university men and clergy to procure an annulment. In January 1533, Henry married Anne

Boleyn and made her his queen. A daughter, Elizabeth, was born to them in September of that same year. To secure his authority in such religious matters, Parliament passed the Act of Supremacy in 1534, recognizing Henry as head of the Church of England.

Henry's church, though severed from Rome, was not **evangelical**.* It did not fully adopt the ideals of the Reformation; Scripture was not subject to individual interpretation. Henry was still a Catholic at heart. The Ten Articles of Faith adopted in 1536 demonstrated his lasting hostility toward Protestantism. The Articles recognized the Bible but also regarded the need for penance and the receiving of Holy Communion at the Mass as "necessary to our salvation." Many Protestants met their death under his reign, but so did Romanists who would not yield to him as the "pope" of England. Sir Thomas More, at once a trusted advisor and friend to Henry, was executed for his refusal to recognize the king as head of the Church.

Determined to rid his country of the pope's control, Henry ordered that all of the monasteries in England be dissolved. Their wealth and land were put into the hands of his supporters. Thomas Cromwell is the man most associated with this work. The aftereffects were both good and bad. The nuns and monks who were accused of gross immoral behavior were exposed and forced to change. But those of the poorer classes who looked to the monasteries for support were left empty-handed. Some of those who lived and farmed on monastic lands were forced from their homes. Suddenly, the state was responsible for the relief of the poor, which was not always possible. The Pilgrimage of Grace in Lincolnshire, involving thirty thousand peasants, was a result of lack of relief caused by the dissolution of the monasteries.

Madonna of the Meadow-1505

To further his reforms and encourage confidence in his decision to break with Rome, Henry authorized the sale of Matthew's Bible in English in 1537. The free circulation of Matthew's Bible was the answer to Tyndale's dying prayer, "O Lord, open the king's eyes!" Although he was not thoroughly reformed in his own understanding of the Scriptures, Henry nevertheless acknowledged that the only way to weed papal authority from the hearts of his people was to give them free access to the Bible. One historian noted that "at one and the same time he published and imposed all over his realm the doctrines of [Catholicism], and circulated without obstacle the Divine Word that overthrew them!" Within three years, another edition based on the work of Tyndale and Miles Coverdale was also authorized. It was called the Great Bible. Its required placement in the cathedral churches throughout England in 1540 effected changes in worship and doctrine that were manifested most clearly in the reign of Edward VI, Henry's son.

As the first and only son of Henry VIII, Edward VI ascended the throne of England in 1547. His mother had been Henry's third wife. Soon after the birth of Elizabeth, Anne Boleyn was executed for treason. The last three of the king's six wives bore him no heirs. Edward and his half-sisters, Mary and Elizabeth, were the last of the Tudor dynasty.

Unlike Mary and Elizabeth, Edward never actually ruled. As a nine-year-old king, Edward's uncle, the Duke of Somerset, became regent, heading a council of sixteen to govern until Edward was of age. The Duke of Somerset was Protestant and sought fervently to establish its doctrines in the Church of England. Early in Edward's reign, the Six Articles Act of 1539 was repealed. This action prohibited the burning of heretics and allowed the Reformation to take a greater hold in England. In 1549, Parliament passed the Act of Uniformity whereby all clergymen were to use *The Book of Common Prayer* as a guide for worship. Progressively Protestant, the prayer book, written by

Archbishop Cranmer, called for the reading of Scripture in English. A second prayer book was issued in 1552, reflecting the increased influence of Calvinists and Lutherans from the Continent. In 1553, Parliament adopted the Forty-Two Articles of the Faith. The document outlined the reformed beliefs of the Church of England. It rejected outright the Catholic doctrine of transubstantiation, seeing the bread and the wine in communion as only spiritual representations of Christ's body and blood. The Articles also removed the altar from the worship service, replacing it with the communion table. This action affirmed and signified the Protestant doctrine of justification by faith alone. A priest was not needed to mediate forgiveness. The only way to the Father was through the Son. All could come freely by faith in Jesus Christ.

Edward, a weak and sickly child, died when he was only fifteen. But before his death, Edward put into motion a plan that would place his Protestant cousin Lady Jane Grey on the throne. Lady Jane Grey reigned as queen for six days, until the rightful heir, Princess Mary, removed her. As the loyal daughter of Spaniard Catherine of Aragon, the new queen was a staunch Catholic. Mary quickly sought to repeal the religious laws enacted during Edward's reign, putting England back into the Catholic fold. Many traditionalists welcomed her counter reforms, but others—especially those who had benefited monetarily from the dissolution of the monasteries—resisted her. To further secure England's return to Catholicism, Mary arranged a marriage with Philip II of Spain. She, like her father, desperately wanted an heir. But the marriage was hated by much of England. The people did not want to be ruled by a foreign power. The possibility of having a Spanish king sparked several rebellions.

The greatest travesty of Mary's reign was her persecution of the Protestants, from whence she gets the name "Bloody Mary." During her short reign of five years, she and her advisors burned at the stake nearly three hundred Protestants. Among those who suffered for the faith were Hugh Latimer, Nicolas Ridley, and Thomas Cranmer. Many Protestants fled to the continent during this time. The Marian Exiles, as they are known, sought refuge in various centers of Protestantism. The scholars and theologians who gathered in Geneva produced the Geneva Bible, the first translation that included commentary notes. It was later to be used widely by the English, especially the Puritans. Other scholars, such as John Foxe, worked to produce an account of the persecution. His *Acts and Monuments*—popularly known as *Foxe's Book of Martyrs*—traced the history of Christian martyrdom from the early church to the reign of Mary. John Knox and others like him struggled to form some kind of ecclesiastical unity among the exiles. Upon his return to Scotland, Knox spread the doctrines of Calvinism and helped to foster the growth of the Presbyterian Church.

Mary died in 1558, allowing Elizabeth to ascend the throne peaceably. As a keen politician, she sought to establish some kind of religious settlement between Protestants and traditionalists. Her parliament passed the Act of Supremacy in 1559. It severed ties with the pope that her half-sister Mary had reestablished. The Act also required all church officials to take an oath of allegiance to Elizabeth as head of the Church of England. The Act of Uniformity followed, requiring that all worship services should be performed in accord with the Edward's Prayer Book. Some revisions had been made to the prayer book that allowed for a more ceremonial form of service, but the Protestant doctrines remained.

When the exiles returned to England, many of them objected to the changes. They accused Queen Elizabeth of being too traditional. Her reforms, they contended, were not thoroughly biblical. But Elizabeth's main concern was not the purity of the church; her concern was for the unity of her nation. The adoption of the Thirty-nine Articles of Faith in 1563 distinguished England as Anglican. It allowed for Lutherans and Catholics to live in harmony under one ruler who was both the head of state and the head of the church.

Elizabeth's religious dealings are only part and parcel of her shrewd politics and reliance on wise counselors. Her desire for unity fostered a fierce spirit of nationalism.

Attractive, intelligent, and headstrong, Elizabeth commanded the attention of much of Europe. As an unmarried queen, she used her foreign suitors to gain power and financial stability for her nation. She always insisted, though, that her spouse was England.

Much of the prosperity in England during Elizabeth's reign was due to the financial endeavors of the middle class, which was the life-blood of the mercantile system. The mercantile system valued gold and silver as the basis for independent wealth. It also encouraged a balance of trade between nations. Much of England's economic power rested on the wool trade. The middle class, as the controllers of the wool trade, enjoyed positions of financial and political power during Elizabeth's reign. The nobility, with its feudal basis of power, had been removed from its ruling position. The parish, rather than the manor house, was the center of control in a community. Men of common birth oversaw courts of law, regulated taxes, and attended the growing number of universities. The ideals of the Reformation dictated these changes. Rich or poor, priest or pauper, all individuals had equal worth in the sight of God. Consequently, all work was valuable. No division existed between secular and sacred. Elizabethan England was very unlike the England of the Middle Ages.

English Renaissance Literature. The literature that resulted during the reign of the Tudors and the Reformation era is nothing short of extraordinary. Many scholars have called it the brightest period of English literature. The flowering of English literature can be attributed to several factors, including the following: an increase in wealth and leisure time, the growth of educational institutions, the use of the printing press, and the perfection of the English language. All of these factors were rooted in the Reformation and the Renaissance that proceeded it.

Unlike the secular humanism that grew out of the Renaissance in Italy, the Reformation saw a unity between the particular and the universal. More simply put, the Reformers saw meaning in everyday life because everyday life was connected to a larger purpose—the span of redemptive history. God was not only sovereign over the "big" events in life, such as wars, but also in control of the growth of a blade of grass. Everything in the universe is ultimately under His direction and control. The belief in the sovereignty of God and man's sinfulness pervaded English culture, shaping the literature that flowed from it. The works of Edmund Spenser, Sir Philip Sidney, and William Shakespeare reflect the ideals of the Reformation.

Within this period we also see the stylistic influences of the Renaissance. The **sonnet*** is chief among the literary devices imported from Italy. Its conventions were originally established by Petrarch (1304–1374) but later modified by other French and English poets. Sir Thomas Wyatt was the writer who introduced the sonnet to England. In its Petrarchian, or Italian, form, the sonnet consists of fourteen lines that are divided into two sets: a set of eight lines, called an **octave**,* and a set of six lines, called a **sestet**.* The octave lines were rhymed *abba abba*. The sestet lines were rhymed *cdecde*. In 1557 Richard Tottel published an anthology of English sonnets written in the Petrarchian form. It was the "channel through which the main currents of European Renaissance poetry flowed into the British Isles." Included in Tottel's *Songs and Sonnets* were poems by Wyatt, the earl of Surrey, and Nicholas Grimald. Later, English writers changed the sonnet structure by incorporating three **quatrains*** and a **couplet**.* The lines rhymed *abab cdcd efef gg*. This form of the sonnet became known as the English, or Shakespearean, sonnet.

Another genre that enjoyed much popularity was the epic. Elizabethans considered it to be at the top of literary forms. Like the medieval forms of the epic, the Elizabethan examples carry assumptions that are distinct to their culture. For example, Spenser's *Faerie Queene* is often difficult for the modern reader to understand because the whole story rests on the assumption that the reader is familiar with both the intrigues of the Elizabethan court and figures from both biblical and classical literature.

On the lower end of the literary spectrum was the **pastoral**.* Pastorals drew images from the world of the shepherd, *pastor* being Latin for "shepherd." Pastoral songs and poetry represented the desire for the simple, idealized life. They were often written in the language of the court. The rural, rustic life was exalted over the life of the city. The pastoral influence was also known to cross over into drama.

The Development of Drama. Dramatic literature changed significantly from 1530–1580. Morality plays such as *Everyman*, though still performed late into the sixteenth century, quickly fell out of vogue. They became unpopular for many reasons. One reason was that the theological basis of the plays had been largely rejected. England was now Protestant; Roman Catholic doctrine would not be tolerated in the pulpit, let alone the stage. Another reason for the unpopularity of morality plays was an increased awareness of classical works.

During the Renaissance in England, students of the New Learning were introduced to the Roman dramatist, Seneca, who wrote in Latin during the time of Nero. He is known for his ten tragedies known as "closet" plays. A closet play is a drama that is not meant to be acted out but rather read or recited. Seneca borrowed much of his form from the Greeks. The origin of Greek drama was religious. The actors were priests who performed a play in honor of the god Dionysus. Seneca did not retain the religious basis of the Greeks but did employ their use of acts or episodes, the chorus, tragic events, and long moral discourses. One critic noted that Seneca was especially appealing to the Elizabethans because he combined classical form with moral value while delighting with horror.

The Elizabethan love for violence and horror on stage was rooted in scenes from their past. The reign of the Tudors had not been peaceful. From the aristocracy to the commoners, life was often tragic. Henry VIII had two of his wives beheaded. His daughter Mary was no less brutal. Known to posterity as "Bloody Mary," she had nearly three hundred Protestants burned at the stake. These types of executions were, in exception to royalty, public events that thousands of people attended. The thrill that this type of violence and horror provided was replicated to some extent in English Senecan tragedies, the first of which was performed before the queen at Whitehall in the 1560s.

Elizabeth's interest in drama was important and helped to foster public interest in the medium. After the publication of Seneca's plays in English, dramatists began to adapt his themes to English culture and society. By 1590, the Senecan tradition was evident in popular plays. A **tragedy*** could be distinguished by its plot structure. It begins with a disturbance in the status quo, then it moves to affliction and ends in destruction, which reestablishes order. Shakespeare imitated Senecan form in many of his plays, of which *Romeo and Juliet, Hamlet,* and *Macbeth* are some of his best known tragedies.

Shakespeare's *Macbeth* also represents another type of drama that was developed significantly during Elizabethan times—the English chronicle play. As a chronicle play, *Macbeth* deals with a period of English history. This link between the Senecan tradition of tragedy and the English chronicle play is important. It demonstrates the application of Senecan form to national themes. However, only scholars used strict Senecan form. Its structure was too academic for the common person. But Shakespeare, and others like him, took the Senecan form and adapted it to popular subjects. National history was a popular subject with the Elizabethans. They were proud of their country and wanted to know more about it. The popularity of English chronicle plays is similar to the popularity of chroniclers such as John Foxe and Ralph Holinshed. Holinshed's *Chronicles of England, Scotland, and Ireland* (1578) provided the historical basis for Shakespeare's *Henry IV* parts I and II and *Henry V*.

Comedy* was also a popular form of drama that experienced development during this period. It, too, was patterned after classical models. Plautus and Terence, both Latin authors, were influential in these changes. Like tragedy, comedy follows a distinct plot structure. It begins with a disturbance, which then progresses to affliction, and ends in restoration. Many of the popular comedies of the time involved the deception of a father by his daughter and her suitor. The first English comedy to be written in the classical form was Nicholas Udall's *Ralph Roister Doister* (1554). Examples of later Elizabethan comedies are Shakespeare's *The Taming of the Shrew* and Ben Jonson's *The Poetaster*.

As one writer has noted, before the establishment of professional public theatres in the late sixteenth century, actors were viewed as vagabonds. In order to avoid imprisonment, actors joined a company, or group of actors and playwrights. Companies were attached to a nobleman, which gave members the status of a noble servant while allowing them to devote their energies to the theater. For their attachment to James I, Shakespeare's company came to be known as the King's Men. Companies were also attached to churches. The Children of the Royal Chapel was one such company. These specifically religious companies usually consisted of boy actors and were successful enough to rival the professional adult companies. All actors were male. It was not socially acceptable for women to act. Boys, before their voices changed, played female roles.

Although noble and ecclesiastical patronage elevated the actor's status in society, financial success was not reached until the opening of public theaters. For fear of the plague and because of restrictions on Sabbath performances, city officials banned the building of public theaters within the city walls. Consequently, large theaters, such as the Globe, were erected in Southwark, a borough of ill repute. But despite their poor location, the theaters drew large crowds that consisted of all classes. Public theaters were oval with several tiers of seating. Wealthy spectators sat in the covered private boxes and galleries encircling the yard in front of the stage. Those that could afford only a penny for a performance stood in the unroofed yard and were known as "groundlings." More privileged spectators were allowed a seat on the stage. Performances were held in the afternoon and were often cancelled because of weather conditions and outbreaks of the plague.

Conclusion. The literature of the Tudor period was a combination of the ideals of the Renaissance and the Reformation. Authors sought to convey universal truths about mankind in an orderly manner. Individuals were valued for their ability to serve God and their country with honor and virtue. Certain pieces of Greek and Roman literature were taught because they proclaimed moral truth. Although they were not Christians, the pagan Greeks and Romans bore witness to the Law of God written in their hearts (Romans 2:14–15); they acknowledged, though imperfectly, moral right and wrong. They also acknowledged that man was inherently imperfect. Man was, as Aristotle said, susceptible to error because of a "certain fallibility." In contrast to the fatalistic thinking of the Greeks was the hopeful Elizabethan mind. Infused with the doctrines of the Reformation, Elizabethan culture and literature acknowledged the power of grace. One critic noted that its most gifted and popular writer, William Shakespeare, recreated in his works a world that was true to the biblical vision. He saw the world as plagued by sin yet a place where grace is active and the possibility of repentance and redemption is real.

 Underline the correct answer in each of the following statements.

1.1 The (Middle Ages, War, Reformation) in England effected changes in religion, government, science, economics, society, art, and literature.

1.2 God worked through the revival of learning and the resurrection of the (classics, Word of God, printing press) to bring about the Reformation in England.

1.3 The (Renaissance, Reformation, Middle Ages) studied truth for its own sake rather than for its relevance to Christianity.

1.4 The (Renaissance, Reformation, Middle Ages) was a man-centered movement.

1.5 The (Cambridge Dons, Oxford Reformers, Oxford Traditionalists) brought the ideals of the Renaissance to England.

1.6 Sir Thomas More and Erasmus were the leading (Protestants, Huguenots, Humanists) during Henry VIII's reign.

1.7 Many Renaissance scholars believed that (human reason, Scripture, the Roman Catholic Church) alone could lead us to the truth.

1.8 Protestant humanists believed that (Scripture, human reason, God) alone could not reveal to us the ultimate answers to life.

1.9 The Roman Catholic Church believes that the interpretation of Scripture must come under the authority of the (individual, church, priest).

1.10 The Protestant Reformers in England believed that (the church, Scripture, the king) alone was the guide to faith and life.

1.11 The (Renaissance, Reformation, Middle Ages) was, in essence, a God-centered movement based on the knowledge of Scripture.

1.12 Erasmus's publication of the New Testament in Greek caused the (poor, ignorant, learned) to examine Scripture afresh.

1.13 (Sir Thomas More, Roger Ascham, William Tyndale) used Erasmus's Greek New Testament to translate the Bible into English.

1.14 Henry VIII (approved, praised, condemned) the sale of Tyndale's English translation of the Bible.

1.15 Henry VIII appealed to the authority of (the church, the pope, Scripture) for his annulment from Catherine.

1.16 After the pope (agreed, refused) to grant an annulment, Henry had Parliament pass the Act of Supremacy, which recognized him as (Defender, Deacon, Head) of the Church of England.

1.17 Although he was severed from Rome, Henry VIII remained faithful to (Protestant, Lutheran, Catholic) doctrine.

1.18 Henry (established, dissolved, supported) the monasteries in England.

1.19 After breaking with Rome, Henry (authorized, condemned, banned) the sale of Matthew's Bible and The Great Bible.

1.20 In 1540, Henry decreed that a copy of (Matthew's, the Geneva, The Great) Bible be placed in every cathedral church throughout England.

1.21 During the reign of (Mary, Edward VI), the Reformation was allowed to take a greater hold in England.

1.22 *The Book of Common Prayer*, first published during Edward's reign, was progressively (Catholic, Protestant, Anglican).

1.23 Mary quickly sought to (reverse, advance, slow) Edward's Protestant reforms.

1.24 During the reign of Mary, nearly three hundred (Protestants, Catholics, Jews) were burned at the stake.

1.25 The Marian exiles fled to various Protestant communities in (Asia, Europe, America).

1.26 To settle religious disputes among her people, Queen Elizabeth distinguished the Church of England as (Anglican, Protestant, Catholic).

1.27 Many exiles believed that the Queen's reforms were not thoroughly (biblical, traditional, conservative).

1.28 The (upper, lower, middle) class was the life-blood of the mercantile system.

1.29 The mercantile system valued gold and silver as the basis for (national, independent, communal) wealth and encouraged the balance of trade between (manor houses, nations, kings).

1.30 The perfection of the English language and the use of the printing press contributed to the flowering of (English, Italian, French) literature.

1.31 The (pastoral, sonnet, short story) was the chief literary device imported from Italy.

1.32 The Petrarchian, or Italian, sonnet consists of (sixteen, fifteen, fourteen) lines that are divided into two sets: an octave and a sestet.

1.33 The (Polish, French, English), or Shakespearean, sonnet consisted of sixteen lines that were divided into three quatrains and a couplet.

1.34 Elizabethans considered the (epic, sonnet, pastoral) to be the top of literary forms.

1.35 The rural, rustic life is exalted in (cavalier, religious, pastoral) songs and poetry.

1.36 The closet plays of (Greece, Dionysus, Seneca) were especially appealing to the Elizabethans because they combined (medieval, classical, modern) form with moral value while delighting with (horror, technology, comedy).

1.37 An English chronicle play deals with (English history, French scandal, German intrigue).

1.38 A (tragedy, comedy) ends in destruction, which reestablishes order.

1.39 To avoid arrest, actors formed companies and attached themselves to a (parish, nobleman, theater).

1.40 Acting was performed only by (men and boys, women and girls, men and women).

1.41 (Public theaters, Private theaters, Private ballrooms) were banned in London for fear of the plague and because of restrictions on Sabbath performances.

1.42 Public theaters were (square, circular, oval) with several tiers of seating.

1.43 Elizabethan culture and literature acknowledged the power of (the church, grace, the will).

1.44 The ideals of the Renaissance and the Reformation shaped (Medieval, Modern, Elizabethan) literature.

THE EARLY RENAISSANCE

Sir Thomas More (1478–1535). "A Man for all Seasons," Thomas More was knighted by his king and canonized by his church. He was educated in the Greek and Latin classics and used his knowledge in the realm of politics, diplomacy, literature, and religion. More was executed by Henry VIII for his unwavering devotion to the Roman Catholic Church.

More, the son of a wealthy lawyer, was born in London and became a page in the household of Cardinal Morton. As a young man, he attended Oxford University, but before receiving his degree he left to study law at the Inns of Court. At this time, he was torn between a life of monastic devotion and one of public service. In 1499, More entered a Carthusian monastery. Eventually, More chose a law career over the priesthood, but he never fully forsook some of the extreme measures of religious devotion practiced by the Carthusian monks. He loved worldly entertainment, but he continued to practice forms of ascetic self-affliction. Beneath his courtly clothes, More wore a shirt made of boar's hair. The practice of wearing a hair shirt was common among Catholics who were attempting to rid themselves of earthly pleasures.

In 1504 More entered public service and became a Member of Parliament. After the death of King Henry VII, he was appointed undersheriff of London. Soon, More's witty and learned ways resulted in his becoming one of Henry VIII's most favored counselors. In 1517 he became a member of the King's Council. Six years later, he was appointed the Speaker of the House of Commons. And in 1529, he became Lord Chancellor, the highest office in England under the crown.

While serving Henry VIII, More became friends with Desiderius Erasmus, the Dutch humanist scholar. The two were members of the second generation of Renaissance humanists. Both of them worked to encourage the Renaissance in England. Erasmus taught at Oxford and at court, while More taught law and wrote works in Latin and English. Among More's first works was the translation of Lucian's Greek into Latin, which he completed with the help of Erasmus. Upon returning to Europe, Erasmus undertook the printing of many of More's Latin works, thus ensuring the spread of More's reputation as a Humanist scholar and statesman. Excepting Henry VIII and Cardinal Wolsey, More was the most famous Englishman of his time.

More wrote many religious and literary works, but his masterpiece is *Utopia*. Published in 1516, nine years after the explorations of Amerigo Vespucci and one year before the posting of Luther's Nine-Five Theses, *Utopia* is a fantastical vision of a New World free of societal ills. As a student of the Renaissance, More was heavily influenced by the philosophical writings of ancient Greece and Rome. Like Plato's *Republic*, *Utopia* offers the use of reason as a means to perfect the human condition. Oddly enough, More's utopian vision is not specifically Catholic, as was More himself. However, when reading More, a person must be aware that he is a witty and often ironic writer. One must look a little deeper to understand what he means. The title *Utopia* means "no place" in Greek. The two characters in whose dialogue the world of Utopia is described are Thomas More and Raphael Hythloday. The name More is close to the Greek word *moros*, which means "fool." Raphael Hythloday in the Greek can be interpreted "healing of God" and "babbler," or, in other words, "divine cure may be found in the words of a babbler." The use of such names hints at an ironic statement by More. He very well might be saying, "This happens nowhere."

From a biblical perspective, More's conclusion is not surprising. In a fallen world, a society without war, greed, and bigotry cannot be achieved solely on the basis of reason. Raphael Hythloday cannot offer us a real cure. Society is made up of individuals. Therefore, before society can be changed, individuals have to be changed. This is the point at which the principles of the Renaissance and the Reformation divide. Change is not bound up in the dispensing of reason or in more education but in the radical transformation of the heart. A utopian society can be effected only by the Spirit, not by pure reason.

Two years after More was appointed Lord Chancellor, he resigned, refusing to support either Henry's defiance of papal authority or his marriage to Anne Boleyn. As a devout Roman Catholic, More did not approve of the reform that was occurring in England. His hatred for the doctrines of the Reformation is well documented in his tracts and books against the works of Tyndale and Luther. More believed that the Catholic Church was the final authority; only the priesthood must interpret Scripture. Staid in his position behind the pope, More was charged with treason in 1534 for his refusal to support Henry VIII as the head of the Church of England. On July 6, 1535, More was beheaded as, he claimed, "the King's good servant, but God's first."

Fill in each of the following blanks with the correct answer.

1.45 Sir Thomas More studied _____ at the Inns of Court.

1.46 After leaving the Carthusian monastery, More continued to practice the extreme forms of ascetic _____ .

1.47   In 1529 More became _____ of England, the highest office in England under the crown.

1.48   With the help of Erasmus, More translated Lucian's Greek into _____.

1.49   More's masterpiece, _____, is a fantastical vision of a New World free of societal ills.

1.50   More's utopian vision offers _____ as a means to perfect the human condition.

1.51   The title *Utopia* means "_____" in Greek.

1.52   More's hatred for the Reformation caused him to write many tracts and books against the works of _____ and Luther.

1.53   More was charged with _____ and subsequently executed for his refusal to support _____ as the Head of the Church of England.

What to Look For:

The Renaissance was a movement that placed great value on the wisdom of the Greeks and Romans, who thought that human reason alone could lead one to truth. As a student of the Renaissance, Sir Thomas More recognized the man-centered ideals of the Renaissance, but he saw difficulty in putting those ideals into action.

Many scholars view *Utopia* as a work of satire. As you read, notice More's use of satire. Whom do you think More is mocking, the commonwealth in which he lives or the Utopian Republic? Do you think that Utopia seems like a very unrealistic world? Can human wisdom create a perfect world? What does the history of the Union of Soviet Socialist Republics tell us about the folly of human reason? (The U.S.S.R. was a communist country that aspired to establish a utopia based on the godless, man-centered teachings of Karl Marx.) In light of 1 Corinthians 2:6–15, upon *whose* wisdom will that perfect place called Heaven be established?

From: *Utopia*—Of the Economy

[THEIR GOLD AND SILVER]

For these reasons, therefore, they have accumulated a vast treasure, but they do not keep it like a treasure. I'm really quite ashamed to tell you how they do keep it, because you probably won't believe me. I would not have believed it myself if someone had just told me about it; but I was there, and saw it with my own eyes. As a general rule, the more different anything is from what people are used to, the harder it is to accept. But considering that all their other customs are so unlike ours, a sensible male will not be surprised that they treat gold and silver quite differently from the way we do. After all, they never do use money among themselves, but keep it only for a contingency that may or may not actually arise. So in the meanwhile they take care that no one shall overvalue gold and silver, of which money is made, beyond what the metals themselves deserve. Anyone can see, for example, that iron is far superior to either; men could not live without iron, by heaven, any more than without fire or water. But gold and silver have, by nature, no function with which we cannot easily dispense. Human folly has made them precious because they are rare. But in fact nature, like a most indulgent mother, has placed her best gifts out in the open, like air, water, and the earth itself; vain and unprofitable things she has hidden away in remote places.

If in Utopia gold and silver were kept locked up in some tower, foolish heads among the common people might concoct a story that the prince and senate six were out to cheat ordinary folk and get some advantage for themselves. Of course, the gold and silver might be put into beautiful plate-ware and such rich handiwork, but then in case of necessity the people would not want to give up such articles, on which they had begun to fix their hearts—only to melt there down for soldiers' pay. To avoid these problems they thought of a plan which conforms with their institutions as clearly as it contrasts with our own. Unless one has actually seen it working, their plan may seem incredible, because we prize gold so highly and are so careful about guarding it. With them it's just the other way. While they eat from earthenware dishes and drink from glass cups, finely made but inexpensive, their chamber pots and all their humblest vessels, for use in common halls and even in private homes, are made of gold and silver. The chains and heavy fetters of slaves are also made of these metals. Finally, criminals who are to bear the mark of some disgraceful act are forced to wear golden rings in their ears and on their fingers, golden chains around their necks, even gold crowns on their heads. Thus they hold up gold and silver to scorn in every conceivable way. As a result, if they had to part with their entire supply of these metals, which other people give up with as much agony as if they were being disemboweled, the Utopians feel it no more than the loss of a penny.

They pick up pearls by the seashore, diamonds and garnets in certain cliffs, but never go out of set purpose to look for them. If they happen to find some, they polish them and give them to the children, who feel proud and pleased with such gaudy decorations when they are small. But after, when they grow a bit older and notice that only babies like such toys, they lay them aside. The parents don't have to say anything, they simply put these trifles away out of a shamefaced sense that they're no longer suitable, just as our children, when they grow up, put away their marbles, rattles, and dolls.

Different customs, different feelings: I never saw the adage better illustrated than in the case of the Anemolian ambassadors, who came to Amaurot while I was there. Because they came to discuss important business, the senate had assembled ahead of time three citizens from each city. The ambassadors from nearby nations, who had visited Utopia before and knew the local customs, realized that fine clothing was not much respected in that land, silk was despised, and gold a badge of contempt; therefore they always came in the very plainest of their clothes. But the Anemolians, who lived farther off and had had fewer dealings with the Utopians, had heard only that they all dressed alike and very simply; so they took for granted that their hosts had nothing to wear that they didn't put on. Being themselves rather more proud than wise, they decided to dress as splendidly as the very gods, and dazzle the eyes of the poor Utopians with their gaudy garb.

Consequently the three ambassadors made a grand entry with a suite of a hundred attendants, all in clothing of many colors, and most in silk. Being noblemen at home, the ambassadors were arrayed in cloth of gold, with heavy gold chains round their necks, gold jewels at their ears and on their fingers, and sparkling strings of pearls and gems on their caps. In fact, they were decked out in all the articles which in Utopia are used to punish slaves, shame wrongdoers, or pacify infants. It was a sight to see how they strutted when they compared their finery with the dress of the Utopians who had poured out into the street to see them pass. But it was just as funny to see how wide they fell of the mark, and how far they were from getting the consideration they expected. Except for a very few Utopians who for some special reason had visited foreign countries, all the onlookers considered this splendid pomp a mark of disgrace. They therefore bowed to the humblest servants as lords, and took the ambassadors, because of their golden chains, to be slaves, passing them by without any reverence at all. You might have seen children, who had themselves thrown away their pearls and gems, nudge their mothers when they saw the ambassadors' jeweled caps, and say: "Look at that big lout, mother, who's still wearing pearls and jewels as if he were a little kid!" But the mother, in all seriousness, would answer, "Quiet, son, I think he is one of the ambassadors' fools."

Others found fault with the golden chains as useless because they were so flimsy any slave could break them, and so loose that he could easily shake them off and run away whenever he wanted.

But after the ambassadors had spent a couple of days among the Utopians, they learned of the immense amounts of gold which were as thoroughly despised there as they were prized at home. They saw too that more gold and silver went into making chains and fetters for a single runaway slave than into costuming all three of them. Somewhat crestfallen, then, they put away all the finery in which they had strutted so arrogantly; but they saw the wisdom of doing so after they had talked with the Utopians enough to learn their customs and opinions.

Answer *true* or *false* for each of the following statements.

1.54 _____ The Utopians treat gold and silver quite differently than we do.

1.55 _____ The Utopians use money for all sorts of transactions.

1.56 _____ The chamber pots and toilet bowls are made of gold and silver.

1.57 _____ Gold and silver is held in high regard and valued most greatly by the people.

1.58 _____ Because the ambassadors of Anemolia came decked out in gold jewels and pearls, the people of Utopia thought they were kings.

From: *Utopia*—The Conclusion

[CONCLUSION]

Now I have described to you as accurately as I could the structure of that commonwealth which I consider not only the best but indeed the only one that can rightfully claim that name. In other places men talk very liberally of the commonwealth, but what they mean is simply their own wealth; in Utopia, where there is no private business, every man zealously pursues the public business. And in both places men are right to act as they do. For elsewhere, even though the commonwealth may flourish, each man knows that unless he makes separate provision for himself, he may perfectly well die of hunger. Bitter necessity, then, forces men to look out for themselves rather than for the people, that is, for other people. But in Utopia, where everything belongs to everybody, no man need fear that, so long as the public warehouses are filled, he will ever lack for anything he needs. Distribution is not one of their problems; in Utopia no men are poor, no men are beggars, and though no man owns anything, everyone is rich.

For what can be greater riches than for a man to live joyfully and peacefully, free from all anxieties, and without worries about making a living? No man is bothered by his wife's querulous complaints about money, no man fears poverty for his son, or struggles to scrape up a dowry for his daughter. Each man can feel secure of his own livelihood and happiness, and of his whole family's as well: wife, sons, grandsons, great-grandsons, great-great-grandsons, and that whole long line of descendants that the gentry are so fond of contemplating. Indeed, even those who once worked but can no longer do so are cared for just as well as if they were still productive.

At this point, I'd like to see anyone venture to compare this justice of the Utopians with the so-called justice that prevails among other nations—among whom let me perish if I can discover the slightest scrap of justice or fairness. What kind of justice is it when a nobleman, a goldsmith, a moneylender, or someone else who makes his living by doing either nothing at all or something completely useless to the commonwealth, gets to live a life of luxury and grandeur, while in the meantime, a laborer, a carter, a carpenter, or a farmer works so hard and so constantly that even beasts of burden would scarcely endure it; and this work of theirs is so necessary that no commonwealth could survive for a year without it? Yet they earn so meager a living and lead such miserable lives that beasts would really seem to be better off. Beasts do not have to work every minute, and their food is not much worse; in fact they like it better, and besides, they do not have to worry about their future. But workingmen must not only sweat and suffer without present reward, but agonize over the prospect of a penniless old age. Their daily wage is inadequate even for present needs, so there is no possible chance of their saving for their declining years.

Now isn't this an unjust and ungrateful commonwealth? It lavishes rich rewards on so-called gentry, loan sharks, and the rest of that crew, who don't work at all or are mere parasites, purveyors of empty pleasures. And yet it makes no provision whatever for the welfare of farmers and colliers, laborers, carters, and carpenters, without whom the commonwealth would simply cease to exist. After society has taken the labor of their best years, when they are worn out by age, sickness, and utter destitution, then the thankless commonwealth, forgetting all their pains and services, throws them out to die a miserable death. What is worse, the rich constantly try to grind out of the poor part of their meager pittance, not only by private swindling but by public laws. It is basically unjust that people who deserve most from the commonwealth should receive least. But now they have distorted and debased the right even further by giving their extortion the form of law; and thus they have palmed injustice off as legal. When I run over in my mind the various commonwealths flourishing today, so help me God, I can see in them nothing but a conspiracy of the rich, who are fattening up their own interests under the name and title of the commonwealth. They invent ways and means to hang onto whatever they have acquired by sharp practice, and then they scheme to oppress the poor by buying up their toil and labor as cheaply as possible. These devices become law as soon as the rich, speaking through the commonwealth—which, of course, includes the poor as well—say they must be observed.

And yet when these insatiably greedy and evil men have divided among themselves goods which would have sufficed for the entire people, how far they remain from the happiness of the Utopian Republic, which has abolished not only money but with it greed! What a mass of trouble was cut away by that one step! What a thicket of crimes was uprooted! Everyone knows that if money were abolished, fraud, theft, robbery, quarrels, brawls, seditious, murders, treasons, poisonings, and a whole set of crimes which are avenged but not prevented by the hangman would at once die out. If money disappeared, so would fear, anxiety, worry, toil, and sleepless nights. Even poverty, which seems to need money more than anything else, would vanish if money were entirely done away with.

Consider if you will this example. Take a barren year of failed harvests, when many thousands of men have been carried off by hunger. If at the end of the famine the barns of the rich were searched, I dare say positively enough grain would be found in them to have kept all those who died of starvation and disease from even realizing that a shortage ever existed—if only it had been divided equally among them. So easily might men get the necessities of life if that cursed money, which is supposed to provide access to them, were not in fact the chief barrier to our getting what we need to live. Even the rich, I'm sure, understand this. They must know that it's better to have enough of what we really need than an abundance of superfluities, much better to escape from our many present troubles than to be burdened with great masses of wealth. And in fact I have no doubt that every man's perception of where his true interest lies, along with the authority of Christ our Savior (whose wisdom could not fail to recognize the best, and whose goodness would not fail to counsel it), would long ago have brought the whole world to adopt Utopian laws, were it not for one single monster, the prime plague and begetter of all others—I mean Pride.

Pride measures her advantages not by what she has but by what other people lack. Pride would not deign even to be made a goddess if there were no wretches for her to sneer at and domineer over. Her good fortune is dazzling only by contrast with the miseries of others, her riches are valuable only as they torruent and tantalize the poverty of others. Pride is a serpent from hell that twines itself around the hearts of men, acting like a suckfish to hold them back from choosing a better way of life.

Pride is too deeply fixed in human nature to be easily plucked out. So I am glad that the Utopians at least have been lucky enough to achieve this Republic which I wish all mankind would imitate. The institutions they have adopted have made their community most happy, and as far as anyone can tell, capable of lasting forever. Now that they have torn up the seeds of ambition and faction at home, along with most other vices, they are in no danger from internal strife, which alone has been the ruin of many other nations that seemed secure. As long as they preserve harmony at home, and keep their institutions healthy, the Utopians can never be overcome or even shaken by their envious neighbors, who have often attempted their ruin, but always in vain.

When Raphael had finished his story, I was left thinking that quite a few of the laws and customs he had described as existing among the Utopians were really absurd. These included their methods of waging war, their religious practices, as well as others of their customs; but my chief objection was to the basis of their whole system, that is, their communal living and their moneyless economy. This one thing alone takes away all the nobility, magnificence, splendor, and majesty which (in the popular view) are the true ornaments and glory of any commonwealth. But I saw Raphael was tired with talking, and I was not sure he could take contradiction in these matters, particularly when I recalled what he had said about certain counsellors who were afraid they might not appear knowing enough unless they found something to criticize in other men's ideas. So with praise for the Utopian way of life and his account of it, I took him by the hand and led him in to supper. But first I said that we would find some other time for thinking of these matters more deeply, and for talking them over in more detail. And I still hope such an opportunity will present itself some day.

Meantime, while I can hardly agree with everything he said (though he is a man of unquestionable learning and enormous experience of human affairs), yet I freely confess that in the Utopian commonwealth there are many features that in our own societies I would like rather than expect to see.

Answer *true* or *false* for each of the following statements.

1.59 _____ In Utopia, there is no private business; everyone purses the public business.

1.60 _____ There are no poor people in Utopia; all men are rich.

1.61 _____ As opposed to Utopia, the commonwealth cares for and rewards the farmers, laborers, and carpenters more than the gentry, bankers, and yellow-money dealers.

1.62 _____ According to the Utopian Republic, when money is abolished, greed, theft, quarrels, murders, treason, worry, fear, and poverty disappear.

1.63 _____ The Utopian Republic is plagued by pride.

1.64 _____ The healthy institutions of Utopia are the cause of its happiness and success.

1.65 _____ The moneyless economy and communal living of the Utopians seemed absurd to More.

1.66 _____ More agrees with everything that Raphael has to say about the Utopian Republic.

1.67 _____ More likes some features of the Utopian Republic, but he does not expect to see them occur in his own society.

> **Roger Ascham (1515–1568).** As a Christian teacher, Roger Ascham taught "God's holy Bible," Cicero, Plato, Aristotle, and the Greek orators Isocrates and Demosthenes. Ascham was a member of the second generation of English humanists who combined the ideals of the Renaissance and the Reformation. He believed that the study of certain Latin and Greek classics in subjection to the authority of Scripture was a means to "truth in religion, honesty of living, and right order in learning."
>
> Born in Yorkshire and educated at St. John's College, Cambridge, Ascham became a prominent Greek scholar. In 1545, he published *Toxophilus*, a book on archery, for which he received a pension from Henry VIII and was given the duty of Public Orator of the University in which he was to give speeches in Latin on special occasions. From 1548–49, he tutored Princess Elizabeth. During Edward VI's reign, Ascham was appointed secretary to Sir Richard Morison, ambassador to the Holy Roman Emperor Charles V. He resumed service to the crown under Elizabeth as a reader of Latin and Greek authors. At the news of his death in 1568, Queen Elizabeth replied, "I would rather have cast ten thousand pounds in the sea than parted from my Ascham."
>
> The reasons for Elizabeth's fondness can be found in his book *The Schoolmaster* (published posthumously in 1570). It is a conduct book for teachers and students. In it, Ascham sets himself apart as an innovator. He is the first person to speak against beating as a means to encourage learning. Instead, he stresses, as one critic has noted, the use of encouragement by focusing on the possible, even with students who have limited abilities. He wrote, "goodness of nature [is to] be joined to the wisdom of the teacher, in leading young wits into a right and plain way of learning" that "children, kept up in God's fear and governed by his grace, may most easily be brought well to serve God and their country, both by virtue and wisdom."
>
> Ascham's gentle love for truth and virtue led him to despise the secular teachings that were developed out of the Italian Renaissance. His concept of Italy as a bastion of immoral behavior later became a commonly held view among Englishmen. As a discerning teacher, Ascham discouraged the reading of immoral literature, whether it was ancient, medieval, or contemporary. He chose to teach certain classic authors because they reinforced biblical concepts of politics and the arts, as well as moral behavior.

Roger Ascham's signature, 1556

Fill in each of the following blanks with the correct answer.

1.68 Roger Ascham believed that the study of certain Latin and Greek classics in subjection to the authority of _____ was a means to "truth in religion, honesty of living, and right order in learning."

1.69 Ascham was a prominent _____ scholar at Cambridge University.

1.70 He was the _____ of Princess Elizabeth.

1.71 At his death, Queen _____ greatly mourned his death.

1.72 Ascham's book _____ is a conduct book for teachers and students.

1.73 Ascham was the first person to condemn _____ as a means to encourage learning.

1.74   Ascham stressed the use of _____ by focusing on the possible.

1.75   Because of the secular teachings that developed out of the Italian Renaissance, Ascham viewed Italy as a bastion of _____ behavior.

What to Look For:

Roger Ascham was a Christian teacher who combined the ideals of the Renaissance and the Reformation. As such, he believed that the study of certain Latin and Greek classics in subjection to the authority of Scripture was a means to "truth in religion, honesty of living, and right order in learning." As you read, notice Ascham's passion for truth and hatred for things immoral. Why do you think he objects to the reading of books that do not encourage virtuous behavior?

From: *The Schoolmaster*—The First Book for the Youth

[METHODS OF TEACHING LATIN]

There is a way, touched in the first book of Cicero, *De oratore,* which I, wisely brought into schools, truly taught, and constantly used, would not only take wholly away this butcherly fear in making of Latins but would also, with ease and pleasure and in short time, as I know by good experience, work a true choice and placing of words, a right ordering of sentences, an easy understanding of the tongue, a readiness to speak, a facility to write, a true judgment both of his own and other men's doings, what tongue soever he doth use.

The way is this. After the three concordances learned, as I touched before, let the master read unto him the epistles of Cicero gathered together and chosen out by Sturmius for the capacity of children.

First let him teach the child, cheerfully and plainly, the cause and matter of the letter; then, let him construe it into English so oft as the child may easily carry away the understanding of it; lastly, parse it over perfectly. This done thus, let the child, by and by, both construe and parse it over again so that it may appear that the child doubteth in nothing that his master taught him before. After this, the child must take a paper book and, sitting in some place where no man shall prompt him, by himself, let him translate into English his former lesson. Then, showing it to his master, let the master take from him his Latin book, arid, pausing an hour at the least, then let the child translate his own English into Latin again in another paper book. When the child bringeth it turned into Latin, the master must compare it with Tully's book and lay them both together, and where the child doth well, either in choosing or true placing of Tully's words, let the master praise him and say, "Here ye do well." For I assure you, there is no such whetstone to sharpen a good wit and encourage a will to learning as is praise.

But if the child miss, either in forgetting a word, or in changing a good with a worse, or misordering the sentence, I would not have the master either frown or chide with him, if the child have done his diligence and used no truantship therein. For I know by good experience that a child shall take more profit of two faults gently warned of than of four things rightly hit. For then the master shall have good occasion to say unto him:

> Child, Tully would have used such a word, not this; Tully would have placed this word here, not there; would have used this case, this number, this person, this degree, this gender; he would have used this mood, this tense, this simple rather than this compound; this adverb here, not there; he would have ended the sentence with this verb, not with that noun or participle, etc.

In these few lines I have wrapped up the most tedious part of grammar and also the ground of almost all the rules that are so busily taught by the master, and so hardly learned by the scholar, in all common schools, which after this sort, the master shall teach without all error, and the scholar shall learn without great pain, the master being led by so sure a guide, and the scholar being brought into so plain and easy a way. And therefore we do not contemn rules, but we gladly teach rules, and teach them more plainly, sensibly, and orderly than they be commonly taught in common schools. For when the master shall compare Tully's book with his scholar's translation, let the master at the first lead and teach his scholar to join the rules of his grammar book with the examples of his present lesson, until the scholar by himself be able to fetch out of his grammar every rule for every example, so as the grammar book be ever in the scholar's hand also used of him, as a dictionary, for every present use. This is a lively and perfect way of teaching of rules, where the common way, used in common schools, to read the grammar alone by itself, is tedious for the master, hard for the scholar, cold and uncomfortable to them both.

Let your scholar be never afraid to ask you any doubt, but use discreetly the best allurements ye can to encourage him to the same, lest his overmuch fearing of you drive him to seek some misorderly shift, as to seek to be helped by some other book, or to be prompted by some other scholar, and so go about to beguile you much and himself more.

Answer *true* or *false* for each of the following statements.

1.76 _____ Roger Ascham recommends the use of Cicero's *De oratore* to work "a readiness to speak" and "a facility to write" in any language.

1.77 _____ To learn Latin grammar, Ascham recommends that the child read the book over and over again.

1.78 _____ Punishment is the best thing to "sharpen a good wit" and "encourage a will to learning."

1.79 _____ Ascham recommends teaching the rules of grammar together with the lessons of translation.

1.80 _____ The teacher should treat the student in such a fearsome way that he is afraid to ask a question.

[*Lady Jane Grey*]

Therefore, to love or to hate, to like or contemn, to ply this way or that way to good or to bad, ye shall have as ye use a child in his youth.

And one example, whether love or fear doth work more in a child for virtue and learning, I will gladly report; which may be heard with some pleasure and followed with more profit. Before I went into Germany, I came to Broadgate in Leicestershire to take my leave of that noble Lady Jane Grey, to whom I was exceeding much beholding. Her parents, the duke and the duchess, with all the household, gentlemen and gentlewomen, were hunting in the park. I found her in her chamber reading Phaedon Platonis in Greek, and that with as much delight as some gentleman would read a merry tale in Boccaccio. After salutation and duty done, with some other talk, I asked her why she would lose such pastime in the park. Smiling she answered me, "Truly, all their sport in the park is but a shadow to that pleasure that I find in Plato. Alas, good folk, they never felt what true pleasure meant." "And how came you, madame," quoth I, "to this deep knowledge of pleasure, and what did chiefly allure you unto it, seeing not many women, but very few men, have attained thereunto?" "I will tell you," quoth she, "and tell you a truth which perchance ye will marvel at. One of the greatest benefits that ever God gave me is that he sent me so sharp and severe parents and so gentle a schoolmaster. For when I am in presence either of father or mother, whether I speak, keep silence, sit, stand, or go, eat, drink, be merry or sad, be sewing, playing, dancing, or doing anything else, I must do it, as it were, in such weight, measure, and number, even so perfectly as God made the world, or else I am so sharply taunted, so cruelly threatened yea, presently sometimes, with pinches, nips, and bobs, and other ways which I will not name for the honor I bear them, so without measure misordered, that I think myself in hell till time come that I must go to Master Aylmer, who teacheth me so gently, so pleasantly, with such fair allurements to learning, that I think all the time nothing whilst I am with him. And when I am called from him, I fall on weeping because whatsoever I do else but learning is full of grief, trouble, fear, and whole misliking unto me. And thus my book hath been so much my pleasure, and bringeth daily to me more pleasure and more, that in respect of it all other pleasures in very deed be but trifles and troubles unto me." I remember this talk gladly, both because it is so worthy of memory and because also it was the last talk that ever I had, and the last time that ever I saw, that noble and worthy lady.

Answer *true* or *false* for each of the following statements.

1.81 _____ Ascham gives Lady Jane Grey's example to prove that fear, more than love, encourages a child toward virtue and learning.

1.82 _____ Ascham found Lady Jane Grey in her room reading with much delight a book by Plato.

1.83 _____ Lady Jane Grey's parents punished her when she did not do something perfectly.

1.84 _____ Lady Jane Grey's teacher, Master Aylmer, taught her so gently and pleasantly that she found it difficult to leave him.

1.85 _____ Everything else but learning brought Lady Jane Grey much grief.

[THE ITALIANATE ENGLISHMAN]

But I am afraid that overmany of our travelers into Italy do not eschew the way to Circe's court but go and ride and run and fly thither; they make great haste to come to her; they make great suit to serve her; yea, I could point out some with my finger that never had gone out of England but only to serve Circe in Italy. Vanity and vice and any license to ill-living in England was counted stale and rude unto them. And so, being mules and horses before they went, returned very swine and asses home again; yet everywhere very foxes with subtle and busy heads and, where they may, very wolves with cruel malicious hearts. A marvelous monster which for filthiness of living, for dullness to learning himself, for wiliness in dealing with others, for malice in hurting without cause should carry at once in one body the belly of a swine, the head of an ass, the brain of a fox, the womb of a wolf. If you think we judge amiss and write too sore against you hear what the Italian saith of the Englishman, what the master reporteth of the scholar, who uttereth plainly what is taught by him and what is learned by you, saying, *Inglese italianato a un diavolo incarnato;* that is to say, "You remain men in shape and fashion but become devils in life and condition." This is not the opinion of one for some private spite but the judgment of all in a common proverb which riseth of that learning and those manners which you gather in Italy, a good schoolhouse of wholesome doctrine, and worthy masters of commendable scholars, where the master had rather defame himself for his teaching than not shame his scholar for his learning. A good nature of the master and fair conditions of the scholars. And now choose you, you Italian Englishmen, whether you will be angry with us for calling you monsters, or with the Italians for calling you devils, or else with your own selves, that take so much pains and go so far to make yourselves both. If some yet do not well understand what is an

Englishman Italianated, I will plainly tell him: he that by living and traveling in Italy bringeth home into England out of Italy the religion, the learning, the policy, the experience, the manners of Italy. That is to say, for religion, papistry or worse; for learning, less, commonly, than they carried out with them; for policy, a factious heart, a discoursing head, a mind to meddle in all men's matters; for experience, plenty of new mischiefs never known in England before; for manners, variety of vanities and change of filthy living.

These be the enchantments of Circe brought out of Italy to mar men's manners in England: much by example of ill life but more by precepts of fond books, of late translated out of Italian into English, sold in every shop in London, commended by honest titles the sooner to corrupt honest manners, dedicated overboldly to virtuous and honorable personages, the easier to beguile simple and innocent wits. It is pity that those which have authority and charge to allow and disallow books to be printed be no more circumspect herein than they are. Ten sermons at Paul's Cross' do not so much good for moving men to true doctrine as one of those books do harm with enticing men to ill-living. Yea, I say further, those books tend not so much to corrupt honest living as they do to subvert true religion. More papists be made by your merry books of Italy than by your earnest books of Louvain. And because our great physicians do wink at the matter and make no count of this score, I, though not admitted one of their fellowship, yet having been many years apprentice to God's true religion, and trust to continue a poor journeyman therein all the days of my life, for the duty I owe and love I bear both to true doctrine and honest living, though I have no authority to amend the sore myself, yet I will declare my good will to discover the sore to others.

St. Paul saith that sects and ill opinions be the works of the flesh and fruits of sins. This is spoken no more truly for the doctrine than sensibly for the reason. And why? For ill-doings breed ill-thinkings, and of corrupted manners spring perverted judgments. And how? There be in man two special things: man's will, man's mind. Where will inclineth to goodness the mind is bent to truth; where will is carried from goodness to vanity the mind is soon drawn from truth to false opinion. And so the readiest way to entangle the mind with false doctrine is first to entice the will to wanton living. Therefore, when the busy and open papists abroad could not by their contentious books turn men in England fast enough from truth and right judgment in doctrine, then the subtle and secret papists at home procured bawdy books to be translated out of the Italian tongue, whereby overmany young wills and wits, allured to wantonness, do now boldly contemn all severe books that sound to honesty and godliness. In our forefathers' tune, when papistry as a standing pool covered and overflowed all England, few books were read in our tongue, saving certain books of chivalry, as they said, for pastime and pleasure, which, as some say, were made in monasteries by idle monks or wanton canons; as one for example, *Le Morte d' Arthur,* the whole pleasure of which book standeth in two special points—in open manslaughter and bold bawdry; in which book those be counted the noblest knights that do kill most men without any quarrel and commit foulest adulteries by subtlest shifts: as Sir Lancelot with the wife of King Arthur his master, Sir Tristram with the wife of King Mark his uncle, Sir Lamorak with the wife of King Lot that was his own aunt. This is good stuff for wise men to laugh at or honest men to take pleasure at. Yet I know when God's Bible was banished, the court and *Le Morte d' Arthur* were received into the prince's chamber.

Answer *true* or *false* for each of the following statements.

1.86 _____ Ascham asserts that Englishmen who live and travel in Italy bring home with them its religion, its learning, its trickery, its experience, and its manners.

1.87 _____ The Italian manners that Englishmen bring back is, namely, "virtuous living."

1.88 _____ Ascham blames the sale of certain Italian books as the prime source of corrupt manners and religion in England.

1.89 _____ According to Ascham, where a man's will is inclined toward goodness then his mind is bent toward falsehood.

1.90 _____ The fastest way to entangle the mind with false doctrine is first to entice the will to immoral living.

1.91 _____ Ascham blames the spread of bawdy books and false religion on the papists.

1.92 _____ *Le Morte d' Arthur,* asserts Ascham, glorifies murder and adultery and should therefore not be read.

1.93 _____ Ascham proves his assertion on the corrupting power of bad books by saying that when the Bible was banned, the prince read *Le Morte d' Arthur*.

John Foxe (1517–1587). An erudite and energetic evangelical, John Foxe wrote *Acts and Monuments* as a historical testament to the fact that evangelicalism has been persecuted throughout the centuries because it embodies the true biblical faith. Educated at Oxford University from 1534–1543, Foxe came into contact with the New Learning. He read the Scriptures in Greek and became convinced that they must be the final authority in regard to faith and life. Impassioned by the doctrines of grace, he protested the Catholic beliefs and practices of his college, insisting upon change. Within a short time, Foxe was removed from his position as fellow of Magdalen College, Oxford. His Lutheran beliefs were at odds with the still very Catholic beliefs of the king. Foxe went on to serve as a tutor in the household of William Lucy, but later he moved to London. While in London, Foxe was providentially offered a tutoring job by the duchess of Richmond, a devout Protestant. Later, Foxe was hired by the duke of Norfolk to tutor his children. In both households, Foxe was allowed to exert an amazing amount of influence on some of England's future leaders.

Foxe, like many of his fellow Protestants, enjoyed much peace during Edward VI's reign. In 1550 he served as an assistant pastor in St. Paul's Cathedral under Bishop Nicholas Ridley. But all things changed when Mary succeeded her half-brother. Foxe, along with many other wealthy and learned Protestants fled to the continent. To stay in England would have meant certain death for one of such a prominent position. Foxe first took his family to the Netherlands but then later came to Strasbourg and settled for a time among a community of Marian exiles. While in Strasbourg, Foxe published a history of the persecutions suffered by the Lollards and the German Lutherans at the hands of the Roman Catholic Church. The book was the beginning of Foxe's massive account of Christian martyrdom over the centuries. As Foxe later came into contact with more and more exiles in Frankfort and Basel, he decided to add to his history of Christian martyrdom the "great persecution and horrible troubles" that were being inflicted upon the Protestants in England during Mary's reign. The result of this expansion amounted to his massive work *Acts and Monuments*.

Upon returning to England in 1559, Foxe gathered more reports of the persecution, adding to and correcting his Latin edition of *Acts and Monuments*. Hoping to destroy any further threat of Catholic persecution, Foxe published an English edition in 1563 so that everyone in England could learn about the great atrocities that had occurred.

Foxe spent the last twenty-five years of his life editing and expanding *Acts and Monuments*. The final version was published in 1587 and amounted to more than 6000 pages bound in several volumes containing four million words. Foxe called it the "crown of his career, the completion of his self-appointed task." So important was his work to the reconstructed Church of England that in 1571 a council of bishops decreed that a copy of *Acts and Monuments,* along with the Bishop's Bible, be placed in every cathedral church in England.

Fill in each of the following blanks with the correct answer.

1.94 While studying at _____ University, John Foxe read the Scriptures in _____ and became convinced that they were the _____ authority in regard to faith and life.

1.95 Foxe served as a _____ to many of England's leaders when they were children.

1.96 During _____ reign, Foxe served as an assistant pastor in St. Paul's Cathedral under Bishop Nicholas Ridley.

1.97 While in exile on the Continent, Foxe published a history of the _____ suffered by the Lollards and the German Lutherans at the hands of the _____ Church.

1.98 After hearing reports of the persecutions of the Protestants in _____, Foxe decided to expand his first history book of Christian martyrdom.

1.99 In 1563 an _____ edition of *Acts and Monuments* was published.

1.100 Foxe spent the last twenty-five years of his life editing and expanding _____.

1.101 The final version of *Acts and Monuments*, published in 1587, contained more than _____ pages.

1.102 In 1571 a council of bishops decreed that a copy of *Acts and Monuments* be placed in every cathedral _____ in England.

1.103 Foxe wrote *Acts and Monuments* as a _____ testament to the fact that _____ has been persecuted throughout the centuries because it embodies the true _____ faith.

What to Look For:

John Foxe wrote *Acts and Monuments* as a historical testament to the fact that evangelicalism has been persecuted throughout the centuries because it embodies the true biblical faith. As you read, notice *how* Foxe presents people who embrace the Protestant faith. How are they different from people who embrace the Catholic faith? How did they respond to persecution? In what ways does Foxe use their ability to persevere as a testimony to the truthfulness of the Protestant faith?

From: *FOXE'S BOOK OF MARTYRS*

Persecutions in England During the Reign of Queen Mary

The premature death of that celebrated young monarch, Edward VI, occasioned the most extraordinary and wonderful occurrences, which had ever existed from the times of our blessed Lord and Savior's incarnation in human shape. This melancholy event became speedily a subject of general regret. The succession to the British throne was soon made a matter of contention; and the scenes which ensued were a demonstration of the serious affliction in which the kingdom was involved. As his loss to the nation was more and more unfolded, the remembrance of his government was more and more the basis of grateful recollection. The very awful prospect, which was soon presented to the friends of Edward's administration, under the direction of his counselors and servants, was a contemplation which the reflecting mind was compelled to regard with most alarming apprehensions. The rapid approaches which were made towards a total reversion of the proceedings of the young king's reign, denoted the advances which were thereby represented to an entire resolution in the management of public affairs both in Church and state.

Alarmed for the condition in which the kingdom was likely to be involved by the king's death, an endeavor to prevent the consequences, which were but too plainly foreseen, was productive of the most serious and fatal effects. The king, in his long and lingering affliction, was induced to make a will, by which he bequeathed the English crown to Lady Jane, the daughter of the duke of Suffolk, who had been married to Lord Guilford, the son of the duke of Northumberland, and was the granddaughter of the second sister of King Henry, by Charles, duke of Suffolk. By this will, the succession of Mary and Elizabeth, his two sisters, was entirely superseded, from an apprehension of the returning system of popery; and the king's council, with the chief of the nobility, the lord-mayor of the city of London, and almost all the judges and the principal lawyers of the realm, subscribed their names to this regulation, as a sanction to the measure. Lord Chief Justice Hale, though a true Protestant and an upright judge, alone declined to unite his name in favor of the Lady Jane, because he had already signified his opinion that Mary was entitled to assume the reins of government. Others objected to Mary's being placed on the throne, on account of their fears that she might marry a foreigner, and thereby bring the crown into considerable danger. Her partiality to popery also left little doubt on the minds of any, that she would be induced to revive the dormant interests of the pope, and change the religion which had been used both in the days of her father, King Henry, and in those of her brother Edward: for in all his time she had manifested the greatest stubbornness and inflexibility of temper, as must be obvious from her letter to the lords of the council, whereby she put in her claim to the crown, on her brother's decease.

When this happened, the nobles, who had associated to prevent Mary's succession, and had been instrumental in promoting, and, perhaps, advising the measures of Edward, speedily proceeded to proclaim Lady Jane Gray, to be queen of England, in the city of London and various other populous cities of the realm. Though young, she possessed talents of a very superior nature, and her improvements under a most excellent tutor had given her many very great advantages.

Her reign was of only five days' continuance, for Mary, having succeeded by false promises in obtaining the crown, speedily commenced the execution of her avowed intention of extirpating and burning every Protestant. She was crowned at Westminster in the usual form, and her elevation was the signal for the commencement of the bloody persecution which followed.

Having obtained the sword of authority, she was not sparing in its exercise. The supporters of Lady Jane Gray were destined to feel its force. The duke of

Northumberland was the first who experienced her savage resentment. Within a month after his confinement in the Tower, he was condemned, and brought to the scaffold, to suffer as a traitor. From his varied crimes, resulting out of a sordid and inordinate ambition, he died unpitied and unlamented.

The changes, which followed with rapidity, unequivocally declared that the queen was disaffected to the present state of religion. Dr. Poynet was displaced to make room for Gardiner to be bishop of Winchester, to whom she also gave the important office of lord-chancellor. Dr. Ridley was dismissed from the see of London, and Bonner was introduced. J. Story was put out of the bishopric of Chichester, to admit Dr. Day. J. Hooper was sent prisoner to the Fleet, and Dr. Heath put into the Sea of Worcester. Miles Coverdale was also excluded from Exeter, and Dr. Vesie placed in that diocese. Dr. Tonstall was also promoted to the see of Durham. These things being marked and perceived, great heaviness and discomfort grew more and more to all good men's hearts; but to the wicked great rejoicing. They that could dissemble took no great care how the matter went; but such, whose consciences were joined with the truth, perceived already coals to be kindled, which after should be the destruction of many a true Christian.

The Words and Behavior of the Lady Jane upon the Scaffold

The next victim was the amiable Lady Jane Gray, who, by her acceptance of the crown at the earnest solicitations of her friends, incurred the implacable resentment of the bloody Mary. When she first mounted the scaffold, she spoke to the spectators in this manner: "Good people, I am come hither to die, and by a law I am condemned to the same. The fact against the queen's highness was unlawful, and the consenting thereunto by me: but, touching the procurement and desire thereof by me, or on my behalf, I do wash my hands thereof in innocency before God, and the face of you, good Christian people, this day:" and therewith she wrung her hands, wherein she had her book. Then said she, "I pray you all, good Christian people, to bear me witness, that I die a good Christian woman, and that I do look to be saved by no other mean, but only by the mercy of God in the blood of His only Son Jesus Christ: and I confess that when I did know the Word of God, I neglected the same, loved myself and the world, and therefore this plague and punishment is happily and worthily happened unto me for my sins; and yet I thank God, that of His goodness He hath thus given me a time and a respite to repent. And now, good people, while I am alive, I pray you assist me with your prayers." And then, kneeling down, she turned to Feckenham,* saying, "Shall I say this Psalm?" and he said, "Yea." Then she said the Psalm of *Miserere mei Deus,** in English, in a most devout manner throughout to the end; and then she stood up, and gave her maid, Mrs. Ellen, her gloves and handkerchief, and her book to Mr. Bruges; and then she untied her gown, and the executioner pressed upon her to help her off with it: but she, desiring him to let her alone, turned towards her two gentlewomen, who helped her off therewith, and also with her frowes, paaft, and neckerchief, giving to her a fair handkerchief to put about her eyes.

Then the executioner kneeled down, and asked her forgiveness, whom she forgave most willingly. Then he desired her to stand upon the straw, which doing, she saw the block. Then she said, "I pray you, despatch me quickly." Then she kneeled down, saying, "Will you take it off before I lay me down?" And the executioner said, "No, madam." Then she tied a handkerchief about her eyes, and feeling for the block, she said, "What shall I do?

by Paul Delaroche

Where is it? Where is it?" One of the standers-by guiding her therunto, she laid her head upon the block, and then stretched forth her body, and said, "Lord, into Thy hands I commend my spirit;" and so finished her life, in the year of our Lord 1554, the twelfth day of February, about the seventeenth year of her age.

Thus died Lady Jane; and on the same day Lord Guilford, her husband, one of the duke of Northumberland's sons, was likewise beheaded, two innocents in comparison with them that sat upon them. For they were both very young, and ignorantly accepted that which others had contrived, and by open proclamation consented to take from others, and give to them.

Touching the condemnation of this pious lady, it is to be noted that Judge Morgan, who gave sentence against her, soon after he had condemned her, fell mad, and in his raving cried out continually to have the Lady Jane taken away from him, and so he ended his life.

On the twenty-first day of the same month, Henry, duke of Suffolk, was beheaded on Tower-hill, the fourth day after his condemnation: about which time many gentlemen and yeomen were condemned, whereof some were executed at London, and some in the country. In the number of whom was Lord Thomas Gray, brother to the said duke, being apprehended not long after in North Wales, and executed for the same. Sir Nicholas Throgmorton, also, very narrowly escaped.

Feckenham - a Catholic priest who had tried to persuade Lady Jane Grey to **recant**.*
Psalm of *Miserere mei Deus* - Psalm 51, a psalm of repentance.

⇒ **Answer *true* or *false* for each of the following statements.**

1.104 _____ Edward VI bequeathed the crown of England to his cousin Lady Jane Grey so that his half-sister Mary would not be allowed to reinstate Roman Catholicism.

1.105 _____ Lady Jane Grey reigned for two years.

1.106 _____ Immediately after ascending the throne, Mary replaced Edward's bishops with her own.

1.107 _____ Upon the scaffold, Lady Jane Grey, a devout Protestant, claimed that she looked to be saved by no other means but by the mercy of God in the blood of Jesus Christ.

1.108 _____ Judge Morgan, who pronounced sentence upon Lady Jane Grey, soon after her death was promoted to Lord Chancellor of England.

Bishops Ridley and Latimer

These reverend prelates suffered October 17, 1555, at Oxford, on the same day that Wolsey and Pygot perished at Ely. Pillars of the church and accomplished ornaments of human nature, they were the admiration of the realm, amiably conspicuous in their lives, and glorious in their deaths.

Dr. Ridley was born in Northumberland, was first taught grammar at Newcastle and afterward removed to Cambridge, where his aptitude in education raised him gradually until he came to be the head of Pembroke College, where he received the title of Doctor of Divinity. Having returned from a trip to Paris, he was appointed chaplain by Henry VIII and bishop of Rochester, and was afterward translated to the see of London* in the time of Edward VI.

To his sermons the people resorted, swarming about him like bees, coveting the sweet flowers and wholesome juice of the fruitful doctrine, which he did not only preach but also showed the same by his life, as a glittering lanthorn to the eyes and senses of the blind, in such pure order that his very enemies could not reprove him in any one jot.

His tender treatment of Dr. Heath, who was a prisoner with him during one year, in Edward's reign, evidently proves that he had no Catholic cruelty in his disposition. In person, he was erect and well proportioned; in temper, forgiving; in self-mortification, severe. His first duty in the morning was private prayer: he remained in his study until ten o'clock and then attended the daily prayer used in his house. Dinner being done, he sat about an hour, conversing pleasantly or playing at chess. His study next engaged his attention, unless business or visits occurred; about five o'clock prayers followed; and after he would recreate himself at chess for about an hour, then retire to his study until eleven o'clock, and pray on his knees as in the morning. In brief, he was a pattern of godliness and virtue, and such he endeavored to make men wherever he came.

His attentive kindness was displayed particularly to old Mrs. Bonner, mother of Dr. Bonner, the cruel bishop of London. Dr. Ridley, when at his manor at Fulham, always invited her to his house, placed her at the head of his table, and treated her like his own mother; he did the same by Bonner's sister and other relatives; but when Dr. Ridley was under persecution, Bonner pursued a conduct diametrically opposite and would have sacrificed Dr. Ridley's sister and her husband, Mr. George Shipside, had not Providence delivered him by the means of Dr. Heath, bishop of Worcester.

Dr. Ridley was first in part converted by reading Bertram's book on the Sacrament and by his conferences with Archbishop Cranmer and Peter Martyr. When Edward VI was removed from the throne and the bloody Mary succeeded, Bishop Ridley was immediately marked as an object of slaughter. He was first sent to the Tower, and afterward, at Oxford, was consigned to the common prison of Bocardo, with Archbishop Cranmer and Mr. Latimer. Being separated from them, he was placed in the house of one Irish, where he remained until the day of his martyrdom, from 1554, until October 16, 1555.

It will easily be supposed that the conversations of these chiefs of the martyrs were elaborate, learned, and instructive. Such indeed they were, and equally beneficial to all of their spiritual comforts. Bishop Ridley's letters to various Christian brethren in bonds in all parts, and his disputations with the mitred enemies of Christ, alike proved the clearness of his head and the integrity of his heart. In a letter to Mr. Grindal (afterward archbishop of Canterbury), he mentions with affection those who had preceded him in dying for the faith and those who were expected to suffer; he regrets that popery is re-established in its full abomination, which he attributes to the wrath of God, made manifest in return for the lukewarmness of the clergy and the people in justly appreciating the blessed light of the Reformation.

This old practiced soldier of Christ, Master Hugh Latimer, was the son of one Hugh Latimer, of Thurkesson in the county of Leicester, a husbandman, of a good and wealthy estimation; where also he was born and brought up until he was four years of age, or thereabout: at which time his parents, having him as then left for their only son, with six daughters, seeing his ready, prompt, and sharp wit, purposed to train him up in erudition, and knowledge of good literature; wherein he so profited in his youth at the common schools of his own country, that at the age of fourteen years, he was sent to the University of Cambridge; where he entered into the study of the school divinity of that day, and was from principle a zealous observer of the Romish superstitions of the time. In his oration when he commenced the bachelor of divinity, he inveighed against the reformer Melancthon* and openly declaimed against good Mr. Stafford, divinity lecturer in Cambridge.

Mr. Thomas Bilney, moved by a brotherly pity toward Mr. Latimer, begged to wait upon him in his study and to explain to him the groundwork of his (Mr. Bilney's) faith. This blessed interview effected his conversion; the persecutor of Christ became his zealous advocate, and before Dr. Stafford died, he became reconciled to him. Once converted, he became eager for the conversion of others and commenced to be public preacher and private instructor in the university. His sermons were so pointed against the absurdity of praying in the Latin tongue, and withholding the oracles of salvation from the people who were to be saved by belief in them, that he drew upon himself the pulpit animadversions of several of the resident friars and heads of houses, whom he subsequently silenced by his severe criticisms and eloquent arguments. This was at Christmas 1529. At length, Dr. West preached against Mr. Latimer at Barwell Abbey, and prohibited him from preaching again in the churches of the university, notwithstanding which, he continued during three years to advocate openly the cause of Christ, and even his enemies confessed the power of those talents he possessed. Mr. Bilney remained here some time with Mr. Latimer, and thus the place where they frequently walked together obtained the name of Heretics' Hill.

Mr. Latimer at this time traced out the innocence of a poor woman, accused by her husband of the murder of her child. Having preached before King Henry VIII at Windsor, he obtained the unfortunate mother's pardon. This, with many other benevolent acts, served only to excite the spleen of his adversaries. He was summoned before Cardinal Wolsey for **heresy,*** but being a strenuous supporter of the king's supremacy, in opposition to the pope's, by favor of Lord Cromwell and Dr. Buts (the king's physician), he obtained the living of West Kingston in Wiltshire. For his sermons here against purgatory, the immaculacy of the Virgin, and the worship of images, he was cited to appear before Warham, archbishop of Canterbury, and John, bishop of London. He was required to subscribe certain articles, expressive of his conformity to the accustomed usages; and there is reason to think, after repeated weekly examinations, that he did subscribe, as they did not seem to involve any important article of belief.

Guided by Providence, he escaped the subtle nets of his persecutors, and at length, through the powerful friends before mentioned, became bishop of Worcester, in which function he qualified or explained away most of the papal ceremonies he was for form's sake under the necessity of complying with. He continued in this active and dignified employment some years.

Beginning afresh to set forth his plow, he labored in the Lord's harvest most fruitfully, discharging his talent as well in divers places of this realm, as before the king at the court. In the same place of the inward garden, which was before applied to lascivious and courtly pastimes, there he dispensed the fruitful Word of the glorious gospel of Jesus Christ, preaching there before the king and his whole court, to the edification of many.

He remained a prisoner in the Tower until the coronation of Edward VI, when he was again called to the Lord's harvest in Stamford and many other places. He also preached at London in the convocation house and before the young king; indeed he lectured twice every Sunday, regardless of his great age (then above sixty-seven years) and his weakness through a bruise received from the fall of a tree. Indefatigable in his private studies, he rose to them in winter and in summer at two o'clock in the morning.

By the strength of his own mind, or of some inward light from above, he had a prophetic view of what was to happen to the church in Mary's reign, asserting that he was doomed to suffer for the truth and that Winchester, then in the Tower, was preserved for that purpose. Soon after Queen Mary was proclaimed, a messenger was sent to summon Mr. Latimer to town, and there is reason to believe it was wished that he should make his escape.

Thus, Master Latimer coming up to London through Smithfield (where merrily he said that Smithfield had long groaned for him) was brought before the Council, where he patiently bore all of the mocks and taunts given him by the scornful papists. He was cast into the Tower, where he, being assisted with the heavenly grace of Christ, sustained imprisonment a long time, notwithstanding the cruel and unmerciful handling of the lordly papists, which thought then their kingdom would never fall; he showed himself not only patient but also cheerful in and above all that which they could or would work against him. Yea, such a valiant spirit the Lord gave him, that he was able not only to despise the terribleness of prisons and torments but also to laugh to scorn the doings of his enemies.

Mr. Latimer, after remaining a long time in the Tower, was transported to Oxford with Cranmer and Ridley, the disputations at which place have been already mentioned in a former part of this work. He remained imprisoned until October, and the principal objects of all of his prayers were three—that he might stand faithful to the doctrine he had professed, that God would restore his gospel to England once again, and that he would preserve the Lady Elizabeth to be queen—all of which happened. When he stood at the stake without the Bocardo gate, Oxford, with Dr. Ridley, and fire was putting to the pile of fagots, he raised his eyes benignantly towards heaven and said, "God is faithful, who will not suffer you to be tempted above that ye are able." His body was forcibly penetrated by the fire, and the blood flowed abundantly from the heart, as if to verify his constant desire that his heart's blood might be shed in defence of the gospel. His polemical and friendly letters are lasting monuments of his integrity and talents. It has been before said that public disputation took place in April 1554, new examinations took place in October 1555, previous to the degradation and condemnation of Cranmer, Ridley, and Latimer. We now draw to the conclusion of the lives of the two last.

Dr. Ridley, the night before execution, was very facetious, had himself shaved, and called his supper a marriage feast; he remarked upon seeing Mrs. Irish (the keeper's wife) weep, "Though my breakfast will be somewhat sharp, my supper will be more pleasant and sweet."

The place of death was on the northside of the town, opposite Baliol College. Dr. Ridley was dressed in a black gown furred, and Mr. Latimer had a long shroud on, hanging down to his feet. Dr. Ridley, as he passed Bocardo, looked up to see Dr. Cranmer, but the latter was then engaged in disputation with a friar. When they came to the stake, Mr. Ridley embraced Latimer fervently and bid him, "Be of good heart, brother, for God will either assuage the fury of the flame, or else strengthen us to abide it." He then knelt by the stake, and after earnestly praying together, they had a short private conversation. Dr. Smith then preached a short sermon against the martyrs, who would have answered him but were prevented by Dr. Marshal, the vice-chancellor. Dr. Ridley then took off his gown and tippet and gave them to his brother-in-law, Mr. Shipside. He gave away also many trifles to his weeping friends, and the populace were anxious to get even a fragment of his garments. Mr. Latimer gave nothing, and from the poverty of his garb, was soon stripped to his shroud, and stood venerable and erect, fearless of death.

Dr. Ridley being unclothed to his shirt, the smith placed an iron chain about their waists, and Dr. Ridley bid him fasten it securely; his brother having tied a bag of gunpowder about his neck, gave some also to Mr. Latimer. Dr. Ridley then requested of Lord Williams, of Fame, to advocate with the queen the cause of some poor men to whom he had, when bishop, granted leases but which the present bishop refused to confirm. A lighted fagot was now laid at Dr. Ridley's feet, which caused Mr. Latimer to say, "Be of good cheer, Ridley, and play the man. We shall this day, by God's grace, light up such a candle in England, as I trust, will never be put out."

When Dr. Ridley saw the fire flaming up toward him, he cried with a wonderful loud voice, "Lord, Lord, receive my spirit!" Master Latimer, cried as vehemently on the other side, "O Father of heaven, receive my soul!" They received the flame as it were embracing of it. After that, he stroked his face with his hands and, as it were, bathed them a little in the fire. He soon died (as it appeared) with very little or no pain.

See of London - ecclesiastical district of London, governed by a bishop; Ridley was once the Bishop of London
Melancthon - Martin Luther's successor

◆ **Answer *true* or *false* for each of the following statements.**

1.109 _____ Bishop Ridley was appointed head of the see of London during the reign of Mary.

1.110 _____ Foxe describes Ridley as the "pattern of godliness and virtue."

1.111 _____ Ridley was converted by reading a book on the Sacrament and by talking to archbishop Cranmer and Peter Martyr.

1.112 _____ Hugh Latimer began studying the doctrines of Roman Catholicism at age fourteen.

1.113 _____ Before his conversion, Latimer was a zealous observer of the "Romish superstitions of the time."

1.114 _____ Latimer was hardened to the gospel after having a conversation with Mr. Thomas Bilney.

1.115 _____ After his conversion, Latimer was fearful about sharing his new faith.

1.116 _____ During Henry VIII's reign, Latimer was named bishop of Worcester and preached the gospel at court many times.

1.117 _____ During Edward's reign, Latimer was banned from preaching at court.

1.118 _____ Latimer cheerfully and patiently endured his various times of imprisonment.

1.119 _____ While awaiting death, Latimer prayed principally for three things: that he might remain faithful to the gospel he had professed, that God would restore the gospel to England once again, and that the Lady Elizabeth would become queen.

1.120 _____ Dr. Ridley called his last supper a funeral meal.

1.121 _____ Upon the lighting of the stake, Latimer said, "Be of good cheer, Ridley; and play the man. We shall this day, by God's grace, light up such a candle in England, as I trust, will never be put out."

1.122 _____ Foxe remarks that Latimer appeared to have suffered greatly in the flames.

Archbishop Cranmer

Dr. Thomas Cranmer was descended from an ancient family and was born at the village of Arselacton in the county of Northampton. After the usual school education, he was sent to Cambridge and was chosen a fellow at Jesus College. There he married a gentleman's daughter, by which he forfeited his fellowship and became a reader in Buckingham College, placing his wife at the Dolphin Inn, the landlady of which was a relation of hers, whence arose the idle

report that he was stableman. His lady shortly after died in childbed. To his credit, he was rechosen a fellow of the college. A few years after, he was promoted to be Divinity Lecturer and appointed one of the examiners over those who were ripe to become Bachelors or Doctors in Divinity. It was his principle to judge of their qualifications by the knowledge they possessed of the Scriptures, rather than of the ancient fathers; hence, many popish priests were rejected, and others were rendered much improved.

While he continued in Cambridge, the question of Henry VIII's divorce with Catherine was agitated. At that time, on account of the plague, Dr. Cranmer removed to the house of a Mr. Cressy, at Waltham Abbey, whose two sons were then educating under him....

It happened that Dr. Gardiner (secretary) and Dr. Fox, defenders of the king in the above suit, came to the house of Mr. Cressy to lodge, while the king removed to Greenwich. At supper, a conversation ensued with Dr. Cranmer, who suggested that the question whether a man may marry his brother's wife, could be easily and speedily decided by the Word of God, and this as well in the English courts as in those of any foreign nation.... Upon relating to the king the conversation which had passed on the previous evening with Dr. Cranmer, his majesty sent for him.... Dr. Cranmer advised that the matter should be referred to the most learned divines of Cambridge and Oxford, as he was unwilling to meddle in an affair of such weight; but the king enjoined him to deliver his sentiments in writing, and to repair for that purpose to the earl of Wiltshire's, who would accommodate him with books and everything requisite for the occasion.

This Dr. Cranmer immediately did, and in his declaration not only quoted the authority of the Scriptures, of general councils, and the ancient writers, but also maintained that the bishop of Rome had no authority whatever to dispense with the Word of God. The king asked him if he would stand by this bold declaration, to which replying in the affirmative, he was deputed ambassador to Rome, in conjunction with the earl of Wiltshire, Dr. Stokesley, Dr. Carne, Dr. Bennet, and others, previous to which, the marriage was discussed in most of the universities of Christendom and at home....

Upon the doctor's return to England, Dr. Warham, archbishop of Canterbury, having quitted this transitory life, Dr. Cranmer was deservedly, and by Dr. Warham's desire, elevated to that eminent station....

At the time that Cranmer was raised to be archbishop, he was king's chaplain, and archdeacon of Taunton; he was also constituted by the pope the penitentiary general of England. It was considered by the king that Cranmer would be obsequious; hence, the latter married the king to Anne Boleyn, performed her coronation, stood godfather to Elizabeth, the first child, and divorced the king from Catherine. Though Cranmer received a confirmation of his dignity from the pope, he always protested against acknowledging any other authority than the king's, and he persisted in the same independent sentiments when before Mary's commissioners in 1555.

One of the first steps after the divorce was to prevent preaching throughout his diocese, but this narrow measure had rather a political view than a religious one, as there were many who inveighed against the king's conduct. In his new dignity, Cranmer agitated the question of supremacy, and by his powerful and just arguments induced the parliament to "render to Caesar the things that are Caesar's." During Cranmer's residence in Germany, 1531, he became acquainted with Ossiander at Nuremberg and married his niece, but he left her with him while on his return to England. After a season, he sent for her privately, and she remained with him until the year 1539, when the Six Articles compelled him to return her to her friends for a time....

In 1538 the Holy Scriptures were openly exposed to sale; and the places of worship overflowed everywhere to hear its holy doctrines expounded. Upon the king's passing into a law the famous Six Articles, which went nearly again to establish the essential tenets of the Romish creed, Cranmer shone forth with all of the luster of a Christian patriot in resisting the doctrines they contained and in which he was supported by the bishops of Sarum, Worcester, Ely, and Rochester, the two former of whom resigned their bishoprics. The king, though now in opposition to Cranmer, still revered the sincerity that marked his conduct. The death of Lord Cromwell in the Tower, in 1540, the good friend of Cranmer, was a severe blow to the wavering Protestant cause, but even now Cranmer, when he saw the tide directly adverse to the truth, boldly waited on the king in person, and by his manly and heartfelt pleading, caused the Book of Articles to be passed on his side, to the great confusion of his enemies, who had contemplated his fall as inevitable....

The death of Edward in 1553 exposed Cranmer to all of the rage of his enemies. Though the archbishop was among those who supported Mary's accession, he was attainted at the meeting of parliament, and in November he was adjudged guilty of high treason at Guildhall and degraded from his dignities. He sent a humble letter to Mary, explaining the cause of his signing the will in favor of Edward, and in 1554 he wrote to the Council, whom he pressed to obtain a pardon from the queen, by a letter delivered to Dr. Weston, but who, when the letter had been opened, and on seeing its contents, basely returned.

Treason was a charge quite inapplicable to Cranmer, who supported the queen's right, while others who had favored Lady Jane were dismissed upon paying a small fine. A calumny was now spread against Cranmer that he complied with some of the popish ceremonies to ingratiate himself with the queen, which he dared publicly to disavow, and justified his articles of faith. The active part which the prelate had taken in the divorce of Mary's mother had ever rankled deeply in the heart of the queen, and revenge formed a prominent feature in the death of Cranmer.

We have in this work noticed the public disputations at Oxford, in which the talents of Cranmer, Ridley, and Latimer shone so conspicuously and tended to their condemnation. The first sentence was illegal, inasmuch as the usurped power of the pope had not yet been re-established by law....

Being sent back to confinement, [Cranmer] received a citation to appear at Rome within eighteen days, but this was impracticable, as he was imprisoned in England; and as he stated, even had he been at liberty, he was too poor to employ an advocate. Absurd as it must appear, Cranmer was condemned at Rome, and on February 14, 1556, a new commission was appointed by which Thirlby, bishop of Ely, and Bonner, of London, were deputed to sit in judgment at Christ-church, Oxford. By virtue of this instrument, Cranmer was gradually degraded, by putting mere rags on him to represent the dress of an archbishop; then stripping him of his attire, they took off his own gown, and put an old worn one upon him instead. This he bore unmoved, and his enemies, finding that severity only rendered him more determined, tried the opposite course, and placed him in the house of the dean of Christ-church, where he was treated with every indulgence.

This presented such a contrast to the three years' hard imprisonment he had received, that it threw him off his guard. His open, generous nature was more easily to be seduced by a liberal conduct than by threats and fetters. When Satan finds the Christian proof against one mode of attack, he tries another; and what form is so seductive as smiles, rewards, and power after a long, painful imprisonment? Thus it was with Cranmer, his enemies promised him his former greatness if he would but **recant***, as well as the queen's favor, and this at the very time they knew that his death was determined in council. To soften the path to apostasy, the first paper brought for his signature was conceived in general terms; this once signed, five others were obtained as explanatory of the first, until finally he put his hand to the following detestable instrument:

"I, Thomas Cranmer, late archbishop of Canterbury, do renounce, abhor, and detest all manner of heresies and errors of Luther and Zuinglius, and all other teachings which are contrary to sound and true doctrine. And I believe most constantly in my heart, and with my mouth I confess one holy and Catholic Church visible, without which there is no salvation; and therefore I acknowledge the Bishop of Rome to be supreme head on earth, whom I acknowledge to be the highest bishop and pope, and Christ's vicar, unto whom all Christian people ought to be subject.

"And as concerning the sacraments, I believe and worship in the sacrament of the altar the body and blood of Christ, being contained most truly under the forms of bread and wine; the bread, through the mighty power of God being turned into the body of our Savior Jesus Christ, and the wine into His blood.

"And in the other six sacraments, also (alike as in this), I believe and hold as the universal Church holdeth and the Church of Rome judgeth and determineth.

"Furthermore, I believe that there is a place of purgatory, where souls departed be punished for a time, for whom the Church doth godily and wholesomely pray, like as it doth honor saints and make prayers to them.

"Finally, in all things I profess, that I do not otherwise believe than the Catholic Church and the Church of Rome holdeth and teacheth. I am sorry that I ever held or thought otherwise. And I beseech Almighty God, that of His mercy He will vouchsafe to forgive me whatsoever I have offended against God or His Church, and also I desire and beseech all Christian people to pray for me.

"And all such as have been deceived either by mine example or doctrine, I require them by the blood of Jesus Christ that they will return to the unity of the Church, that we may be all of one mind, without schism or division.

"And to conclude, as I submit myself to the Catholic Church of Christ, and to the supreme head thereof, so I submit myself unto the most excellent majesties of Philip and Mary, king and queen of this realm of England, etc., and to all other their laws and ordinances, being ready always as a faithful subject ever to obey them. And God is my witness, that I have not done this for favor or fear of any person, but willingly and of mine own conscience, as to the instruction of others."

"Let him that standeth take heed lest he fall!" said the apostle, and here was a falling off indeed! The papists now triumphed in their turn; they had acquired all that they wanted short of his life. His recantation was immediately printed and dispersed, that it might have its due effect upon the astonished Protestants. But God counter worked all the designs of the Catholics by the extent to which they carried the implacable persecution of their prey. Doubtless, the love of life induced Cranmer to sign the preceeding declaration; yet death may be said to have been preferable to life to him who lay under the stings of a goaded conscience and the contempt of every gospel Christian; this principle he strongly felt in all of its force and anguish.

The queen's revenge was only to be satiated by Cranmer's blood; therefore, she wrote an order to Dr. Pole to prepare a sermon to be preached March 21, directly before his martyrdom, at St. Mary's, Oxford. Dr. Pole visited him the day previous and was induced to believe that he would publicly deliver his sentiments in confirmation of the articles to which he had subscribed. About nine in the morning of the day of sacrifice, the queen's commissioners, attended by the magistrates, conducted the amiable unfortunate to St. Mary's Church. His torn, dirty garb, the same in which they habited him upon his degradation, excited the commiseration of the people. In the church he found a low mean stage, erected opposite to the pulpit, on which being placed, he turned his face, and fervently prayed to God.

The church was crowded with persons of both persuasions, expecting to hear the justification of the late apostasy: the Catholics rejoicing, and the Protestants deeply wounded in spirit at the deceit of the human heart. Dr. Pole, in his sermon, represented Cranmer as having been guilty of the most atrocious crimes; encouraged the deluded sufferer not to fear death, not to doubt the support of God in his torments, nor that Masses would be said in all the churches of Oxford for the repose of his soul. The doctor then noticed his conversion, and which he ascribed to the evident working of Almighty power and, that the people might be convinced of its reality, asked the prisoner to give them a sign. This Cranmer did, and begged the congregation to pray for him, for he had committed many and grievous sins; but, of all, there was one which awfully lay upon his mind, of which he would speak shortly.

During the sermon, Cranmer wept bitter tears, lifting up his hands and eyes to heaven, and letting them fall, as if unworthy to live. His grief now found vent in words; before his confession he fell upon his knees, and, in the following words, unveiled the deep contrition and agitation that harrowed up his soul.

"O Father of heaven! O Son of God, Redeemer of the world! O Holy Ghost, three persons all one God! have mercy on me, most wretched coward and miserable sinner. I have offended both against heaven and earth, more than my tongue can express. Whither then may I go, or whither may I flee? To heaven I may be ashamed to lift up mine eyes and in earth I find no place of refuge or succor. To Thee, therefore, O Lord, do I run; to Thee do I humble myself, saying, O Lord, my God, my sins be great, but yet have mercy upon me for Thy great mercy. The great mystery that God became man, was not wrought for little or few offenses. Thou didst not give Thy Son, O Heavenly Father, unto death for small sins only, but for all the greatest sins of the world, so that the sinner return to Thee with his whole heart, as I do at present. Wherefore, have mercy on me, O God, whose property is always to have mercy, have mercy upon me, O Lord, for Thy great mercy. I crave nothing for my own merits, but for Thy name's sake, that it may be hallowed thereby, and for Thy dear Son, Jesus Christ's sake. And now therefore, O Father of Heaven, hallowed be Thy name," etc.

Then, rising, he said he was desirous before his death to give them some pious exhortations by which God might be glorified and themselves edified. He then descanted upon the danger of a love for the world, the duty of obedience to their majesties, of love to one another and the necessity of the rich administering to the wants of the poor. He quoted the three verses of the fifth chapter of James and then proceeded, "Let them that be rich ponder well these three sentences: for if they ever had occasion to show their charity, they have it now at this present, the poor people being so many and victual so dear.

"And now forasmuch as I am come to the last end of my life, whereupon hangeth all my life past, and all my life to come, either to live with my master Christ for ever in joy, or else to be in pain for ever with the wicked in hell, and I see before mine eyes presently, either heaven ready to receive me, or else hell ready to swallow me up; I shall therefore declare unto you my very faith how I believe, without any color of dissimulation: for now is no time to dissemble, whatsoever I have said or written in times past.

"First, I believe in God the Father Almighty, Maker of heaven and earth, etc. And I believe every article of the Catholic faith, every word and sentence taught by our Savior Jesus Christ, His apostles and prophets, in the New and Old Testament.

"And now I come to the great thing which so much troubleth my conscience, more than any thing that ever I did or said in my whole life, and that is the setting abroad of a writing contrary to the truth, which now here I renounce and refuse, as things written with my hand contrary to the truth which I thought in my heart, and written for fear of death, and to save my life, if it might be; and that is, all such bills or papers which I have written or signed with my hand since my degradation, wherein I have written many things untrue. And forasmuch as my hand hath offended, writing contrary to my heart, therefore my hand shall first be punished; for when I come to the fire it shall first be burned.

"And as for the pope, I refuse him as Christ's enemy, and Antichrist, with all his false doctrine."

Upon the conclusion of this unexpected declaration, amazement and indignation were conspicuous in every part of the church. The Catholics were completely foiled, their object being frustrated, Cranmer, like Samson, having completed a greater ruin upon his enemies in the hour of death than he did in his life.

Cranmer would have proceeded in the exposure of the popish doctrines, but the murmurs of the idolaters drowned his voice, and the preacher gave an order to "lead the heretic away!" The savage command was directly obeyed, and the lamb about to suffer was torn from his stand to the place of slaughter, insulted all the way by the revilings and taunts of the pestilent monks and friars.

With thoughts intent upon a far higher object than the empty threats of man, he reached the spot dyed with the blood of Ridley and Latimer. There he knelt for a short time in earnest devotion and then arose that he might undress and prepare for the fire. Two friars who had been parties in prevailing upon him to abjure, now endeavored to draw him off again from the truth, but he was steadfast and immovable in what he had just professed and publicly taught. A chain was provided to bind him to the stake, and after it had tightly encircled him, fire was put to the fuel, and the flames began soon to ascend.

Then were the glorious sentiments of the martyr made manifest; then it was that, stretching out his right hand, he held it unshrinkingly in the fire until it was burnt to a cinder, even before his body was injured, frequently exclaiming, "This unworthy right hand."

His body did abide the burning with such steadfastness that he seemed to have no more than the stake to which he was bound; his eyes were lifted up to heaven, and he repeated "this unworthy right hand" as long as his voice would suffer him; and using often the words of Stephen, "Lord Jesus, receive my spirit," in the greatness of the flame, he gave up the ghost.

Answer *true* or *false* for each of the following statements.

1.123 _____ While a doctor of divinity at Cambridge, Cranmer judged doctoral candidates on their knowledge of the Scriptures rather than on knowledge of the ancient church fathers.

1.124 _____ Cranmer advised King Henry to obey the pope's authority in regard to his marriage to Catherine.

1.125 _____ For his bold denial of the pope's authority, Henry appointed Cranmer ambassador to Rome.

1.126 _____ While he was archbishop of Canterbury, Cranmer served as Queen Mary's chaplain.

1.127 _____ Cranmer resisted the Catholic doctrines of King Henry's Six Articles.

1.128 _____ After Edward VI's death, Cranmer supported Mary as the rightful heir.

1.129 _____ According to Foxe, Mary sought to execute Cranmer for his part in her parents' divorce.

1.130 _____ Cranmer retained the dignity and dress of an archbishop throughout his imprisonment.

1.131 _____ Though much tempted by the love of life, Cranmer never signed papers denouncing the doctrines of the Reformation.

1.132 _____ Before being burned at the stake, Cranmer denounced his recantation as a lie and called the pope Christ's enemy.

1.133 _____ For "writing contrary to his heart," Cranmer held his right hand directly in the fire until it was burned to a cinder.

1.134 _____ Cranmer exclaimed, "This unworthy right hand" until he was consumed by the flame.

Review the material in this section in preparation for the Self Test, which will check your mastery of this particular section. The items that you miss on this Self Test will indicate specific areas in which restudy is needed for mastery.

SELF TEST 1

Underline the correct answer in each of the following statements (each answer, 1 point).

1.01 The (Middle Ages, War, Reformation) in England effected changes in religion, government, science, economics, society, art, and literature.

1.02 God worked through the revival of learning and the resurrection of the (classics, Word of God, printing press) to bring about the Reformation in England.

1.03 The (Renaissance, Reformation, Middle Ages) was a man-centered movement.

1.04 The Roman Catholic Church believes that the interpretation of Scripture must come under the authority of the (individual, church, priest).

1.05 The Protestant Reformers in England believed that (the church, Scripture, the king) alone was the guide to faith and life.

1.06 The (Renaissance, Reformation, Middle Ages) was in essence a God-centered movement based on the knowledge of Scripture.

1.07 (Sir Thomas More, Roger Ascham, William Tyndale) used Erasmus's Greek New Testament to translate the Bible into English.

1.08 Although he was severed from Rome, Henry VIII remained faithful to (Protestant, Lutheran, Catholic) doctrine.

1.09 During the reign of (Mary, Edward VI), the Reformation was allowed to take a greater hold in England.

1.010 During the reign of Mary, nearly three hundred (Protestants, Catholics, Jews) were burned at the stake.

1.011 To settle religious disputes between her people, Queen Elizabeth distinguished the Church of England as (Anglican, Protestant, Catholic).

1.012 The mercantile system valued gold and silver as the basis for (national, independent, communal) wealth and encouraged the balance of trade between (manor houses, nations, kings).

1.013 The perfection of the English language and the use of the printing press contributed to the flowering of (English, Italian, French) literature.

1.014 The (pastoral, sonnet, short story) was the chief literary device imported from Italy.

1.015 The Petrarchian or Italian sonnet consists of (sixteen, fifteen, fourteen) lines that are divided into two sets: an octave and a sestet.

1.016 The (Polish, French, English), or Shakespearean, sonnet consisted of sixteen lines that were divided into three quatrains and a couplet.

1.017 The rural, rustic life is exalted in (cavalier, religious, pastoral) songs and poetry.

1.018 The closet plays of (Greece, Dionysus, Seneca) were especially appealing to the Elizabethans because they combined (medieval, classical, modern) form with moral value while delighting with (horror, technology, comedy).

1.019 An English chronicle play deals with (English history, French scandal, German intrigue).

1.020 A (tragedy, comedy) ends in (destruction, restoration), which reestablishes order.

1.021 Public theaters were (square, circular, oval) shaped with several tiers of seating.

1.022 The ideals of the Renaissance and the Reformation shaped (Medieval, Modern, Elizabethan) literature.

Fill in each of the blanks using items from the following word list (each answer, 3 points).

> *The Schoolmaster*   Scriptures   Lord Chancellor
> Greek   *Utopia*   Henry VIII
> evangelicalism   treason   Oxford
> England   Roger Ascham   biblical
> no place   reason   faith
> historical

1.023   In 1529 More became _____ of England, the highest office in England beneath the crown.

1.024   More's masterpiece, _____, is a fantastical vision of a New World free of societal ills.

1.025   More's utopian vision offers _____ as a means to perfect the human condition.

1.026   The title *Utopia* means in Greek "_____."

1.027   More was charged with _____ and executed for his refusal to support _____ as the Head of the Church of England.

1.028   Roger Ascham believed that the study of certain Latin and Greek classics in subjection to the authority of _____ was a means to "truth in religion, honesty of living, and right order in learning."

1.029   _____ was the tutor of Princess Elizabeth.

1.030   Ascham's book _____ is a conduct book for teachers and students.

1.031   While studying at _____ University, John Foxe read the Scriptures in _____ and became convinced that they were the final authority in regard to _____ and life.

1.032   After hearing reports of the persecutions of the Protestants in _____, Foxe decided to expand his first history book of Christian martyrdom.

1.033   Foxe wrote *Acts and Monuments* as a _____ testament to the fact that _____ has been persecuted throughout the centuries because it embodies the true _____ faith.

Answer *true* or *false* for each of the following statements (each answer, 2 points).

1.034   _____   The Utopians in More's book valued gold and silver highly.

1.035   _____   There are no poor people in Utopia; all men are rich.

1.036   _____   According to the Utopian Republic, when money is abolished so greed, theft, quarrels, murders, treason, worry, fear, and poverty disappear.

1.037   _____   The healthy institutions of Utopia are the cause of its happiness and success.

1.038   _____   More comments that he likes some features of the Utopian Republic, but he does not expect to see them occur in his own society.

1.039   _____   In *The Schoolmaster*, Roger Ascham recommends punishment as the best thing to "sharpen a good wit" and "encourage a will to learning."

1.040   _____   Ascham gives Lady Jane Grey's example to prove that fear, more than love, encourages a child toward virtue and learning.

1.041 _____ Ascham blames the sale of certain Italian books as the prime source of corrupt manners and religion in England.

1.042 _____ According to Ascham, the fastest way to entangle the mind with false doctrine is first to entice the will to immoral living.

1.043 _____ *Acts and Monuments* contains the account where, upon the scaffold, Lady Jane Grey, a devout Protestant, claimed that she looked to be saved by no other mean but by the mercy of God in the blood of Jesus Christ.

1.044 _____ John Foxe described Bishop Nicholas Ridley as the "pattern of godliness and virtue."

1.045 _____ Before his conversion, Latimer was a zealous observer of the "Romish superstitions of the time."

1.046 _____ Latimer cheerfully and patiently endured his various times of imprisonment.

1.047 _____ Upon the lighting of the stake, Latimer said, "Be of good cheer, Ridley; and play the man. We shall this day, by God's grace, light up such a candle in England, as I trust, will never be put out."

1.048 _____ Thomas Cranmer advised King Henry to obey the pope's authority in regard to his marriage to Catherine.

1.049 _____ Before being burned at the stake, Cranmer denounced his earlier recantation as a lie and called the pope Christ's enemy.

1.050 _____ For "writing contrary to his heart," Cranmer held his right hand directly in the fire until it was burned to a cinder.

For Thought and Discussion:

Explain to a Parent/Teacher Sir Thomas More's book *Utopia*. Be sure to point out that Utopia is an idealistic world based upon human reason and where gold is scorned and crime is nonexistent. In light of 1 Corinthian 2:6–15, discuss the possibility of a perfect world based upon human wisdom. How does the history of the Union of Soviet Socialist Republics relate to the truth of Scripture?

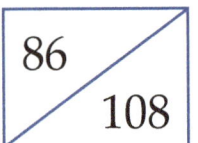

Score _____

Adult Check _____
                   Initial   Date

II. RENAISSANCE POETS

Sir Thomas Wyatt the Elder (1503–1542). As a trusted courtier, Sir Thomas Wyatt spent many of his adult years abroad serving his king, Henry VIII. Born at Allington Castle in Kent and educated at St. John's College, Cambridge, Wyatt was well equipped by the age of twenty-five to perform his duties as diplomat to France and Italy. He also served as ambassador to Spain. During his career as a courtier, Wyatt rose, fell, and rose again in favor. In 1536 he was imprisoned after quarreling with the duke of Suffolk. But Wyatt soon regained the king's favor and was knighted the following year. From 1537 to 1539, he served as ambassador to the Holy Roman Emperor Charles V. In 1541 Wyatt was charged with treason and sent to the Tower to await execution. But Henry again relented of his anger and reinstated Wyatt.

Wyatt's travels bore more than diplomatic fruits for England. Wyatt was particularly interested in the literature of the countries in which he visited. His trips to Italy during the High Renaissance proved to be of great importance to the future of English literature. Much of Wyatt's poetry is based on Italian models. Especially influential on Wyatt's choice of theme were the sonnets of Petrarch (1304–1374). A Petrarchian sonnet usually focuses on the despairing feelings of a lover. The lover, a man, is desperate to have his love returned. Enslaved by his love for his lady, he muses over her beauty by comparing it to other forms of natural beauty. The comparisons used within a sonnet are called **conceits**.* For example, a poet might compare the brightness of the lady's eyes to the sun, or he might compare his feelings of love to a warrior or a ship.

The form that Wyatt introduced into England was Italian but not exclusively Petrarchian. The Italian, or Petrarchian, sonnet contains fourteen lines, which are arranged into an octave and a sestet. The eight lines of the octave follow the rhyme scheme *abbaabba*. The six lines of the sestet follow one of three schemes, *cdecde*, *cdcdcd*, or *cdedce*. The octave and the sestet are not merely ornamental but follow a rhetorical format. The question or proposition stated in the octave is then answered or solved in the sestet. The meter or rhythm that is heard in the stressed syllables of a line of the Italian sonnet is iambic pentameter. Iambic pentameter consists of five stressed syllables per line.

Many of Wyatt's sonnets show an alteration of the Italian form, hinting at changes that would be made later by the English. His changes to the sestet placed a couplet at the end. His rhyme schemes often appear as such—*abbaabba cddcee*. Wyatt's successor, Henry Howard, the earl of Surrey, adapted the Italian sonnet further. He structured the sonnet into three quatrains and a couplet—*abab cdcd efef gg*. The rhyme scheme was much more flexible than the Italian form. Consequently, the English rhyme scheme became the most popular sonnet form of the Elizabethan period.

Fill in each of the following blanks with the correct answer.

2.1 Sir Thomas Wyatt was a trusted courtier of _____.

2.2 Wyatt was educated at St. John's College, _____.

2.3 Wyatt introduced the Italian sonnet into _____.

2.4 A(n) _____ sonnet usually focuses on the despairing feelings of a lover.

2.5 A _____ is an elaborate comparison made by the poet within the sonnet.

2.6 The Petrarchian, or _____, sonnet contains _____ lines, which are arranged into an _____ and a sestet.

2.7 The Italian sonnet follows a rhetorical format in which the _____ or proposition stated in the octave is then answered or solved in the _____.

2.8 The meter of a poem is its _____.

2.9 The meter of the Italian sonnet is _____ pentameter.

2.10 Iambic pentameter consists of _____ stressed syllables per _____.

2.11 Wyatt altered the Italian sonnet by altering the rhyme scheme of the _____.

2.12 Henry Howard, the earl of Surrey, structured the sonnet into _____ quatrains and a couplet—abab cdcd efef gg.

2.13 The _____ rhyme scheme became the most popular sonnet form of the Elizabethan period.

What to Look For:

Wyatt often imitated the sonnets of the Italian poet, Petrarch. He translated many of Petrarch's sonnets into English. However, Wyatt's sonnets do not always follow the Italian model exactly. As you read, notice the difference between the Italian rhyme scheme (*abbaabba cddcdc*) and Wyatt's rhyme scheme. What has he changed? Is it the number of lines? Is it the rhyme scheme? Notice carefully the lines of the sestet.

This is a translation of Petrarch's Sonnetto in Vita 137. *All of the lines that are designated with matching letters rhyme. For example, lines 1 and 4 are designated with an "a" to indicate that they rhyme with one another.*

MY GALLEY

a	My galley* charged with forgetfulness	*an ancient ship
b	Thorough* sharp seas, in winter nights doth pass	*through
b	'Tween rock and rock; and eke* mine enemy,* alas	*also *feelings of love
a	That is my lord, steereth with cruelness,	
a	And every oar a thought in readiness,	5
b	As though that death were light in such a case.	
b	An endless wind doth tear the sail apace	
a	Of forced sighs and trusty fearfulness.*	*fearful trust
c	A rain of tears, a cloud of dark disdain,	
d	Hath done the wearied cords great hinderance;	10
d	Wreathed with error and eke with ignorance.	
c	The stars be hid that led me to this pain.	
e	Drowned is reason that should me consort,*	*accompany
e	And I remain despairing of the port.	

Answer *true* or *false* for each of the following statements.

2.14 _____ The sonnet is a translation of one of Petrarch's sonnets.

2.15 _____ "My galley" is a conceit or comparison of the poet himself.

2.16 _____ "Mine enemy" is a conceit of his feelings of hatred for his beloved.

2.17 _____ Like a ship out at sea, the poet says that "the stars" led him to this pain.

2.18 _____ Reason, as opposed to feelings, is drowned and unable to help the poet.

2.19 _____ The poet is content and happy with his condition.

2.20 _____ The sestet of the sonnet is similar to the sestet of the Italian model.

What to Look For:

Henry Howard, the earl of Surrey, was Wyatt's poetical successor. He made further adaptations to the Italian sonnet and is credited with inventing the form that is now known as the English sonnet. As you read, notice the differences between the rhyme scheme of the earl of Surrey and that of Wyatt. How many lines does the earl of Surrey's sonnet have? What rhyme scheme does the earl of Surrey use?

Love, That Doth Reign and Live Within My Thought

This is a translation of Petrarch's Sonnetto in Vita 91. *Wyatt also translated this work. However, Surrey's rhyme scheme structure lends a more fluid rendering. True to classic examples, the sonnet follows an ordered flow of thought and experience. Each* **quatrain** *contains a distinct thought. The sonnet ends with a couplet that contains a resolution to the lover's problems.*

a	Love, that doth reign and live within my thought,
b	And built his seat within my captive breast,
a	Clad in the arms wherein with me he fought,
b	Oft in my face he doth his banner rest.
c	But she that taught me love and suffer pain, 5
d	My doubtful hope and eke my hot desire
c	With shamefast look to shadow and refrain,
d	Her smiling grace converteth straight to ire.* *bitter anger*
e	And coward Love, then, to the heart apace
f	Taketh his flight, where he doth lurk and plain,* *complain* 10
e	His purpose lost, and dare not show his face.* *he is humiliated*
f	For my lord's guilt thus faultless bide I pain,
g	Yet from my lord shall not my foot remove:
g	Sweet is the death that taketh end by love.

Answer *true* or *false* for each of the following statements.

2.21 _____ The sonnet is a translation of an English sonnet.

2.22 _____ The sonnet contains fourteen lines, similar to an Italian sonnet.

2.23 _____ The rhyme scheme is similar to an Italian sonnet.

2.24 _____ Each quatrain of the sonnet contains a vague and meaningless thought.

2.25 _____ According to lines 1–4, love is presumed to be reigning.

2.26 _____ According to last line of the second quatrain, the poet is rejected by his beloved.

2.27 _____ According to the third quatrain, the poet is proud of the rejection that he has suffered.

2.28 _____ The sonnet ends in the resolution that death is bitter that ends by love.

2.29 _____ The first quatrain contains a resolution of the lover's problems.

Sir Philip Sidney (1554–1586). As a man "kept up in God's fear and governed by his grace," Sir Philip Sidney was most nearly that ideal gentleman that the Christian humanists sought to develop. Whether it was in the field of battle or in the presence of the Queen, Sidney sought to "serve God and his country, both by virtue and wisdom." Sidney was *the* Renaissance man, the near perfect courtier, the pride of his age.

Sidney grew up at his family's castle in Kent. His father, Sir Henry Sidney, was the lord deputy of Ireland, and his uncles were the earls of Warwick and Leicester. Before

Sidney's entrance to Shrewsbury School in 1564, he, alongside his sister, Mary, was partially educated by his mother. As a woman of noble birth, she had received an unusually advanced education. In 1568 Sidney entered Christ Church College, Oxford, but left for Europe before finishing his degree. From 1571–75, Sidney visited various countries, perfecting his mastery of languages and making important contacts with other Protestant nobles abroad. While in Paris, Sidney witnessed the St. Bartholomew's Day Massacre. The horrible event, incited by Queen Catherine de Medici and some of her nobles, lasted more than a month, killing thousands of Huguenots (French Calvinists). No doubt such a sight enflamed Sidney's desire to see Protestantism prevail in Europe.

When Sidney returned to England in 1576, he began his career as a courtier. Elizabeth, liking what she saw in Sidney, appointed him Cupbearer. The position brought him in daily contact with the Queen during which times she could enjoy his company and mold him into an effective minister of the state. In 1577 Elizabeth sent him on diplomatic missions to Germany and Holland. He was to test support for the formation of a Protestant alliance. While abroad, Sidney received news that Elizabeth was considering marriage with the Duke of Anjou. The thought of his Queen and his country in alliance with a Catholic nation was too much for Sidney. He wrote an open letter to the Queen in opposition to the marriage. For his outspoken behavior, Sidney was dismissed from his position at court and relieved of his diplomatic mission.

While waiting for the return of his Queen's favor, Sidney retreated to Wilton House, the estate of his sister, the Countess of Pembroke. The Countess was a patron of the arts who enjoyed the company of musicians and writers. During that time, many gentlemen and ladies would compose poetry and plays but never with the intention of publication. Their literary works were for private entertainment. In 1578 Sidney began work on a pastoral romance intended only for his sister's eyes. Basing it on an Italian model, Sidney called it the *Arcadia*. In 1580 Sidney completed what is now known as the *Old Arcadia*. In 1582 he began a major revision to style and content, which he never finished. After his death, the Countess continued to work on the *Arcadia*. The new version was completed sometime before its publication in 1590. It was titled *The Countess of Pembroke's Arcadia,* or the *New Arcadia*. Critics have considered both new and old versions of the *Arcadia* "the most important original work of English prose fiction produced before the eighteenth century."

Another important literary work of Sidney's was the sonnets of *Astrophil and Stella*. The sonnets were written as a sequence after the Petrarchian model. This was the first time that a sonnet sequence had been done in English. According to the Petrarchian form, a sonnet sequence is a series of poems or songs written about a single subject. In this case, it is about a lover and his beloved, namely, Astrophil and Stella. Filled with Petrarchian conceits, the fictional story is loosely based upon Sidney's romantic involvement with Penelope Devereux. When the two were young, there was much talk of an engagement, but that never happened. Penelope married Lord Robert Rich in 1581, and Sidney married Frances Walsingham in 1583. In later years, Sidney denounced the motivations behind *Astrophil and Stella* as "vanity." Nevertheless, the sequence was extremely influential in the development of English poetry. One critic has noted that the personal presence felt in Sidney's poems laid the groundwork for a new form that can be seen most readily in the poetry of John Donne.

As a devout Protestant and a gifted poet, Sidney was passionate about the use of the arts for the benefit of religion. In the Elizabethan age, some Christians questioned the necessity and goodness of such literary forms as fiction and poetry. With much gentleness and power of articulation, Sidney answered this narrow point of view. The essay *The Defense of Posey* was the only major piece of literary criticism published during the Elizabethan age. In it, Sidney encouraged the use of poetry and fiction as a

> means of vigorously encouraging the hatred of vice and bolstering a love for virtue. Literature was to delight and to teach wisdom.
>
> Sidney's childhood friend, Fulke Greville, once said of him, "Though I lived with him and knew him from a child, yet I never knew him other than a man." Sidney carried within him that grace that made him exemplary. The circumstances surrounding his death were no less a confirmation of his greatness. While leading a charge through enemy lines, Sidney was mortally wounded. It is said that while he lay suffering, he offered his water to another man in a worse condition, saying, "Thy necessity is yet greater than mine." At the news of Sidney's death, all of England mourned.

✝ Underline the correct answer in each of the following statements.

2.30 Sir Philip Sidney's father was the lord deputy of (France, Ireland, Spain).

2.31 Sidney was educated at Christ Church College, (Oxford, Cambridge, London).

2.32 While in (Holland, Paris, Geneva), Sidney witnessed the St. Bartholomew's Day Massacre.

2.33 As a courtier, Sir Philip Sidney was appointed (Personal Guard, Lord Chancellor, Cupbearer) to Queen Elizabeth.

2.34 (King James, Queen Mary, Queen Elizabeth) sent Sidney on diplomatic missions to Germany and Holland to test support for the formation of a Protestant alliance.

2.35 Sidney was dismissed from court because he openly opposed the alliance that would be formed with a (Protestant, Catholic, Irish) nation if Queen Elizabeth married the Duke of Anjou.

2.36 The *Arcadia* is a (pastoral romance, short story, science fiction novel).

2.37 Sidney's work on the *Arcadia* is known to us today as the (*Old Arcadia, New Arcadia, Utopia*).

2.38 Sidney completed the first (epic, play, sonnet sequence) in English—*Astrophil and Stella*.

2.39 A (play, sonnet trivial, sonnet sequence) is a series of poems or songs written about a single subject.

2.40 (*Arcadia, Astrophil and Stella, The Defense of Posey*) is loosely based upon Sidney's romantic involvement with Penelope Devereux.

2.41 (*Arcadia, Astrophil and Stella, The Defense of Posey*) argues for the necessity and goodness of such literary forms as fiction and poetry.

2.42 Sidney was (mortally, slightly, not) wounded while leading a charge through enemy lines.

2.43 During his time, Sidney was considered the near perfect (writer, courtier, soldier).

What to Look For:

Astrophil and Stella is the first sonnet sequence written in English. A sonnet sequence focuses on a love relationship, usually a romantic one. In Sidney's work, Astrophil is helplessly in love with Stella. She is to him like a "star," unreachable and removed from his earthly desires. As a courtly lover, he can only hope for a loving glance or a kind word. Their love can never be consummated. Consequently, the sonnet sequence is filled with trials and heartache on the part of Astrophil. The sequence ends without any kind of resolution. As you read, pay attention to Astrophil's state of mind. What is he feeling in each sonnet? Hope? Despair? Bitterness? Exultation? What causes his mood to change?

1

Loving in truth, and fain* in verse my love to show,   *eager*
That the dear she might take some pleasure of my pain,
Pleasure might cause her read, reading might make her know,
Knowledge might pity win, and pity grace obtain,
    I sought fit words to paint the blackest face of woe:
Studying inventions fine,* her wits to entertain,   *good poetry*
Oft turning others' leaves,* to see if thence would flow   *reading other poets' work*
Some fresh and fruitful showers upon my sunburned brain.
    But words came halting forth, wanting Invention's stay;
Invention, Nature's child, fled step-dame Study's blows,
And others' feet still seemed but strangers in my way.
Thus great with child to speak, and helpless in my throes,
    Biting my trewand* pen, beating myself for spite,   *truant*
    "Fool," said my Muse to me, "look in thy heart and write."

20

Fly, fly, my friends—I have my death wound—fly!
See there that boy,* that murdering boy, I say,   *Cupid*
Who, like a thief, hid in dark bush doth lie
Till bloody bullet get him wrongful prey.
So tyrant he no fitter place could spy,
Nor so fair level in so secret stay,
As that sweet black which veils the heavenly eye;
There himself with his shot he close doth lay.
Poor passenger, pass now thereby I did,
And stayed, pleased with the prospect of the place,
While that black hue from me the bad guest hid;
But straight I saw motions of lightning grace,
    And then descried the glistering of his dart;
    But ere I could fly thence, it pierced my heart.

37

Any references to rich or riches are a pun on the name of the man Penelope Devereux ("Stella") was forced to marry, Lord Robert Rich.

My mouth doth water, and my breast doth swell,
    My tongue doth itch, my thoughts in labour be;
    Listen then, lordings, with good ear to me,
For of my life I must a riddle tell.
Towards Aurora's court,* a nymph doth dwell,   *Aurora's court is in the east; Penelope Devereux's home was in Essex or east.*
    Rich in all beauties which man's eye can see,
    Beauties so far from reach of words, that we
Abase her praise, saying she doth excell:
    Rich in treasure of deserved renown,
Rich in the riches of a royal heart,
Rich in those gifts which give the eternal crown;
Who though most rich in these and every part,
    Which make the parents of true worldly bliss,
    Hath no misfortune, but that Rich she is.

71

Who will in fairest book of Nature know
How virtue may best lodged in beauty be,

Let him but learn of love to read in thee,
Stella, those fair lines which true goodness show,
There shall he find all vices overthrow,
Not by rude force, but sweetest sovereignty
Of reason, from whose light those night-birds fly,
That inward sun in thine eyes shineth so.
And, not content to be perfection's heir
Thyself, dost strive all minds that way to move,
Who mark in thee what is in thee most fair.
So while thy beauty draws the heart to love,
    As fast thy virtue bends that love to good.
    But, ah, Desire still cries, 'Give me some food.'

⇒ **Answer *true* or *false* for each of the following statements.**

2.44 _____ According to Sonnet 1, Astrophil is hopeful to win Stella through writing poetry.

2.45 _____ When he is unable to write, Astrophil is told to look in his mind and write.

2.46 _____ The "murdering boy" in Sonnet 20 is Cupid.

2.47 _____ According to Sonnet 20, Astrophil was able to escape Cupid's "bloody bullets."

2.48 _____ According to Sonnet 37, the "riddle" that the poet must tell is about his life.

2.49 _____ The "rich" in Sonnet 37 is a pun on Lord Robert Rich, Penelope Devereaux's brother.

2.50 _____ According to Sonnet 71, one might learn what hatred and ugliness are by looking at Stella.

2.51 _____ Stella's beauty and virtue encourage Astrophil to love and goodness.

What to Look For:

Sidney's *Defense of Posey* was the only piece of literary criticism written during the Elizabethan era. In it, he stresses the importance of fiction and poetry. Posey can be a help, he says, to encourage us to virtue and good deeds. As you read, pay close attention to Sidney's line of argument. How does Sidney use the example of biblical authors to support his point?

From: *The Defense of Posey*

[The Poet, Poetry]

Since the authors of most of our sciences were the Romans, and before them the Greeks, let us a little stand upon their authorities, but even so far as to see what names they have given unto this now scorned skill.

Among the Romans a poet was called vates, which is as much as a diviner, foreseer, or prophet, as by his conjoined words *vaticinium* and *vaticinate* is manifest: so heavenly a title did that excellent people bestow upon this heart-ravishing knowledge. And so far were they carried into the admiration thereof, that they thought in the chanceable hitting upon any such verses great foretokens of their following fortunes were placed. Whereupon grew the word of Sortes Virgilianae, when by sudden opening Virgil's book they lighted upon any verse of his making, whereof the histories of the emperors' lives are full: as of Albinus, the governor of our island, who in his childhood met with this verse, *Arma amens capio nec sat rationis in armis,* and in his age performed it. Which, although it were a very vain and godless superstition, as also it was to think spirits were commanded by such verses whereupon this word charms, derived of carmina, cometh—so yet serveth it to show the great reverence those wits were held in; and altogether not without ground, since both the oracles of Delphos and Sibylla's prophecies were wholly delivered in verses. For that same exquisite observing of number and measure in the words, and that high-flying liberty of conceit proper to the poet, did seem to have some divine force in it.

And may not I presume a little further, to show the reasonableness of this word vates, and say that the holy David's Psalms are a divine poem? If I do, I shall not do it without the testimony of great learned men, both ancient and modern. But even the name of *Psalms* will speak for me, which being interpreted, is nothing but "songs"; then that it is fully written in metre, as all learned hebricians agree, although the rules be not yet fully found; lastly and principally, his handling his prophecy, which is merely poetical: for what else is the awaking his musical instruments, the often and free changing of persons, his notable prosopopoeia, when he maketh you, as it were, see God coming in His majesty, his telling of the beasts' joyfulness and hills leaping, but a heavenly poesy, wherein almost he showeth himself a passionate lover of that unspeakable and everlasting beauty to be seen by the eyes of the mind, only cleared by faith? But truly now having named him, I fear me I seem to profane that holy name, applying it to poetry, which is among us thrown down to so ridiculous an estimation. But they that with quiet judgements will look a little deeper into it, shall find the end and working of it such as, being rightly applied, deserveth not to be scourged out of the Church of God.

But now let us see how the Greeks named it, and how they deemed of it. The Greeks called him a "poet," which name hath, as the most excellent, gone through other languages. It cometh of this word *poiein,* which is, "to make": wherein, I know not whether by luck or wisdom, we Englishmen have met with the Greeks in calling him a maker: which name, how high and incomparable a title it is, I had rather were known by marking the scope of other sciences than by any partial allegation.

There is no art delivered to mankind that hath not the works of nature for his principal object, without which they could not consist, and on which they so depend, as they become actors and players, as it were, of what nature will have set forth. So doth the astronomer look upon the stars, and, by that he seeth, set down what order nature hath taken therein. So doth the geometrician and arithmetician in their diverse sorts of quantities. So doth the musicians in time tell you which by nature agree, which not. The natural philosopher thereon hath his name, and the moral philosopher standeth upon the natural virtues, vices, or passions of man; and follow nature (saith he) therein, and thou shalt not err. The lawyer saith what men have determined; the historian what men have done. The grammarian speaketh only of the rules of speech; and the rhetorician and logician, considering what in nature will soonest prove and persuade, thereon give artificial rules, which still are compassed within the circle of a question according to the proposed matter. The physician weigheth the nature of man's body, and the nature of things helpful or hurtful unto it. And the metaphysic, though it be in the second and abstract notions, and therefore be counted supernatural, yet doth he indeed build upon the depth of nature. Only the poet, disdaining to be tied to any such subjection, lifted up with the vigour of his own invention, doth grow in effect another nature, in making things either better than nature bringeth forth, or, quite anew, forms such as never were in nature, as the Heroes, Demigods, Cyclops, Chimeras, Furies, and such like: so as he goeth hand in hand with nature, not enclosed within the narrow warrant of her gifts, but freely ranging only within the zodiac of his own wit. Nature never set forth the earth in so rich tapestry as divers poets have done; neither with so pleasant rivers, fruitful trees, sweet-smelling flowers, nor whatsoever else may make the too much loved earth more lovely. Her world is brazen, the poets only deliver a golden.

But let those things alone, and go to man—for whom as the other things are, so it seemeth in him her uttermost cunning is employed—and know whether she have brought forth so true a lover as Theagenes, so constant a friend as Pylades, so valiant a man as Orlando, so right a prince as Xenophon's Cyrus, so excellent a man every way as Virgil's Aeneas. Neither let this be jestingly conceived, because the works of the one be essential, the other in imitation or fiction, for any understanding knoweth the skill of each artificer standeth in that idea or fore-conceit of the work, and not in the work itself. And that the poet hath that idea is manifest, by delivering them forth in such excellency as he had imagined them. Which delivering forth also is not wholly imaginative, as we are wont to say by them that build castles in the air; but so far substantially it worketh, not only to make a Cyrus, which had been but a particular excellency as nature might have done, but to bestow a Cyrus upon the world to make many Cyruses, if they will learn aright why and how that maker made him.

Neither let it be deemed too saucy a comparison to balance the highest point of man's wit with the efficacy of nature; but rather give right honour to the heavenly Maker of that maker, who, having made man to His own likeness, set him beyond and over all the works of that second nature: which in nothing he showeth so much as in poetry, when with the force of a divine breath he bringeth things forth surpassing her doings—with no small arguments to the credulous of that first accursed fall of Adam, since our erected wit maketh us know what perfection is, and yet our infected will keepeth us from reaching unto it. But these arguments will by few be understood, and by fewer granted. This much (I hope) will be given me, that the Greeks with some probability of reason gave him the name above all names of learning.

Now let us go to a more ordinary opening of him, that the truth may be the more palpable: and so I hope, though we get not so unmatched a praise as the etymology of his names will grant, yet his very description, which no man will deny, shall not justly be barred from a principal commendation.

Poesy therefore is an art of imitation, for so Aristotle termeth it in the word *mimesis*—that is to say, a representing, counterfeiting, or figuring forth—to speak metaphorically, a speaking picture—with this end, to teach and delight.

Now therein of all sciences (I speak still of human, and according to the human conceit) is our poet the monarch. For he doth not only show the way, but giveth so sweet a prospect into the way, as will entice any man to enter into it. Nay, he doth, as if your journey should lie through a fair vineyard, at the first give you a cluster of grapes, that full of that taste, you may long to pass further. He beginneth not with obscure definitions, which must blur the margin with interpretations, and load the memory with doubtfulness; but he cometh to you with words set in delightful proportion, either accompanied with, or prepared for, the well enchanting skill of music; and with a tale forsooth he cometh unto you, with a tale which holdeth children from play, and old men from the chimney corner. And, pretending no more, doth intend the winning of the mind from wickedness to virtue—even as the child is often brought to take most wholesome things by hiding them in such other as have a pleasant taste, which, if one should begin to tell them the nature of aloes or rhabarbarum they should receive, would sooner take their physic at their ears than at their mouth. So is it in men (most of which are childish in the best things, till they be cradled in their graves): glad will they be to hear the tales of Hercules, Achilles, Cyrus, Aeneas.

By these, therefore, examples and reasons, I think it may be manifest that the poet, with that same hand of delight, doth draw the mind more effectually than any other art doth: and so a conclusion not unfitly ensueth, that, as virtue is the most excellent resting place for all worldly learning to make his end of, so poetry, being the most familiar to teach it, and most princely to move toward it, in the most excellent work is the most excellent workman.

[Answers to Charges against Poetry]

Now then go we to the most important imputations laid to the poor poets. For aught I can yet learn, they are these. First, that there being many other more fruitful knowledges, a man might better spend his time in them than in this. Secondly, that it is the mother of lies. Thirdly, that it is the nurse of abuse, infecting us with many pestilent desires; with a siren's sweetness drawing the mind to the serpent's tail of sinful fancies (and herein, especially, comedies give the largest field to earl as Chaucer saith); how, both in other nations and in ours, before poets did soften us, we were full of courage, given to martial exercises, the pillars of manlike liberty, and not lulled asleep in shady idleness with poets' pastimes. And lastly, and chiefly, they cry out with open mouth as if they had overshot Robin Hood, that Plato banished them out of his commonwealth. Truly, this is much, if there be much truth in it.

First, to the first. That a man might better spend his time, is a reason indeed; but it doth (as they say) but *petere principium*. For if it be as I affirm, that no learning is so good as that which teacheth and moveth to virtue; and that none can both teach and move thereto so much as poetry: then is the conclusion manifest that ink and paper cannot be to a more profitable purpose employed. And certainly, though a man should grant their first assumption, it should follow (methinks) very unwillingly, that good is not good, because better is better. But I still and utterly deny that there is sprung out of earth a more fruitful knowledge.

To the second, therefore, that they should be the principal liars, I will answer paradoxically, but truly, I think truly, that of all writers under the sun the poet is the least liar, and, though he would, as a poet can scarcely be a liar. The astronomer, with his cousin the geometrician, can hardly escape, when they take upon them to measure the height of the stars. How often, think you, do the physicians lie, when they aver things good for sicknesses, which afterwards send Charon a great number of souls drowned in a potion before they come to his ferry? And no less of the rest, which take upon them to affirm. Now, for the poet, he nothing affirms, and therefore never lieth. For, as I take it, to lie is to affirm that to be true which is false. So as the other artists, and especially the historian, affirming many things, can, in the cloudy knowledge of mankind, hardly escape from many lies. But the poet (as I said before) never affirmeth. The poet never maketh any circles about your imagination, to conjure you to believe for true what he writes. He citeth not authorities of other histories, but even for his entry calleth the sweet Muses to inspire into him a good invention; in truth, not labouring to tell you what is or is not, but what should or should not be. And therefore, though he recount things not true, yet because he telleth them not for true, he lieth not—without we will say that Nathan lied in his speech before-alleged to David; which as a wicked man durst scarce say, so think I none so simple would say that Aesop lied in the tales of his beasts; for who thinks that Aesop wrote it for actually true were well worthy to have his name chronicled among the beasts he writeth of. What child is there, that, coming to a play, and seeing Thebes written in great letters upon an old door, doth believe that it is Thebes? If then a man can arrive to that child's age to know that the poets' persons and doings are but pictures what should be, and not stories what have been, they will never give the lie to things not affirmatively but allegorically and figuratively written.

To the third...but what, shall the abuse of a thing make the right use odious? Nay truly, though I yield that poetry may not only be abused, but that being abused, by the reason of his sweet charming force, it can do more hurt than any other army of words, yet shall it be so far from concluding that the abuse should give reproach to the abused, that contrariwise it is a good reason, that whatsoever, being abused, doth most harm, being rightly used (and upon the right use each thing conceiveth his title) doth most good.

Answer *true* or *false* for each of the following statements.

2.52 _____ The Romans hated their poets because they spread all sort of lies.

2.53 _____ Sidney calls David's psalms divine poems.

2.54 _____ The principle object of art is nature.

2.55 _____ The poet corrupts the image of nature, making it seem uglier than it really is.

2.56 _____ Our "erected wit," or renewed mind, helps us to understand what perfection is, yet our "infected will" keeps us from wanting it.

2.57 _____ The purpose of writing posey is to teach and delight.

2.58 _____ Poetry is not wholly imaginative.

2.59 _____ The poet not only shows the way to virtue but also entices people to be virtuous.

2.60 _____ Sidney asserts that poetry is one of the most profitable ways to spend your time because it "teacheth and moveth to virtue."

2.61 _____ Sidney affirms that poets are liars because they mislead people into believing that what they are saying is scientific or historical truth.

2.62 _____ Poets labor to tell us what the world should or should not be, not what is or what is not.

2.63 _____ Poetry, though it can be abused and used in a most powerful way for evil, does the most good when it is rightly used.

> **Edmund Spenser (1552–1599).** C. S. Lewis wrote, "To read Spenser is to grow in mental health." Edmund Spenser's poetry, metrically diverse and joyfully imbued with the goodness of morality, no doubt fulfills Sidney's wishes for the use of *posey*—to teach wisdom with much delight. As a Christian humanist, Spenser stretches the imagination and broadens the heart. His "new poetry" is the delight of the Elizabethan age.

> Like his much-imitated predecessor, Geoffrey Chaucer, Spenser was born to a middle class family living in London. As a boy, he attended Merchant Taylors' School and studied under Richard Mulcaster. Mulcaster was known throughout England for his teaching methods, which included the novel study of English as an important and learned language. In 1569, Spenser entered Pembroke Hall, Cambridge, as a sizar, a poor student who helped pay for his education by working odd jobs on campus. Spenser finished his bachelor's degree in 1573. Three years later, he completed his master's degree.

> After finishing his education at Cambridge, Spenser became the secretary to the bishop of Rochester, Dr. John Young. Dr. Young had been the master of Spenser's college, Pembroke Hall. During his short employment with the bishop (1578–79), Spenser began and finished his work on *The Shepherd's Calendar*. Published in 1579, the *Calendar* revealed Spenser's resistance to abandoning everything medieval. Although he was educated in the progressive environment of the Puritans and the humanists, Spenser did not did go as far as they did in reforming or reviving. In religion, he is considered a moderate Anglican. In regard to literature, he is "more medieval than classical." The *Calendar* demonstrates that Spenser is a radical conservative; he did not want to forsake fully the conventions of the past. As a pastoral eclogue (a formal pastoral poem), the poem is modeled after the classical tradition of Virgil, the much-imitated ancient Roman writer. However, the language of the

poem is archaic, written after the "rustic" dialect of Chaucer, as one critic has noted. Many of Spenser's contemporaries did not appreciate his combination of the classical and the medieval. However, they enjoyed the poem nonetheless for its innovative verse forms. Within the *Calendar* alone Spenser uses thirteen different verse forms.

In 1579 Spenser married Machabyas Childe and was employed as secretary and aide to the earl of Leicester. Often, men of importance would hire a poet of some renown to handle various administrative duties, most importantly letter writing. It was difficult and not socially acceptable for a gentleman to make a living from his publications. While working in the House of Leicester, Spenser met the earl's nephew, Sir Philip Sidney. Impressed with Sidney's person and abilities as a poet, Spenser dedicated the *Calendar* to him. Later in 1580, Lord Grey of Wilton employed Spenser. Lord Grey's duties as Deputy of Ireland took Spenser to Dublin. Under English domination, Ireland was not allowed to govern itself. Needless to say, the presence of Lord Grey and his staff was often protested.

While in Ireland, Spenser lived in Kilcolman Castle in the county of Cork. Its beautiful countryside shaped the setting of *The Faerie Queene,* which Spenser had already started before he moved to Ireland. Not too far from Spenser's residence was the estate of Sir Walter Raleigh. The two men often visited with one another, sharing their works of poetry. In 1589 Raleigh took Spenser back to London to introduce him at court and present the Queen with the first three books of *The Faerie Queene.* Elizabeth was so impressed with Spenser's work that she awarded him £50 per year for the rest of his life. It was a good sum but not the position in England that Spenser desperately wanted.

However, what awaited Spenser in Ireland proved to be more inspiring than a new job. In 1591 he began to court Elizabeth Boyle. She was significantly younger than Spenser. Therefore, he tried all the harder to win her. As an expression of his love, he began to write a sonnet sequence. He gave the "Amoretti" and the "Epithalamion," a marriage song, to Elizabeth as wedding presents in 1594, and they were published a year later. Spenser's second marriage (his first wife had died) brought him much joy in Ireland.

In 1595 Spenser made another trip to London to deliver the manuscript for Books IV–VI of *The Faerie Queene.* A year later, the work was published in a six-volume edition. *The Faerie Queene* demonstrates further that Spenser is a radical conservative. The work is an epic—the epitome of the classical literary tradition—yet it employs the use of archaic language and medieval symbols of chivalry. Spenser does this to heighten the effect of the epic—a celebration of past and present national power. One critic has noted that Spenser used the conventions of the past to justify England's current policies, be they ecclesiastical, political, or otherwise. He did so by using allegory. In *The Faerie Queene,* Queen Elizabeth is portrayed as a glorious, divine monarch in the Arthurian tradition who rules with righteousness and power. Spenser also uses biblical imagery, borrowing heavily from the book of Revelation.

Unfortunately, Spenser's romantic visions of English rule were not a reality. In 1598 a band of Irish rebels, under the earl of Tyrone, destroyed Kilcolman Castle. Spenser's family, suffering the loss of their home and a child, left Ireland. In January of 1599, three months after arriving back in England, Spenser died an impoverished man. He was buried next to Chaucer in what is now known as the Poets Corner of Westminster Abbey. He has been honored with a marble monument with the inscription, "The Prince of Poets in His Tyme."

➤ **Fill in each of the following blanks with the correct answer.**

2.64 Edmund Spenser was born into a _____ class family.

2.65 As a boy, he studied under _____.

2.66 As a poor student, Spenser helped pay for his education at _____ by working odd jobs on campus.

2.67 Spenser earned his _____ from Cambridge in 1576.

2.68 *The Shepheardes Calendar* is a pastoral _____, modeled after the classical tradition of Virgil.

2.69 The language of the *Calendar* is similar to the "rustic" dialect of _____.

2.70 Many of Spenser's contemporaries appreciated his innovative _____ forms in the *Calendar*.

2.71 Spenser dedicated the *Calendar* to _____.

2.72 The setting of *The Faerie Queene* is based on the _____ countryside.

2.73 _____ introduced Spenser at court so that he could present the Queen with the first three books of *The Faerie Queene*.

2.74 The _____ is a sonnet sequence that expresses Spenser's love for Elizabeth Boyle.

2.75 *The Faerie Queene* is an epic that uses _____ language and medieval symbols of _____.

2.76 Spenser's use of allegory in *The Faerie Queene* borrows heavily from the book of _____.

2.77 In *The Faerie Queene*, _____ is figured as a glorious, divine monarch in the Arthurian tradition who rules with righteousness and power.

2.78 Spenser is buried next to _____ in the Poets Corner of _____ Abbey.

What to Look For:

Sir Philip Sidney, in his essay *Defense of Posey,* stated that the poet holds up an image of what the world should or should not be by speaking in allegorical and figurative language. As you read, pay close attention to Spenser's use of allegory. Read Genesis 3, Matthew 21:1–11, Ephesians 6, and Revelation 16:13. As you read, notice the similarities between Spenser's story and these Bible passages. How do the characters illustrate biblical truth?

From: *The Faerie Queene*—Book 1, Canto 1

The various characters in this section are on the side of either good or evil. The Red Cross Knight represents the Christian as he struggles to resist temptation and live a life that is pleasing to his Lord. The lovely lady represents both truth and true religion, as opposed to the Catholic faith. Her white donkey is symbolic of the pure church, which carries truth to the corners of the world. The monster Error is the personification of evil. Like the serpent in the garden, Error strives against God by perverting the truth and ensnaring His children in sin.

Canto 1

The Patron of true Holinesse, Foule Errour doth defeate: Hypocrisie him to entrappe, Doth to his home entreate.

1

    A Gentle Knight was pricking* on the plaine,   *cantering*
        Ycladd in mightie armes and silver shielde,
        Wherein old dints of deepe wounds did remaine,
        The cruell markes of many a bloudy fielde;
5   Yet armes till that time did he never wield:
        His angry steede did chide his foming bitt,
        As much disdayning to the curbe to yield:
        Full jolly knight he seemd and faire* did sitt,   *gallant*
    As one for knightly giusts* and fierce encounters fitt.   *tourneys, jousts*

2

10   But on his brest a bloudie Crosse he bore,
        The deare remembrance of his dying Lord,
        For whose sweete sake that glorious badge he wore,
        And dead as living ever him adored:
        Upon his shield the like was also scored,
15   For sovereign hope, which in his helpe he had:
        [Right faithful] true he was in deede and word,
        But of his cheers did seeme too solemne* sad;   *grave*
    Yet nothing did be dread, but ever was ydrad.*   *dreaded, feared*

3

    Upon a great adventure he was bond,*   *bound*
20   That greatest Gloriana to him gave,
        That greatest Glorious Queene of Faerie Lond,
        To winne him worship,* and her grace to have,   *honor*
        Which of all earthly things he most did crave;
        And ever as he rode, his hart did earne*   *yearn*
25   To prove his puissance* in battell brave   *might*
        Upon his foe, and his new force to learne;
    Upon his foe, a Dragon horrible and stearne.

4

    A lovely Ladie rode him faire beside,
        Upon a lowly Asse more white than snow,
30   Yet she much whiter, but the same did hide
        Under a vele, that wimpled* was full low,   *lying in folds*
        And over all a blacke stole she did throw,
        As one that inly mournd: so was she sad,
        And heavie sat upon her palfrey slow:
35   Seemed in heart some hidden care she had,
    And by her in a line a milke white lambe she lad.

5

    So pure an innocent, as that same lambe,
        She was in life and every vertuous lore,
        And by descent from Royall lynage came

40 Of ancient Kings and Queenes, that had of yore
    Their scepters stretcht from East to Westerne shore,
    And all the world in their subjection held;
    Till that infernall feend with foule uprore
    Forwasted* all their land, and them expeld: *laid waste*
45 Whom to avenge, she had this Knight from far compeld.* *summoned*

6

  Behind her farre away a Dwarfe did lag,
    That lasie seemd in being ever last,
    Or wearied with bearing of her bag
    Of needments at his backe. Thus as they past,
50 The day with cloudes was suddeine overcast,
    And angry Jove an hideous storme of raine
    Did poure into his Lemans' lap so fast,
    That every wight* to shrowd* it did constrain, *creature/cover*
  And this faire couple eke* to shroud themselves were fain.* *also/content*

7

55 Enforst to seeke some covert nigh at hand,
    A shadie grove not far away they spide,
    That promist ayde the tempest to withstand:
    Whose loftie trees yclad with sommers pride,
    Did spred so broad, that heavens light did hide,
60 Not perceable* with power of any starre: *penetrable*
    And all within were pathes and alleies wide,
    With footing worne, and leading inward farre:
  Faire harbour that them seemes; so in they entred arre.

8

  And foorth they passe with pleasure forward led,
65   as toying to heare the birdes sweete harmony,
    Which therein shrouded from the tempest dred,* *fearful*
    Seemd in their song to scone the cruel sky.
    Much can* they prayse the trees, so straight and by, *did*
    The sayling Pine, the Cedar proud and tall,
70 The vine-prop Elme, the Poplar never dry,
    The builder Oake, sole king of forrests all,
  The Aspine good for staves, the Cypresse funerall.

9

  [The Laurel], meed* of mightie Conquerours *reward*
    And Poets sage, the Firre that weepeth still,
75 The Willow worne of forlorne Paramours,
    The Eugh* obedient to the benders will, *yew*
    The Birch for shaftes, the Sallow' for the mill,
    The Mirrhe sweete bleeding in the bitter wound,
    The warlike Beech, the Ash for nothing ill,
80 [The fruitful] Olive and the Platane* round, *plane-tree*
  The carver Holme, the Maple seeldom inward sound.

10

  Led with delight, they thus beguile the way,
    Untill the blustring storme is overblowne;

When weening* to returne whence they did stray,   *supposing*
85 They cannot finde that path, which first was showne,
But wander too and fro in wayes unknowne,
Furthest from end then, when they neerest weene,
That makes them doubt, their wits be not their owne:
So many pathes, so many turnings scene
90 That which of them to take, in diverse doubt they been.

11

At last resolving forward still to fare,
Till that some end they finde or* in or out,   *either*
That path they take, that beaten seemed most bare,
And like to lead the labyrinth about;   *out of*
95 Which when by tract they hunted had throughout,
At length it brought them to a hollow cave,
Amid the thickest woods. The Champion stout
Eftsoones* dismounted from his courser brave,   *forthwith*
And to the Dwarfe a while his needlesse spere he gave.

12

100 "Be well aware," quoth then that Ladie milde,
"Least suddaine* mischiefe ye too rash provoke: *sudden*
The danger hid, the place unknowne and wilde,
Breedes dreadfull doubts: Oft fire is without smoke,
And perill without show: therefore your stroke
toy Sir knight with-hold, till further triall made."
"Ah Ladie," said he, "shame were to revoke
The forward footing for an hidden shade:
Vertue gives her selfe light, through darkenesse for to wade."

13

"Yea but," quoth she, "the perill of this place
110 I better wot than you, though now too late
To wish you backe returne with foule disgrace,
Yet wisedome warnes, whilest foot is in the gate,
To stay the stepe, ere forced to retreat.
This is the wandring wood, this Errours den,
115 A monster vile, whom God and man does hate:
Therefore I read* beware." "Fly fly," quoth then   *advise*
The fearefull Dwarfe: "this is no place for living men."

14

But full of fire and greedy hardiment,*   *boldness*
The youthfull knight could not for ought be staide,*   *stayed*
120 But forth unto the darksome hole he went,
And looked in: his glistring armor made
A litle glooming light, much like a shade,
By which he saw the ugly monster plaine,
Halfe like a serpent horribly displaide,
125 But th' other halfe did woman's shape retaine,
Most lothsom, filthie, foule, and full of vile
  disdaine.*   *loathsomeness*

15

     And as she lay upon the durtie* ground,   *dirty*
        Her huge long taile her den all overspred,
        Yet was in knots and many boughtes* upwound,   *coils*
130   Pointed with mortall sting. Of her there bred
     A thousand yong ones, which she dayly fed,
        Sucking upon her poisonous dugs, each one
        Of sundry shapes, yet all ill favored:
        Soone as that uncouth* light upon them shone,   *unfamiliar*
135 Into her mouth they crept, and suddain all were gone.

16

     Their dam upstart, out of her den effraide,*   *alarmed*
        And rushed forth, hurling her hideous taile
        About her cursed head, whose folds displaid
     Were stretcht now forth at length without entraile.*   *coiling*
140   She lookt about, and seeing one in mayle*   *mail*
        Armed to point, sought backe to turne againe;
        For light she hated as the deadly bale,*   *evil*
        Ay wont in desert darknesse to remain,
     Where plaine none might her see, nor she see any plaine.

17

145 Which when the valiant Elfes perceived, he lept
        As Lyon fierce upon the flying pray,
        And with his trenchand* blade her boldly kept   *cutting*
        From turning backe, and forced her to stay:
     Therewith enraged she loudly gan to bray,
150   I so and turning fierce, her speckled taile advaunst,*   *advanced*
        Threatning her angry sting, him to dismay:
        Who nough* aghast, his mightie hand enhaunst: *now/lifted up*
     The stroke down from her head unto her shoulder glaunst.

18

     Much daunted with that dint,* her sence was dazd,   *blow*
155   Yet kindling rage, her selfe she gathered round,
        And all attonce her beastly body raizd
        With doubled forces high above the ground:
        Tho* wrapping up her wrethed sterne arownd,   *then*
     Lept fierce upon his shield, and her huge traine*   *tail*
160   All suddenly about his body wound,
        That hand or foot to stirre he strove in vaine:
     God helpe the man so wrapt in Errours endlesse traine.

19

     His Lady sad to see his sore constraint,*   *fettered state*
        Cride out, "Now now Sir knight, shew what ye bee,
165   Add faith unto your force, and be not faint:
        Strangle her, else she sure will strangle thee."
        That when he heard, in great perplexitie,
        His gall did grate for griefe* and high disdaine,   *wrath*
     And knitting all his force got one hand free,

20

170 Wherewith he grypt her gorge* with so great paine,	*neck*
That soone to loose her wicked bands did her constraine.	

20

Therewith she spewd out of her filthy maw*   *mouth*
    A floud of poyson horrible and blacke,
    Full of great lumpes of flesh and gobbets raw,
175 Which stunck so vildly, that it forst him slacke
    His grasping hold, and from her turne him backe:
    Her vomit full of bookes and papers was,
    With loathly frogs and toades, which eyes did lacke,
    And creeping sought way in the weedy gras:
180 Her filthy parbreake* all the place defiled has.   *vomit*

21

As when old father Nilus gins to swell
    With timely pride above the Aegyptian vale,
    His fattie* waves do fertile slime outwell,   *rich*
    And overflow each plaine and lowly dale:
185 But when his later spring gins to avale,*   *subside*
    Huge heapes of mudd he leaves, wherein there breed
    Ten thousand kindes of creatures, partly male
    And partly female of his fruitfull seed;
Such ugly monstrous shapes elswhere may no man reed.*   *see*

22

190 The same so sore annoyed has the knight,
    That welnigh* choked with the deadly stinke,   *almost*
    His forces faile, ne can no longer fight.
    Whose corage when the feend perceived to shrinke,
    She poured forth out of her hellish sinke
195 Her fruitfull cursed spawne of serpents small,
    Deformed monsters, fowle, and blacke as inke,
    Which swarming all about his legs did crall,*   *crawl*
And him encombred sore, but could not hurt at all.

23

As gentle Shepheard in sweete even-tide,
200 When ruddy Phoebus gins to welke* in west,   *sink*
    High on an hill, his flocke to vewen wide,
    Markes* which do byte their hasty supper best;   *observes*
    A cloud of combrous* gnattes do him molest,   *encumbering*
    All striving to infixe their feeble stings,
205 That from their noyance he no where can rest,
    But with his clownish* hands their tender wings   *rough*
He brusheth oft, and oft doth mar their murmurings.

24

Thus ill bestedd,* and fearful more of shame,   *situated*
    Then of the certaine perill he stood in,
210 Halfe furious unto his foe he came,
    Resolved in minde all suddenly to win,
    Or soone to lose, before he once would lin;
    And strooke at her with more then manly force,

BRITISH LITERATURE

two

LIFEPAC TEST

83/104

Name _____

Date _____

Score _____

BRITISH LITERATURE LIFEPAC TWO TEST

Fill in each of the blanks using items from the following word list (each answer, 2 points).

                Protestant Reformers   sonnet sequence   Sir Walter Raleigh
                fall   Stratford-on-Avon   Queen Mary
                Geneva   sonnet   William Tyndale
                courtier   Reformation   comedy
                King James Version   wicked   First Folio
                literature   Renaissance
                oval

1. The _____ in England believed that Scripture alone was the guide to faith and life.

2. The _____ was a man-centered movement.

3. The ideals of the Renaissance and the Reformation shaped Elizabethan _____ .

4. During his time, Sir Philip Sidney was considered the near-perfect _____ .

5. Sidney completed the first _____ in English—*Astrophil and Stella*.

6. A _____ seeks primarily to amuse.

7. The _____ was the chief literary device imported from Italy.

8. _____ used Erasmus's Greek New Testament to translate the Bible into English.

9. During the reign of _____ , nearly three hundred Protestants were burned at the stake for their faith.

10. In her rendering of Psalm 58, the Countess of Pembroke compares the _____ to snakes.

11. _____ was a soldier and a seaman as well as a philosopher, a historian and a poet.

12. During Elizabethan times, the public theaters were _____ shaped with several tiers of seating.

13. William Shakespeare was born in _____ .

14. The tragedies *Hamlet*, *Macbeth*, *King Lear*, and *Othello* dramatize the _____ of man.

15. *The Complete Edition of Shakespeare's Works,* also known as the _____ , was first published in 1623.

16. The English _____ was a revolution of heart and mind based on the teachings of a single book, the Bible.

17. First published in 1560, The _____ Bible was the first translation to include marginal notes and divide the passages by numbered verses.

18. The editors of the _____ avoided the most literal or direct translation, inserting words or phrases that would be most clearly understood by all of the people.

Answer *true* or *false* for each of the following statements (each answer, 2 points).

19. _____ The Utopians of Sir Thomas More's book did not value gold and silver highly.

20. _____ Before being burned at the stake, Thomas Cranmer announced his love for the Roman Catholic faith.

21. _____ In *The Schoolmaster*, Roger Ascham recommends praise as the best thing to "sharpen a good wit" and "encourage a will to learning."

22. _____ According to Ascham, the fastest way to encourage the mind to believe in right doctrine is first to entice the will to immoral living.

23. _____ Before he was burned at the stake, John Foxe turned to Nicholas Ridley and said, "Be of good cheer, Ridley, and play the man. We shall this day, by God's grace, light up such a candle in England, as I trust, will never be put out."

24. _____ The "murdering boy" in Sonnet 20 of Sidney's sonnet sequence *Astrophil and Stella* is William Shakespeare.

25. _____ In *Defense of Posey*, Sidney asserts that the purpose of writing fiction and poetry is to entice people to idleness and immoral living.

26. _____ In *The Faerie Queene*, the lovely lady is representative of error and false religion.

27. _____ The lovely lady instructs the knight to add determination to his force so that he might be able to escape the power of Error.

28. _____ In the last stanza of Sir Walter Raleigh's "The Nymph's Answer to the Shepherd," the speaker has been moved by the beauties of nature to become the shepherd's love.

29. _____ In his *History of the World,* Raleigh comments that man has divine understanding so that he may serve God.

30. _____ Raleigh stated in his *History of the World* that man has the intellect of angels and the sensual nature of animals.

31. _____ *The Taming of the Shrew* is a comedy that is a play within a play.

32. _____ In *The Taming of the Shrew*, Petruccio is dressed up in his lord's clothes and told that he has been insane for many years.

33. _____ Baptista will not allow Bianca to be courted until Katherine is married.

34. _____ Katherine and Petruccio never fight over the meanings of various words.

35. _____ Petruccio says that taming Kate is like training a dog.

36. _____ At the end of the play, Bianca tells the other women that a husband is the "head" of the wife and the "one that cares for" her.

Underline the correct answer in each of the following statements (each answer, 2 points).

37. John Foxe wrote (*Utopia*, *Acts and Monuments*, *The Faerie Queene*) as a historical testament to the fact that evangelicalism has been persecuted throughout the centuries because it embodies the true biblical faith.

38. Sir Thomas More's masterpiece (*Acts and Monuments*, *The Taming of the Shrew*, *Utopia*) is a fantastical vision of a new world free of societal ills.

39. Roger Ascham believed that the study of certain Latin and Greek classics in subjection to the authority of (Scripture, the church, the state) was a means to "truth in religion, honesty of living, and right order in (worship, learning, exercise)."

40. Sir Thomas Wyatt introduced the Italian sonnet into (Poland, Holland, England).

41. The (conceit, sonnet, octave) is an elaborate comparison made by the poet within the sonnet.

42. *The Faerie Queene* is an epic that uses (elaborate, classical, archaic) language and medieval symbols of (chivalry, astrology, magic).

43. (Sir Philip Sidney, The Countess of Pembroke, Sir Walter Raleigh) was known the "divine poet."

44. The Countess edited and completed works by her brother, (Sir Walter Raleigh, Edmund Spenser, Sir Philip Sidney).

45. According to line 5 of Shakespeare's Sonnet 116, true love is "(a temporary, an ever-fixed, an altering) mark."

46. Despite her "imperfections," the poet thinks that his mistress is "(common, rare, ugly)."

47. In the selected readings from Isaiah, the last sentence of the King James text matches the last two sentences of the (Latin Vulgate, Geneva, Douay-Rheims) Bible.

48. The (Italian, English, French) rhyme scheme became the most popular sonnet form of the Elizabethan period.

49. (Sir Walter Raleigh, Sir Philip Sidney, Henry Howard) structured the sonnet into three quatrains and a couplet—abab cdcd efef gg.

50. The (English, Italian, French) sonnet contains fourteen lines, which are arranged into an octave and a sestet.

Thinking and Writing:

Choose one of the following "Thought and Discussion" topics. Write your answer on a separate piece of paper.

1. Explain Sir Thomas More's book *Utopia*. Be sure to point out it that Utopia is an idealistic world based upon human reason and where gold is scorned and crime is nonexistent. In light of 1 Corinthian 2:6-15, discuss the possibility of a perfect world based upon human wisdom. Relate your answer to the history of the Union of Soviet Socialist Republics.

2. Explain the section you read from *The Faerie Queene*. Be sure to describe the Red Cross Knight, the "lovely lady," and the monster Error along with the various things they symbolize. Discuss the similarities between Spenser's story and the Christian's struggle to resist error and sin. How important is faith to this battle?

3. Explain briefly William Shakespeare's play *The Taming of the Shrew*. Be sure to describe the relationship between Petruccio and Katherine. In light of Ephesians 5:22-33, discuss who Petruccio and Katherine resemble? Give examples of the way in which Petruccio "sanctifies and cleanses" Katherine?

	That from her body full of filthie sin	
215	He raft* her hatefull head without remorse;	*cut off*
	A streame of cole black blood forth gushed from her corse.*	*corpse*

25

	Her scattred brood, soone as their Parent deare	
	They saw so rudely* falling to the ground,	*with great force*
	Groning full deadly, all with troublous feare,	
220	Gathred themselves about her body round,	
	Weening* their wonted entrance to have found	*thinking*
	At her wide mouth: but being there withstood	
	They flocked all about her bleeding wound,	
	And sucked up their dying mothers blood,	
225	Making her death their life, and eke* her hurt their good.	*also*

26

	That detestable sight him much amazde,*	*amazed*
	To see th' unkindly Impes of heaven accurst,	
	Devoure their dam; on whom while so he gazd,	
	Having all satisfide their bloudy thurst,	
230	Their bellies swolne he saw with fulnesse burst,	
	And bowels gushing forth: well worthy end	
	Of such as drunke her life, the which them nurst;	
	Now needeth him no lenger labour spend,	
	His foes have slaine themselves, with whom he should contend.	

27

	His Ladie seeing all, that chaunst,* from farre	*chance*
235	Approcht in hast to greet* his victorie,	*congratulate*
	And said, "Faire knight, borne under happy starre,	
	Who see your vanquisht foes before you lye;	
	Well worthy be you of that Armoric,	
240	Wherein ye have great glory wonne this day,	
	And prooved your strength on a strong enimie,	
	Your first adventure: many such I pray,	
	And henceforth ever wish, that like succeed it may."	

Answer *true* or *false* for each of the following statements.

2.79 _____ The Red Cross Knight represents the unbeliever.

2.80 _____ According to the second stanza, the knight's help is the sovereign grace of God.

2.81 _____ The lovely lady represents truth and true religion.

2.82 _____ The white donkey is symbolic of the English throne.

2.83 _____ Error is a white lamb.

2.84 _____ On the breastplate and the shield of the knight is a red cross.

2.85 _____ According to the third stanza, the earthly things that the knight craved the most were the honor and favor of the queen of Fairyland.

2.86 _____ An old man with a dark cloak rode beside the knight on a black horse.

2.87 _____ The lovely lady was as pure and innocent as the "milk white lamb."

2.88 _____ The three travelers were forced to seek shelter because of a bad storm.

2.89 _____ According to stanza 10, fear drove the travelers farther into the woods.

2.90 _____ While in the woods, the travelers lose their way.

2.91 _____ The knight warns the lovely lady to beware while in the Wandering Wood.

2.92 _____ The monster Error is half serpent and half woman.

2.93 _____ Upon the knight's entrance into the cave, a thousand of Error's children crawl back into her mouth.

2.94 _____ The sting of Error's tail can inflict a mortal wound.

2.95 _____ According to lines 142–144, Error hates light because it reveals who she is.

2.96 _____ Error wraps herself around the dwarf.

2.97 _____ The lovely lady instructs the knight to add faith to his force so that he might be able to escape the power of Error.

2.98 _____ The vomit of Error is full of books and papers.

2.99 _____ The lovely lady kills Error by cutting off the monster's head.

2.100 _____ After Error is dead, her children run from the cave and attack the dwarf.

2.101 _____ In the last stanza, the lovely lady hints that more such trials are in the future.

Mary (Sidney) Herbert, Countess of Pembroke (1562–1621). During the Elizabethan era, many aristocratic women helped spread the ideals of the Renaissance and the Reformation with the use of their own money and talents. Chief among these was Mary Herbert, Countess of Pembroke. She translated many religious works into English and completed and expanded the work of her brother, Sir Philip Sidney.

As a patron of the arts, the Countess of Pembroke supported a large group of poets and musicians in her household. Sir Philip Sidney, her brother, was one of the first people to stay and work at Wilton House. During his intermittent visits with the Countess, he began to write the "Arcadia." He intended his "idle work" for her eyes only. But the Countess could not keep the pleasure to herself. After Sidney's death in 1586, she began to edit the work, seeing it through to publication in 1593.

Like many of her male peers, she trained herself by "imitation and exercise in the arts of poetry." She developed from the writing of prose to poetry. In addition to her work on the "Arcadia," the Countess also finished Sidney's versification of the Psalms. Sidney had completed only forty-two psalms, leaving the Countess with 107 psalms to translate. Her poetical renderings display a variety of verse forms and meter. For her work on the Psalms, she has been called the "divine poet."

As a woman author, and not strictly a translator, the Countess made advances into a field that had before been reserved for men. Her poetry idealizes virtue and seeks perfect lyric articulation, noted one critic. As a poet of great religious zeal, we find in the Countess a writer who desired the rebirth of both religion and the arts. She, like other Christian humanists, combined the ideals of the Renaissance and the Reformation.

Fill in each of the following blanks with the correct answer.

2.102 As a patron of the arts, Mary Herbert, Countess of Pembroke, supported a large group of _____ and _____ in her household.

2.103 Her brother, _____ , began to write the "Arcadia" while he stayed at Wilton House.

2.104　After Sidney's death, the Countess edited the _____ and saw it through to publication.

2.105　The Countess was known as the "_____ poet" for her translation of the Psalms into verse.

2.106　Her poetical renderings of the Psalms display a variety of _____ forms and _____ .

2.107　As a woman _____ , and not strictly a translator, the Countess made advances into a field that before had been reserved for _____ .

2.108　As a poet of great religious zeal, the Countess was a writer who desired the rebirth of both _____ and the _____ .

What to Look For:

The poetical work of Mary Herbert, the Countess of Pembroke, is a combination of the ideals of the Renaissance and the Reformation. It demonstrates a rebirth of both the arts and religion. Her poetical renderings of the Psalms were important because they do two things, as John Donne noted: "They tell us *why*, and teach us *how* to sing." As you read, think about Donne's statement. *Why* and *how* are we being taught to sing? Does her work show a relationship between poetic beauty and truth? Compare the Countess's rendering with the corresponding biblical text.

Psalm 52

1　Tyrant, why swell'st thou thus,
2　Of mischief vaunting?
3　Since help from God to us
4　Is never wanting.

5　Lewd lies the tongue contrives
6　Loud lies it soundeth;
7　Sharper than sharpest knives
8　With lies it woundeth.

9　Falsehood thy wit approves,
10　All truth rejected:
11　Thy will all vices loves,
12　Virtue neglected.

13　Not words from cursed thee,
14　But gulfs are poured;
15　Gulfs wherein daily be
16　Good men devoured.

17　Thinks't thou to bear it so?
18　God shall displace thee;
19　God shall thee overthrow,
20　Crush thee, deface thee.

21　The just shall fearing see
22　These fearful chances,
23　And laughing shoot at thee
24　With scornful glances.

25	Lo, lo, the wretched wight,
26	Who, God disdaining,
27	His mischief made his might,
28	His guard his gaining.
29	I as an olive tree
30	Still green shall flourish:
31	God's house the soil shall be
32	My roots to nourish.
33	My trust on his true love
34	Truly attending,
35	Shall never thence remove,
36	Never see ending.
37	Thee will I honour still,
38	Lord, for this justice;
39	There fix my hopes I will
40	Where they saint's trust is.
41	Thy saints trust in thy name,
42	Therein they joy them:
43	Protected by the same,
44	Naught can annoy them.

Underline the correct answer in each of the following statements.

2.109 The Countess renders the enduring goodness of God in verse 1 as "Since help from God to us is never (wanting, there, lacking)."

2.110 Verses 3 is rendered, "(Truthfulness, Falsehood) thy wit approves, All truth (accepted, rejected): Thy will all vices (loves, hates), Virtue neglected."

2.111 According to line 27, the wicked made his might in his "(faith, lies, mischief)."

2.112 The psalmist describes himself as an (apple, olive, orange) tree.

2.113 According to lines 40–41, the saints are protected by the same name in which they "(believe, trust, hope)."

Psalm 58

AND call ye this to utter what is just,
    You that of justice hold the sovereign throne?
And call ye this to yield, O sons of dust,
    To wronged brethren every man his own?
O no: it is your long malicious will   5
    Now to the world to make by practice known,
With whose oppression you the balance fill,
    Just to yourselves, indifferent else to none.

But what could they, who even in birth declined,
    From truth and right to lies and injuries?   10
To show the venom of their cancered mind
    The adder's* image scarcely can suffice;   *snake's*
Nay scarce the aspic* may with them contend,   *a small poisonous snake*
    On whom the charmer all in vain applies
His skilful'st spells: ay missing of his end,   15
While she self-deaf and unaffected lies.

> Lord, crack their teeth; Lord, crush these lions' jaws,
> > So let them sink as water in the sand.
> When deadly bow their aiming fury draws,
> > Shiver the shaft ere past the shooter's hand.   20
> So make them melt as the dis-housed snail
> > Or as the embryo, whose vital band
> Breaks ere it holds, and formless eyes do fail
> > To see the sun, though brought to lightful land.
>
> O let their brood, a brood of springing thorns,   25
> > Be by untimely rooting overthrown,
> Ere bushes waxed they push with pricking horns,
> > As fruits yet green are oft by tempest blown.
> The good with gladness this revenge shall see,
> > And bathe his feet in blood of wicked one;   30
> While all shall say: the just rewarded be;
> > There is a God that carves to each his own.

Underline the correct answer in each of the following statements.

2.114   The Countess translates the phrase "sons of men" as "sons of (God, dust, earth)."

2.115   From birth the wicked have gone from "(truth, lies) and right to (truth, lies) and injuries."

2.116   In lines 11–16, the image of the (donkey, rabbit, snake) is used to describe the wicked.

2.117   In line 21, God is asked to make the wicked "(melt, die, grow)" as a snail without his shell.

2.118   The righteous shall wash their (hands, feet, face) in the blood of the wicked.

2.119   God (judges, saves, loves) men by carving to "each his own."

Review the material in this section in preparation for the Self Test, which will check both your mastery of this particular section and your knowledge of the previous section.

SELF TEST 2

Fill in each of the blanks using items from the following word list (each answer, 2 points).

Amoretti	Petrarchian	*Utopia*
England	Queen Elizabeth	"Arcadia"
archaic	three	fourteen
Cambridge	historical	sestet
Sir Philip Sidney	question	Chaucer
chivalry	Sir Walter Raleigh	divine
conceit	octave	English
rhyme scheme	Scripture	pastoral

2.01. Sir Thomas More's masterpiece, _____, is a fantastical vision of a New World free of societal ills.

2.02 Roger Ascham believed that the study of certain Latin and Greek classics in subjection to the authority of _____ was a means to "truth in religion, honesty of living, and right order in learning."

2.03 John Foxe wrote *Acts and Monuments* as a _____ testament to the fact that evangelicalism has been persecuted throughout the centuries because it embodies the true biblical faith.

2.04 Sir Thomas Wyatt was a trust courtier of _____.

2.05 Wyatt introduced the Italian sonnet into _____.

2.06 A _____ is an elaborate comparison made by the poet within the sonnet.

2.07 The _____, or Italian, sonnet contains _____ lines, which are arranged into an _____ and a sestet.

2.08 The Italian sonnet follows a rhetorical format in which the _____ or proposition stated in the octave is then answered or solved in the _____.

2.09 Wyatt altered the Italian sonnet by altering the _____ of the sestet.

2.010 Henry Howard, the Earl of Surrey, structured the sonnet into _____ quatrains and a couplet—*abab cdcd efef gg*.

2.011 The _____ rhyme scheme became the most popular sonnet form of the Elizabethan period.

2.012 As a poor student, Spenser helped pay for his education at _____ by working odd jobs on campus.

2.013 *The Shepheardes Calendar* is a _____ eclogue modeled after the classical tradition of Virgil.

2.014 The language of the *Calendar* is similar to the "rustic" dialect of _____.

2.015 _____ introduced Spenser at court so that he could present the Queen with the first three books of *The Faerie Queene*.

2.016 The _____ is a sonnet sequence that expresses Spenser's love for Elizabeth Boyle.

2.017 *The Faerie Queene* is an epic that uses _____ language and medieval symbols of _____.

2.018 The Countess of Pembroke edited and completed works by her brother, _____.

2.019 The Countess was known as the "_____ poet."

Answer *true* **or** *false* **for each of the following statements** (each answer, 1 point).

2.020 _____ The Utopians in Sir Thomas More's book valued gold and silver highly.

2.021 _____ According to Roger Ascham, the fastest way to entangle the mind with false doctrine is first to entice the will to immoral living.

2.022 _____ Before being burned at the stake, Cranmer denounced his recantation as a lie and called the pope Christ's enemy.

2.023 _____ Sir Thomas Wyatt's poem "My Galley" is a translation of one of Petrarch's sonnets.

2.024 _____ In the poem "My Galley," the speaker compares himself to a galley, or a ship.

2.025 _____ The speaker in "My Galley" is content and happy with his condition.

2.026 _____ The rhyme scheme of "Love, That Doth Reign and Live Within My Thought" is similar to an Italian sonnet.

2.027 _____ Each quatrain of "Love, That Doth Reign and Live Within My Thought" contains a vague and meaningless thought.

2.028 _____ In "Love, That Doth Reign and Live Within My Thought," the first quatrain contains a resolution of the lover's problems.

2.029 _____ According to Sonnet 1 of Sidney's sonnet sequence *Astrophil and Stella*, Astrophil is hopeful to win Stella through writing poetry.

2.030 _____ The "murdering boy" in Sonnet 20 of *Astrophil and Stella* is Cupid.

2.031 _____ The "rich" in Sonnet 37 of Sidney's sonnet sequence is a pun on Lord Robert Rich, Penelope Devereaux's brother.

2.032 _____ According to Sonnet 71 of *Astrophil and Stella*, one might learn what hatred and ugliness are by looking at Stella.

2.033 _____ In *Defense of Posey*, Sidney calls David's psalms divine poems.

2.034 _____ The purpose of writing posey is to teach and delight.

2.035 _____ Sidney asserts that poetry is one of the most profitable ways to spend your time because it "teacheth and moveth to virtue."

2.036 _____ In *The Faerie Queene*, the Red Cross Knight represents the unbeliever.

2.037 _____ The lovely lady in *The Faerie Queene* represents truth and true religion.

2.038 _____ While in the woods, the travelers lose their way.

2.039 _____ The monster Error is half serpent and half woman.

2.040 _____ Upon the knight's entrance into the cave, a thousand of Error's children crawl back into her mouth.

2.041 _____ Error wraps herself around the dwarf.

2.042 _____ The lovely lady instructs the knight to add faith to his force so that he might be able to escape the power of Error.

2.043 _____ The vomit of Error is full of books and papers.

2.044 _____ The lovely lady kills Error by cutting off the monster's head.

Underline the correct answer in each of the following statements (each answer, 3 points).

2.045   The (Renaissance, Reformation, Middle Ages) was a man-centered movement.

2.046   The Protestant Reformers in England believed that (the church, Scripture, the king) alone was the guide to faith and life.

2.047   The (pastoral, sonnet, short story) was the chief literary device imported from Italy.

2.048   The ideals of the Renaissance and the Reformation shaped (Elizabethan, Classical, Modern) literature.

2.049   Sir Philip Sidney was dismissed from court because he openly opposed the alliance that would be formed with a (Protestant, Catholic, Irish) nation if Queen Elizabeth married the Duke of Anjou.

2.050   The "Arcadia" is a (pastoral romance, short story, science fiction novel).

2.051   Sidney completed the first (epic, play, sonnet sequence) in English—*Astrophil and Stella*.

2.052   ("Arcadia," *Astrophil and Stella*, *The Defense of Posey*) argues for the necessity and goodness of such literary forms as fiction and poetry.

2.053   During his time, Sidney was considered the near-perfect (writer, courtier, soldier).

2.054   In her poetic version of Psalm 52, the Countess of Pembroke renders the enduring goodness of God as "Since help from God to us in never (wanting, there, lacking)."

2.055   According to line 32 of the Countess's rendering of Psalm 52, the wicked made his might in his "(faith, lies, mischief)."

2.056   In lines 11–16 of Psalm 58, the image of the (donkey, rabbit, snake) is used to describe the wicked.

For Thought and Discussion:

Explain to a Parent/Teacher the section you read from *The Faerie Queene*. Be sure to describe the Red Cross Knight, the "lovely lady," and the monster Error along with the various things that they symbolize. Read Genesis 3, Matthew 21:1–11, Ephesians 6, and Revelation 16:13. Discuss the similarities between Spenser's story and these Bible passages. How do the characters illustrate biblical truth?

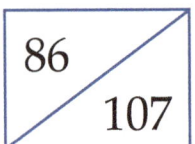

Score _____

Adult Check _____
             Initial   Date

III. RENAISSANCE PROSE AND DRAMA

Sir Walter Raleigh (1554–1618). A prominent figure in the court of Queen Elizabeth I, Sir Walter Raleigh was not only a gallant seaman and explorer but also a philosopher, historian, and poet. Born in Devonshire and educated at Oriel College, Oxford, Raleigh took the path to power and fame as a soldier. During the French religious wars, he fought on the side of the Huguenots (French Calvinists). He later returned to London to study law. In 1578 Raleigh accompanied his half brother Sir Humphrey Gilbert on a voyage to the Americas. It was the first of many colonization and explorations trips that Raleigh made. For his attempt to establish a colony on Roanoke Island in 1585, he was credited with the founding of Virginia.

As a dashing courtier, Raleigh quickly became one of Elizabeth's most trusted advisors, making him one of the most powerful men in England. Raleigh first approached the Queen in 1580 as an expert in Irish affairs. He had served as a soldier in that country and was familiar with their tactics of war. However, he was no expert. Nonetheless, the Queen liked him and made him a knight. In 1587 he was appointed Captain of the Queen's guard, which afforded close, daily contact with Elizabeth. She looked to him for advice in many matters. But in 1592, Raleigh's indiscreet behavior and a secret marriage to the Queen's maid of honor, Elizabeth Throckmorton, put him out of favor with the Queen. Consequently, Raleigh was imprisoned.

Elizabeth would not be the first monarch to treat Raleigh so harshly. Elizabeth's successor, James I, did not like Raleigh's associations with the Puritans. The Puritans' staunch religious views were offensive to the king and his diplomatic policies. James wished to establish peaceful relations with the Catholic Spanish. But Raleigh, as a Protestant, had fought bitterly against Spain and disliked James's diplomatic policy. In 1603 James had Raleigh imprisoned in the Tower of London on charges of treason. Although the evidence was not convincing, Raleigh was condemned to die. However, by either an act of grace or guilt, James relented and granted Raleigh a life sentence. Raleigh and his family remained in the Tower for thirteen years, during which time Raleigh busied himself with the completion of the first volume of the *History of the World* (1641). He also wrote poems and studied scientific theories.

The death of his friend, Prince Henry, in 1612 dashed Raleigh's hopes of regaining favor with the crown. Desperate and frustrated, he made a proposal to King James that would bring England wealth and him freedom. James agreed to allow Raleigh to return to Guiana (Venezuela) to search for gold on one condition: Raleigh could not offend the Spanish. While seeking out the lost city of gold, El Dorado, Raleigh's son and an aide attacked a Spanish colony. Raleigh's son, Walter, was killed, and Raleigh's own death was determined. Upon his return to London, King James reinvoked Raleigh's death sentence and had him beheaded on October 29, 1618.

Underline the correct answer in each of the following statements.

3.1 Sir Walter Raleigh was educated at Oriel College, (Oxford, Cambridge, Manchester).

3.2 Raleigh was not only a soldier and a seaman but also a philosopher, a historian, and a (prince, merchant, poet).

3.3 Raleigh fought in the French religious wars on the side of the (French government, Huguenots, Catholics).

3.4 Raleigh is credited with the founding of (Massachusetts, Virginia, Florida).

3.5 In 1587 Raleigh was appointed Captain of the (Queen's guard, Queen's fleet, King's Navy).

3.6 Raleigh was (King James's, Queen Mary's, Queen Elizabeth's) most trusted advisors.

3.7 (King James, Queen Mary, Queen Elizabeth) imprisoned Raleigh on charges of treason.

3.8 While he was in (America, Guiana, prison), Raleigh wrote the first volume of the *History of the World*.

3.9 King James allowed Raleigh to return to Guiana to search for (coal, gold, his son).

3.10 Upon returning to London from Guiana, Raleigh was (beheaded, rewarded, knighted).

What to Look For:

As a philosopher and an amateur scientist, Sir Walter Raleigh could not appreciate emotions based on non-reason. His philosophical papers and his poetry were the products of logical thinking. Truth was important to Raleigh in all spheres of life. As you read, notice Raleigh's line of thought. On what is it based? Emotions? Facts? Experience? History? Biblical revelation?

Around 1599, Christopher Marlowe, the great poet and playwright, wrote "The Passionate Shepherd to His Love." It is a pastoral poem that exalts nature. Moved by the beautiful countryside, the shepherd asks his beloved to base her love for him on nature's "pleasures." He says to his beloved, "If these delights thy mind may move, Then live with me and be my love."

Sometime after the publication of Marlowe's poem, Raleigh penned an antiromantic reply. In his poem, Raleigh is painfully realistic. He turns the bidding of Marlowe's shepherd inside out by explaining that love based on the pleasures of nature is fleeting. It is no more than a romantic feeling that will come and go with the changing of the seasons. It is not just a criticism of Marlowe's work; it is a letter of revulsion to those who base their decisions on emotion rather than logic.

Answer to Marlowe, or The Nymph's Reply to the Shepherd

If all the world and love were young,
And truth in every shepherd's tongue,
These pretty pleasures might me move
To live with thee and be thy love.

Time drives the flocks from field to fold   5
When rivers rage and rocks grow cold,
And Philomel* becometh dumb;   *the nightingale
The rest complains of cares to come.

The flowers do fade, and wanton fields
To wayward winter reckoning yields;   10
A honey tongue, a heart of gall,
Is fancy's spring, but sorrow's fall.

Thy gowns, thy shoes, thy beds of roses,
Thy cap, thy kirtle,* and thy posies   *dress
Soon break, soon wither, soon forgotten—   15
In folly ripe, in reason rotten.

Thy belt of straw and ivy buds,
Thy coral clasps and amber studs,
All these in me no means can move
To come to thee and by thy love.   20

But could youth last and love still breed,
Had joys no date* nor age no need,   *no end*
Then these delights my mind might move
To live with thee and be thy love.

Answer *true* or *false* for each of the following statements.

3.11 _____ Christopher Marlowe's poem is a pastoral poem that exalts the beauties of nature.

3.12 _____ In Sir Walter Raleigh's response to Marlowe, the shepherd bids his beloved to be his love based on the pleasures of nature.

3.13 _____ In lines 1-4, the speaker says that if every shepherd spoke the truth then she might be moved to be his love.

3.14 _____ In the poem, nature is described an exalted manner.

3.15 _____ In the fourth stanza, the poet says that the flowers and tokens of romance are soon forgotten.

3.16 _____ Romantic tokens and nature's fleeting beauty cannot persuade the speaker to be the shepherd's love.

3.17 _____ According to the last stanza, if the joys of romance never ended then the speaker might be moved to be the shepherd's love.

From: *The History of the World*
That Man Is, As It Were, A Little World: With A Digression Touching Our Mortality

Man, thus compounded and formed by God, was an abstract or model, or brief story of the universal, in whom God concluded the creation and work of the world, and whom he made the last and most excellent of his creatures, being internally endued with a divine understanding, by which lie might contemplate and serve his Creator, after whose image he was formed, and endued with the powers and faculties of reason and other abilities, that thereby also he might govern and rule the world, and all other God's creatures therein. And whereas God created three sorts of living natures, to wit, angelical, rational, and brutal; giving to angels an intellectual, and to beasts a sensual nature, he vouchsafed unto man both the intellectual of angels, the sensitive of beasts, and the proper rational belonging unto man, and therefore, saith Gregory Nazianzen, *Homo est utriusque naturae vinculum:* "Man is the bond and chain which tieth together both natures." And because in the little frame of man's body there is a representation of the universal, and (by allusion) a kind of participation of all the parts thereof, therefore was man called microcosmos, or the little world. *Deus igitur hominem factum, velut alterum quendam mundum, in brevi magnum, atque exiguo totum, in terris statuit:* "God therefore placed in the earth the man whom he had made, as it were another world, the great and large world in the small and little world." For out of earth and dust was formed the flesh of man, and therefore heavy and lumpish; the bones of his body we may compare to the hard rocks and stones, and therefore strong and durable, of which Ovid:

> *Inde genus durum sumus, experiensque laborum,*
> *Et documenta damus qua simus origine nati.*

> From thence our kind hard-hearted is,
>   Enduring pain and care,
> Approving, that our bodies of
>   A stony nature are.

His blood, which disperseth itself by the branches of veins through all the body, may be resembled to those waters which are carried by brooks and rivers over all the earth; his breath to the air; his natural heat to the enclosed warmth which the earth hath in itself—which, stirred up by the heat of the sun, assisteth nature in the speedier procreation of those varieties which the earth bringeth forth; our radical moisture, oil, or balsamum (whereon the natural heat feedeth and is maintained) is resembled to the fat and fertility of the earth; the hairs of man's body, which adorns, or overshadows it, to the grass, which covereth the upper face and skin of the earth; our generative power, to nature, which produceth all things; our determinations, to the light, wandering, and unstable clouds, carried every where with uncertain winds; our eyes, to the light of the sun and moon; and the beauty of our youth, to the flowers of the spring, which either in a very short time, or with the sun's heat, dry up and wither away, or the fierce puffs of wind blow them from the stalks; the thoughts of our mind, to the motion of angels; and our pure understanding (formerly called mens, and that which always looketh upwards) to those intellectual natures which are always present with God; and, lastly, our immortal souls (while they are righteous); are by God himself beautified with the title of his own image and similitude. And although, in respect of God, there is no man just, or good, or righteous (for, *in angelis deprehensa est stultitia,* "Behold, he found folly in his angels," saith Job) yet, with such a kind of difference as there is between the substance and the shadow, there may be found a goodness in man: which God being pleased to accept, hath therefore called man the image and similitude of his own righteousness. In this also is the little world of man compared, and made more like the universal (man being the measure of all things—*Homo est mensura omnium rerum,* saith Aristotle and Pythagoras) that the four complexions resemble the four elements, and the seven ages of man the seven planets; whereof our infancy is compared to the moon, in which we seem only to live and grow, as plants; the second age to Mercury, wherein we are taught and instructed; our third age to Venus, the days of love, desire, and vanity; the fourth to the sun, the strong, flourishing, and beautiful age of man's life; the fifth to Mars, in which we seek honor and victory, and in which our thoughts travel to ambitious ends; the sixth age is ascribed to Jupiter, in which we begin to take account of our times, judge of ourselves, and grow to the perfection of our understanding; the last and seventh to Saturn, wherein our days are sad, and overcast, and in which we find by dear and lamentable experience, and by the loss which can never be repaired, that of all our vain passions and affections past, the sorrow only abideth: our attendants are sicknesses, and variable infirmities; and by how much the more we are accompanied with plenty, by so much the more greedily is our end desired, whom when time hath made unsociable to others, we become a burden to ourselves: being of no other use, than to hold the riches we have from our successors. In this time it is, when (as aforesaid) we, for the most part, and never before, prepare for our eternal habitation, which we pass on unto with many sighs, groans, and sad thoughts, and in the end, by the workmanship of death, finish the sorrowful business of a wretched life; towards which we always travel both sleeping and waking; neither have those beloved companions of honor and riches any power at all to hold us any one day by the glorious promise of entertainments; but by what crooked path soever we walk, the same leadeth on directly to the house of death, whose doors lie open at all hours, and to all persons. For this tide of man's life, after it once turneth and declineth, ever runneth with a perpetual ebb and falling stream, but never floweth again: our leaf once fallen, springeth no more; neither doth the sun or the summer adorn us again, with the garments of new leaves and flowers.

Redditur arboribus florens revirentibus actas;
Ergo non homini, quod fuit ante, redit.

To which I give this sense.

The plants and trees made poor and old

> By winter envious,
> The spring-time bounteous
> Covers again from shame and cold:
> But never man repaired again
> His youth and beauty lost,
> Though art, and care, and cost,
> Do promise nature's help in vain.

And of which Cattillus, Epigram 53.

> *Soles occidere et redire possunt:*
> *Nobis cum semel occidit brevis lax,*
> *Nox est perpetua Una dormienda.*

> The sun may set and rise:
> But we contrarywise
> Sleep after our short light
> One everlasting night.

For if there were any baiting place, or rest, in the course or race of man's life, then, according to the doctrine of the Academics, the same might also perpetually be maintained. But as there is a continuance of motion in natural living things, and as the sap and juice, wherein the life of plants is preserved, doth evermore ascend or descend; so is it with the life of man, which is always either increasing towards ripeness and perfection, or declining and decreasing towards rottenness and dissolution.

Answer *true* or *false* for each of the following statements.

3.18 _____ Man is the last and most excellent of God's creatures.

3.19 _____ Man is given divine understanding so that he may serve himself.

3.20 _____ The three kinds of living creatures that God created are the angelical, the rational, and the brutal.

3.21 _____ Animals have the intellect of angels and the sensual nature of man.

3.22 _____ Because man was created from the dust of the earth, he is considered a macrocosm, or large world.

3.23 _____ The only goodness in man is that he bears the image of God.

3.24 _____ The nine ages of man are similar to the nine planets.

3.25 _____ Man's life is always either increasing toward ripeness and perfection or declining and decreasing toward rottenness and dissolution.

William Shakespeare (1564–1616). When William Shakespeare was born on April 23, 1564 (traditional date), in Stratford-on-Avon, the earth did not shake with the advent of the most gifted literary genius the world has known. The new baby boy was just the third child born to John and Mary Shakespeare, middle class citizens of a farming community. Like other normal children of the period, William was baptized several days after his birth. The entry of his name in the church register on April 26, 1564, is the first record that we have of him.

Much speculation surrounds the life of Shakespeare. Because of the scant records we have of his personal life, many skeptics and mythmakers have propounded theories as to his true identity and the origin of his works. With such greatness often comes much disbelief. Despite the haze of doubt and fantasy, we can draw an outline of his life from the public and literary accounts of his contemporaries.

On November 27, 1582, Shakespeare appears again in the records after eighteen years of obscurity. The entry in the Register of the Bishop of Worcester is of the marriage of William Shakespeare and "Anne Whateley." *Whateley* was probably a misprint and should have read "Hathwey," or, as we know it, "Hathaway." Anne was from a village not far from Stratford and was eight years Shakespeare's senior. On May 26, 1583, the christening of Shakespeare's first child, Susanna, was recorded in the register of the Stratford parish church. Two years later, Anne gave birth to twins. "Hamnet & Judeth sonne and daughter to William Shakespeare" were baptized on Candlemas Day (February 2) 1585.

After this, Shakespeare disappears from the record books for many years. Many people consider these his "lost years." We find him again in the complaints of a Robert Greene, a struggling dramatist and poet in London. Apparently, Shakespeare had made his way in London as a playwright, rivaling even the much-talented Christopher Marlowe. Greene bitterly describes Shakespeare's achievements to his colleagues in *A Groatsworth of Wit:*

"Base minded men all three of you, if by my misery you be not warned: for unto none of you (like me) sought those burrs to cleave: those Puppets (I mean) that spake from our mouths, those Antics garnished in our colours. Is it not strange, that I, to whom they all have been beholding: is it not like that you, to whom they all have been beholding, shall (were ye in that case as I am now) be both at once of them forsaken, that with his Tyger's heart wrapt in a Player's hide, supposes he is as well able to bombast out a blank verse as the best of you: and being, an absolute Iohannes fac totum, is in his own conceit the only Shake-scene in a country."

Greene, like many other players and playwrights, had by 1592 fallen into the magnificent shadow of Shakespeare. At that time, we find records of his connection with the Lord Chamberlain's Men, an immensely popular troupe that later became the King's Men under the support of James I.

In 1593 Shakespeare published his first work, a narrative poem, *Venus and Adonis*. Although he had already written or contributed to various plays, they had not been published. Plays during that period were significant only in their performance, and even then they were not much more than a means of entertainment. Shakespeare's writing of *Venus and Adonis* and later *The Rape of Lucrece*, published in 1594, was an attempt to establish himself as a serious poet. The two long poems were written during an outbreak of the plague in London, which caused the public theaters to be closed for several years. Shakespeare dedicated the works to the earl of Southampton, a friend and patron of his literary endeavors.

In 1596 Shakespeare was touched by both personal tragedy and honor. On August 11 of that year, his son, Hamnet, died and was buried in Stratford. Later in October, Shakespeare's father was granted a coat of arms. John Shakespeare had served Stratford as bailiff (mayor) and alderman while maintaining a successful business trading leather and wool. The honor bestowed upon his father made Shakespeare a gentleman, only adding to his prominence that the accumulation of wealth had already afforded him.

In May 1597, records showed the purchase of New Place by a William Shakespeare. New Place was the second largest residence in Stratford, and it's possession marked its owner as well to do. This purchase, though, did not mean the removal of Shakespeare from the London theater scene. He must have divided his time between the two places, for in September of the same year we find him cast in Ben Jonson's play *Every Man in his Humour*.

Records also reveal his increasing fame during this time. Francis Meres' comments, written in 1598, give us the idea that Shakespeare's contemporaries were becoming aware that the poet in their midst "was not of an age, but for all time!" Meres wrote, "As Plautus and Seneca are accounted the best for Comedy and Tragedy among the Latins: so Shakespeare among the English is the most excellent in both kinds for the stage: for Comedy, witness his *Gentlemen of Verona*, his *Errors*, his *Love Labours's Lost*, his *Love Labour's Won*, his *Midsummer's Night Dream*, and his *Merchant of Venice*: for Tragedy his *Richard the 2*, *Richard the 3*, *Henry the 4*, *King John*, *Titus Andronicus* and his *Romeo and Juliet*." Meres' catalogue gives us a list of Shakespeare's great works, excepting those of the next decade—*Hamlet*, *King Lear*, *Macbeth*, *Anthony and Cleopatra*, and *Othello*.

Meres also noted Shakespeare's sonnets, which were not published until 1609, as "his sugared sonnets among his private friends." The writing of these sonnets conformed to the current vogue perpetuated by Sidney and Spenser. However, Shakespeare was an innovator. As he did his plays, with his sonnets he took the standard form and molded it to shape something more startlingly beautiful. The dominant subject of his sonnet sequence is love, but it is not necessarily a romantic love. He writes about love between friends, love between a man and a woman, and a triangle of love involving two men and a woman. The rhyme scheme that Shakespeare uses is *abab cdcd efef gg*. It is also known as the English sonnet, but it came to be known as the Shakespearean sonnet because of the popularity and profundity of his work.

After losing the property lease for their theater in London, the Lord Chamberlain's Company erected the Globe Theater in 1599. On the list of shareholders, Shakespeare is distinguished as one-tenth owner. At the death of Queen Elizabeth in 1603, the Lord Chamberlain's Company became the King's Men. Shakespeare and the other players were clothed with liveries of James I.

During this time, Shakespeare was residing in London, instead of Stratford, with a Huguenot (French Calvinist) tradesman, Christopher Mountjoy. This fact is interesting considering the biblical parameters within which some of plays are written. One can only speculate as to the influence that this relationship might have had on the plays he wrote during this time and later. Among the plays that might bear this influence are *Hamlet*, *Macbeth*, *King Lear*, and *Othello*. These tragedies dramatize, as one critic has noted, the fall of man followed by either the path to destruction or redemption.

In 1607 Shakespeare's daughter, Susanna, married a prominent physician, John Hall, who was known to hold Puritan beliefs. The following year, the couple bore Shakespeare a granddaughter and named her after the favorite queen, Elizabeth. In 1610, Shakespeare retired to New Place, living out the rest of his life in the country of his family and at times lending his talents to the aid of other playwrights. He is said to have written part of *Henry VIII* (c. 1613) and *Two Noble Knights* (c.1613). On April 23, 1616, exactly fifty-two years after his birth, Shakespeare died. He was buried in the same parish church in which he had been christened.

In 1623 John Hemings and Henry Condell published the *Complete Edition of Shakespeare's Works* in a folio format, giving it the name the First Folio. (A folio was a large sheet of paper folded once, creating two leaves.) The thirty-six plays that were compiled by Shakespeare's colleagues were, in their opinion, authentically his. *Pericles* was in later editions considered a part of the canon, crediting Shakespeare with the completion of thirty-seven plays. Before Shakespeare's death, only eighteen of his plays had been published in "quartos" or smaller editions. (A quarto was a large sheet of paper folded twice, creating four leaves.) Some of these quartos were unauthorized editions, reproduced merely from the memory of an actor or a spectator. The First Folio is the best and most accurate early edition of his plays.

Shakespeare's writing career, astonishingly prolific, can be divided into four periods. The first period includes the years up to 1594. It is characterized by experimentation and includes many historical chronicle works such as *Henry VI*, Parts 1, 2, and 3 (c. 1590-92) and *Richard the III* (c. 1593) as well as the comedies *The Comedy of Errors* (c. 1592) and *The Taming of the Shrew* (c. 1593).

The second period includes the years 1594–1600. During this time, Shakespeare wrote some of his most important plays. The historical plays of the period include *Richard II* (c. 1595) and *Henry V* (c. 1598); the comedies include *A Midsummer Night's Dream* (c. 1595) and *Much Ado About Nothing* (c. 1599). *The Merchant of Venice* (c. 1596) is categorized as a tragicomedy of the period. *Romeo and Juliet* (c. 1595) and *Julius Caesar* (c. 1599) complete the list, serving as precursors to some of Shakespeare's greatest tragedies.

The third period extends from 1600 to 1608. During this time, Shakespeare wrote a rapid succession of tragedies that are of unparalleled significance. Included in this period are *Hamlet* (c. 1601), *Othello* (c. 1604), *King Lear* (c. 1605), and *Antony and Cleopatra* (c. 1606).

The fourth period includes the years 1608–1616. This era is viewed as Shakespeare's tragicomedy period. As tragicomedies, the plays *Pericles, Prince of Tyre* (c. 1608), and *The Tempest* (c. 1611) seem to embody the author's feelings of finality as he nears the end of his life. Although they are comedies, they carry with them the burden of grave sobriety, as one critic has noted.

 Underline the correct answer in each of the following statements.

3.26   William Shakespeare was born in (Stratford-on-Avon, London, Edinburgh).

3.27   Shakespeare was married to (Anne Burton, Anne Hathaway, Queen Elizabeth).

3.28   Shakespeare had (five, two, three) children.

3.29   By 1592, Shakespeare was known in London as a (poet, playwright, farmer).

3.30   As an actor and a playwright, Shakespeare was a member of the (Lord Stratford's Men, Lord Leicester's Men, Lord Chamberlain's Men).

3.31   Shakespeare's first published work was a (narrative poem, play, sonnet sequence) titled *Venus and Adonis*.

3.32   In October 1596, Shakespeare's father was granted a (castle, new home, coat of arms).

3.33   Shakespeare purchased (New Place, Old Manor, Wilton House), the second largest residence in Stratford, in May 1597.

3.34   The popular sonnet sequences of Shakespeare's time focused on (friendship, romantic, erotic) love.

3.35   Shakespeare's sonnet sequence focused on (three, two, four) kinds of love.

3.36   The English sonnet came to be known as the (Petrarchian, Shakespearean, Italian) sonnet.

3.37   The Lord Chamberlain's men built the (Globe, World, London) Theater in 1599.

3.38   The tragedies *Hamlet*, *Macbeth*, *King Lear*, and *Othello* dramatize the (fall, success, triumph) of man followed by either the path to destruction or (self-exaltation, redemption, condemnation).

3.39   In (1599, 1623, 1603), seven years after Shakespeare's death, the (*Second, Third, First*) *Complete Edition of Shakespeare's Works* was published by two of his colleagues.

3.40   *The Complete Edition of Shakespeare's Works* is also known as the (First Folio, First Quarto, First Book).

3.41   Shakespeare's writing career can be divided into (two, three, four) periods.

3.42   The first period (up to 1594) includes many historical chronicle plays and is characterized by (experimentation, sadness, comedy).

3.43   *Romeo and Juliet* and *Julius Caesar* were written during the (first, second, third) period of Shakespeare's career (1594–1600).

3.44 During the third period (1600–1608) Shakespeare wrote a rapid succession of (tragedies, comedies, history chronicles), including *Hamlet*, *King Lear*, and *Othello*.

3.45 The fourth period (1608–1616) is viewed as Shakespeare's (comedy, tragicomedy, tragedy) period.

What to Look For:

As you read the following selections, pay attention to Shakespeare's understanding of various human relationships. How do his sonnets differ from the sonnets of Wyatt and Sidney (see pages 40ff)?

Sonnet 116

Let me not to the marriage of true minds
Admit impediments: love is not love
Which alters when it alteration finds,
Or bends with the remover to remove.
5   Oh no! it is an ever-fixèd mark
That looks on tempests and is never shaken;
It is the star to every wand'ring bark,
Whose worth's unknown, although his height be taken.
Love's not Time's fool, though rosy lips and cheeks
10 Within his bending sickle's compass come;
Love alters not with his brief hours and weeks,
But bears it out even to the edge of doom.
    If this be error and upon me proved,
    I never writ, nor no man ever loved.

Sonnet 130

My mistress'* eyes are nothing like the sun;   *beloved
Coral is far more red than her lips' red;
If snow be white, why then her breasts are dun;*   *tan
If hairs be wires, black wires grow on her head;
5   I have seen roses damasked,* red and white,   *pink roses
But no such roses see I in her cheeks;
And in some perfumes is there more delight
Than in the breath that from my mistress reeks;
I love to hear her speak, yet well I know
10 That music hath a far more pleasing sound;
I grant I never saw a goddess go
(My mistress when she walks treads on the ground).
    And yet by heaven I think my love as rare
    As any she belied with false compare.

➡ **Fill in each of the following blanks with the correct answer.**

3.46 According to line 5 of Sonnet 116, true love is an "_____ mark."

3.47 _____ "is the star to every wandering bark."

3.48 If the poet is wrong in his assessment of love, then "no man ever _____."

3.49 According to line 6 of Sonnet 130, the poet's mistress does not have _____ in her cheeks.

3.50 _____ is far more pleasing than the sound of his mistress's voice.

3.51 Despite her "imperfections," the poet thinks that his mistress is "_____."

What to Look For:

As a comedy, *The Taming of the Shrew* is a story that develops from affliction to restoration. As one critic has noted, it is, in essence, a "redemption story." As you read, pay close attention to the relationship between Petruccio and Katherine (or "Kate"). In light of Ephesians 5:22-33, who does Petruccio resemble? Who does Kate resemble? How does Petruccio "sanctify and cleanse" Kate?

The Taming of the Shrew

The Taming of the Shrew *is a comedy. However, it is not a comedy in the modern sense. It is much more complex than a television situation comedy or a funny movie. As a comedy, it has a plot that progresses in a U shape. The play begins with some disturbance, then progresses to affliction, and ends in restoration as noted by one writer. It is not simply a silly love story filled with humor and wit. The possibility of tragedy is real. Throughout the play you are kept guessing as to how the play will end.*

Because comedy ends in restoration, it can be likened to the story of redemption. Peter Leithart has noted, "Just as every drama that shows the consequences of sin bears some resemblance to the story of the fall of Adam, so every drama that involves a rescue from tragedy and ends with reconciliation and happiness reflects, if only vaguely, the reality of redemption, and every comic hero who wins his bride bears some likeness to the Divine Bridegroom." From a biblical worldview, the reading of comedies may remind us of our own salvation.

Petruccio and Katherine are the central characters in The Taming of the Shrew. *Petruccio is desirous of a wife. Katherine, the eldest daughter of the wealthy Baptista, becomes the object of his "love." But Katherine is not a kind, gentle person. Like an unloved and undisciplined child, she throws fits and lashes out with the cruelest of words. In the city of Padua, she has earned for herself a reputation as a shrew, a tiny, mouse-like creature that possesses a violent manner. Upon seeing her behavior, Petruccio determines to change her by "education." He is a man who loves a challenge. But Petruccio's friends warn him that Kate is a "fiend of hell," and any attempt to make her his gentle, obedient bride will only bring him to a tragic end.*

The subplot of the play concerns the relationship between Lucentio and Bianca. Lucentio has come to Padua to learn. But he falls in love with Bianca, the younger sister of Katherine. Lucentio cannot court Bianca openly until Katherine has a suitor. Thinking that Katherine will never be married, Lucentio devises a plan by which he can secretly court Bianca.

The main plot and subplots are actually parts of a play within a play. The Induction with Christopher Sly is a story within itself. It introduces some of the play's themes: transformation of life and changed identities.

DRAMATIS PERSONAE

A Lord
CHRISTOPHER SLY, *a drunker Tinker.* } *Persons in the Induction*
A Hostess Page, Players, Huntsmen, *and* Servants

BAPTISTA, *a rich Gentleman of Padua.*
VINCENTIO, *an old Gentleman of Pisa.*
LUCENTIO, *Son to Vincentio, in love with Bianca.*
PERTRUCCIO, *a Gentleman of Verona, a Suitor to Katherine.*

GREMIO, } *Suitors to* BIANCA.
HORTENSIO

TRANIO, } *Servants to* LUCENTIO.
BIONDELLO

GRUMIO, } *Servants to* PERTRUCCIO.
CURTIS

Pedant, *an old fellow set up to personate* VINCENTIO

KATHERINE, *the shrew* } *Daughters to* BAPTISTA.
BIANCA

Widow

Tailor, Haberdasher, *and* Servants *attending on* BAPTISTA *and* PETRUCCIO

SCENE, —*Sometimes in* PADUA, *and sometimes in* PETRUCCIO'S *House in the Country.*

INDUCTION
SCENE I
Before an alehouse on a heath.
[Enter Hostess and SLY]

Sly
I'll pheeze you, in faith.

Hostess
A pair of stocks, you rogue!

Sly
Ye are a baggage: the Slys are no rogues; look in the Chronicles; we came in with Richard Conqueror. Therefore *paucas pallabris*; let the world slide. Sessa!

Hostess
You will not pay for the glasses you have burst?

Sly
No, not a denier. Go by, Saint Jeronimy! Go to thy cold bed and warm thee.

Hostess
I know my remedy; I must go fetch the headborough.

[Exit]

Sly
Third, or fourth, or fifth borough, I'll answer him by law. I'll not budge an inch, boy. Let him come, and kindly.

[Falls asleep]
[Horns sounded Enter a Lord from hunting, with his train]

Lord
Huntsman, I charge thee, tender well my hounds.
Brach Merriman, the poor cur is emboss'd;
And couple Clowder with the deep-mouth'd brach.
Saw'st thou not, boy, how Silver made it good
At the hedge-corner, in the coldest fault?
I would not lose the dog for twenty pound.

First Huntsman
Why, Belman is as good as he, my lord;
He cried upon it at the merest loss
And twice to-day pick'd out the dullest scent:
Trust me, I take him for the better dog.

Lord
Thou art a fool: if Echo were as fleet,
I would esteem him worth a dozen such.
But sup them well, and look unto them all:
Tomorrow I intend to hunt again.

First Huntsman
I will, my lord.

Lord
What's here? One dead, or drunk? See, doth he breathe?

Second Huntsman
He breathes, my lord. Were he not warm'd with ale,
This were a bed but cold to sleep so soundly.

Lord
O monstrous beast! How like a swine he lies!
Grim death, how foul and loathsome is thine image!
Sirs, I will practise on this drunken man.
What think you, if he were convey'd to bed,
Wrapp'd in sweet clothes, rings put upon his fingers,
A most delicious banquet by his bed,
And brave attendants near him when he wakes,
Would not the beggar then forget himself?

First Huntsman
Believe me, lord, I think he cannot choose.

Second Huntsman
It would seem strange unto him when he waked.

Lord
Even as a flattering dream or worthless fancy.
Then take him up and manage well the jest:
Carry him gently to my fairest chamber
And hang it round with all my wanton pictures:
Balm his foul head in warm distilled waters
And burn sweet wood to make the lodging sweet:
Procure me music ready when he wakes,
To make a dulcet and a heavenly sound;
And if he chance to speak, be ready straight
And with a low submissive reverence
Say 'What is it your honour will command?'
Let one attend him with a silver basin
Full of rose-water and bestrew'd with flowers,
Another bear the ewer, the third a diaper,
And say 'Will't please your lordship cool your hands?'
Some one be ready with a costly suit
And ask him what apparel he will wear;
Another tell him of his hounds and horse,
And that his lady mourns at his disease:
Persuade him that he hath been lunatic;
And when he says he is, say that he dreams,
For he is nothing but a mighty lord.
This do, and do it kindly, gentle sirs:
It will be pastime passing excellent,
If it be husbanded with modesty.

First Huntsman
My lord, I warrant you we will play our part,
As he shall think by our true diligence
He is no less than what we say he is.

Lord
Take him up gently, and to bed with him;
And each one to his office when he wakes.

[Some bear out SLY. A trumpet sounds]
Sirrah, go see what trumpet 'tis that sounds.

[Exit Servingman]
Belike, some noble gentleman that means,
Travelling some journey, to repose him here.

[Re-enter Servingman]
How now! Who is it?

Servant
An't please your honour, players
That offer service to your lordship.

Lord
Bid them come near.

[Enter Players]
Now, fellows, you are welcome.

Players
We thank your honour.

Lord
Do you intend to stay with me tonight?

A Player
So please your lordship to accept our duty.

Lord
With all my heart. This fellow I remember,
Since once he play'd a farmer's eldest son:
'Twas where you woo'd the gentlewoman so well:

I have forgot your name; but sure that part
Was aptly fitted and naturally perform'd.

A Player
I think 'twas Soto that your honour means.

Lord
'Tis very true: thou didst it excellent.
Well, you are come to me in a happy time;
The rather for I have some sport in hand
Wherein your cunning can assist me much.
There is a lord will hear you play tonight:
But I am doubtful of your modesties;
Lest over-eyeing of his odd behavior,—
For yet his honour never heard a play—
You break into some merry passion
And so offend him; for I tell you, sirs,
If you should smile he grows impatient.

A Player
Fear not, my lord: we can contain ourselves,
Were he the veriest antic in the world.

Lord
Go, sirrah, take them to the buttery,
And give them friendly welcome every one.
Let them want nothing that my house affords.

[Exit one with the Players]

Sirrah, go you to Barthol'mew, my page,
And see him dress'd in all suits like a lady:
That done, conduct him to the drunkard's chamber;
And call him 'madam,' do him obeisance.
Tell him from me, as he will win my love,
He bear himself with honourable action,
Such as he hath observed in noble ladies
Unto their lords, by them accomplished.
Such duty to the drunkard let him do
With soft low tongue and lowly courtesy,
And say 'What is't your honour will command,
Wherein your lady and your humble wife
May show her duty and make known her love?'
And then with kind embracements, tempting kisses,
And with declining head into his bosom,
Bid him shed tears, as being overjoy'd
To see her noble lord restored to health,
Who for this seven years hath esteem'd him
No better than a poor and loathsome beggar.
And if the boy have not a woman's gift
To rain a shower of commanded tears,
An onion will do well for such a shift,
Which, in a napkin being close convey'd,
Shall in despite enforce a watery eye.
See this dispatch'd with all the haste thou canst:
Anon I'll give thee more instructions.

[Exit a Servingman]

I know the boy will well usurp the grace,
Voice, gait, and action of a gentlewoman.
I long to hear him call the drunkard husband,
And how my men will stay themselves from laughter
When they do homage to this simple peasant.
I'll in to counsel them. Haply my presence
May well abate the over-merry spleen
Which otherwise would grow into extremes.

[Exeunt]

INDUCTION
SCENE II
A bedchamber in the Lord's house.

[Enter aloft SLY, with Attendants; some with apparel, others with basin and ewer and appurtenances; and Lord]

Sly
For God's sake, a pot of small ale.

First Servant
Will't please your lordship drink a cup of sack?

Second Servant
Will't please your honour taste of these conserves?

Third Servant
What raiment will your honour wear today?

Sly
I am Christophero Sly; call not me 'honour' nor 'lordship.' I ne'er drank sack in my life, and if you give me any conserves, give me conserves of beef. Ne'er ask me what raiment I'll wear; for I have no more doublets than backs, no more stockings than legs, nor no more shoes than feet; nay, sometimes more feet than shoes, or such shoes as my toes look through the over-leather.

Lord
Heaven cease this idle humour in your honour!
O, that a mighty man of such descent,
Of such possessions and so high esteem,
Should be infused with so foul a spirit!

Sly
What, would you make me mad? Am not I Christopher Sly, old Sly's son of Burton Heath, by birth a pedlar, by education a cardmaker, by transmutation a bear-herd, and now by present profession a tinker? Ask Marian Hacket, the fat ale-wife of Wincot, if she know me not. If she say I am not fourteen pence on the score for sheer ale, score me up for the lyingest knave in Christendom. What! I am not bestraught: here's—

Third Servant
O, this it is that makes your lady mourn!

Second Servant
O, this is it that makes your servants droop!

Lord
Hence comes it that your kindred shuns your house,
As beaten hence by your strange lunacy.
O noble lord, bethink thee of thy birth.
Call home thy ancient thoughts from banishment,
And banish hence these abject lowly dreams.
Look how thy servants do attend on thee,
Each in his office, ready at thy beck.
Wilt thou have music? Hark! Apollo plays,

[Music]

And twenty cagèd nightingales do sing.
Or wilt thou sleep? We'll have thee to a couch
Softer and sweeter than the lustful bed
On purpose trimm'd up for Semiramis.
Say thou wilt walk; we will bestrew the ground:
Or wilt thou ride? Thy horses shall be trapp'd,
Their harness studded all with gold and pearl.
Dost thou love hawking? Thou hast hawks will soar
Above the morning lark. Or wilt thou hunt?
Thy hounds shall make the welkin answer them

And fetch shrill echoes from the hollow earth.

First Servant
Say thou wilt course; thy greyhounds are as swift
As breathèd stags, ay, fleeter than the roe.

Second Servant
Dost thou love pictures? We will fetch thee straight
Adonis painted by a running brook,
And Cytherea all in sedges hid,
Which seem to move and wanton with her breath,
Even as the waving sedges play with wind.

Lord
We'll show thee Io as she was a maid,
And how she was beguiled and surprised,
As lively painted as the deed was done.

Third Servant
Or Daphne roaming through a thorny wood,
Scratching her legs that one shall swear she bleeds,
And at that sight shall sad Apollo weep,
So workmanly the blood and tears are drawn.

Lord
Thou art a lord, and nothing but a lord.
Thou hast a lady far more beautiful
Than any woman in this waning age.

First Servant
And till the tears that she hath shed for thee
Like envious floods o'er-run her lovely face,
She was the fairest creature in the world;
And yet she is inferior to none.

Sly
Am I a lord? And have I such a lady?
Or do I dream? Or have I dream'd till now?
I do not sleep. I see, I hear, I speak;
I smell sweet savours, and I feel soft things.
Upon my life, I am a lord indeed
And not a tinker, nor Christophero Sly.
Well, bring our lady hither to our sight;
And once again, a pot o' the smallest ale.

Second Servant
Will't please your mightiness to wash your hands?
O, how we joy to see your wit restored!
O, that once more you knew but what you are!
These fifteen years you have been in a dream;
Or when you waked, so waked as if you slept.

Sly
These fifteen years! By my fay, a goodly nap.
But did I never speak of all that time?

First Servant
O, yes, my lord, but very idle words,
For though you lay here in this goodly chamber,
Yet would you say ye were beaten out of door;
And rail upon the hostess of the house,
And say you would present her at the leet,
Because she brought stone jugs and no seal'd quarts:
Sometimes you would call out for Cicely Hacket.

Sly
Ay, the woman's maid of the house.

Third Servant
Why, sir, you know no house nor no such maid,
Nor no such men as you have reckon'd up,
As Stephen Sly and old John Naps of Greece
And Peter Turph and Henry Pimpernell
And twenty more such names and men as these,
Which never were, nor no man ever saw.

Sly
Now Lord be thankèd for my good amends!

All
Amen.

Sly
I thank thee. Thou shalt not lose by it.

[Enter the Page as a lady, with attendants]

Page
How fares my noble lord?

Sly
Marry, I fare well for here is cheer enough.
Where is my wife?

Page
Here, noble lord: what is thy will with her?

Sly
Are you my wife and will not call me husband?
My men should call me 'lord.' I am your goodman.

Page
My husband and my lord, my lord and husband;
I am your wife in all obedience.

Sly
I know it well. What must I call her?

Lord
Madam.

Sly
Al'ce madam, or Joan madam?

Lord
'Madam,' and nothing else: so lords
call ladies.

Sly
Madam wife, they say that I have dream'd
And slept above some fifteen year or more.

Page
Ay, and the time seems thirty unto me,
Being all this time abandon'd from your bed.

Sly
'Tis much. Servants, leave me and her alone.
Madam, undress you and come now to bed.

Page
Thrice-noble lord, let me entreat of you
To pardon me yet for a night or two,
Or, if not so, until the sun be set:
For your physicians have expressly charged,
In peril to incur your former malady,
That I should yet absent me from your bed.
I hope this reason stands for my excuse.

Sly
Ay, it stands so that I may hardly
tarry so long. But I would be loath to fall into
my dreams again. I will therefore tarry in
despite of the flesh and the blood.

[Enter a Messenger]

Messenger
Your honour's players, hearing your amendment,
Are come to play a pleasant comedy;
For so your doctors hold it very meet,
Seeing too much sadness hath congeal'd your blood,

And melancholy is the nurse of frenzy.
Therefore they thought it good you hear a play
And frame your mind to mirth and merriment,
Which bars a thousand harms and lengthens life.

Sly
Marry, I will, let them play it. Is not a comonty a Christmas gambol or a tumbling-trick?

Page
No, my good lord; it is more pleasing stuff.

Sly
What, household stuff?

Page
It is a kind of history.

Sly
Well, we'll see't. Come, madam wife, sit by my side, and let the world slip. We shall ne'er be younger.

[Flourish]

ACT I
SCENE I

Padua. A public place.

[Enter LUCENTIO and his man TRANIO]

Lucentio
Tranio, since fore the great desire I had
To see fair Padua, nursery of arts,
I am arrived for fruitful Lombardy,
The pleasant garden of great Italy;
And by my father's love and leave am arm'd
With his good will and thy good company,
My trusty servant, well approved in all,
Here let us breathe and haply institute
A course of learning and ingenious studies.
Pisa, renown'd for grave citizens
Gave me my being and my father first,
A merchant of great traffic through the world,
Vincetino come of Bentivolii.
Vincetino's son brought up in Florence,
It shall become to serve all hopes conceived
To deck his fortune with his virtuous deeds.
And therefore, Tranio, for the time I study,
Virtue and that part of philosophy
Will I apply that treats of happiness
By virtue specially to be achieved.
Tell me thy mind; for I have Pisa left
And am to Padua come, as he that leaves
A shallow plash to plunge him in the deep
And with satiety seeks to quench his thirst.

Tranio
Mi perdonato, gentle master mine.
I am in all affected as yourself;
Glad that you thus continue your resolve
To suck the sweets of sweet philosophy.
Only, good master, while we do admire
This virtue and this moral discipline,
Let's be no stoics nor no stocks, I pray;
Or so devote to Aristotle's cheques
As Ovid be an outcast quite abjured.
Balk logic with acquaintance that you have,
And practise rhetoric in your common talk;
Music and poesy use to quicken you;
The mathematics and the metaphysics,
Fall to them as you find your stomach serves you;
No profit grows where is no pleasure ta'en:
In brief, sir, study what you most affect.

Lucentio
Gramercies, Tranio, well dost thou advise.
If, Biondello, thou wert come ashore,
We could at once put us in readiness,
And take a lodging fit to entertain
Such friends as time in Padua shall beget.
But stay a while: what company is this?

Tranio
Master, some show to welcome us to town.

[Enter Baptista, Katherine, Bianca, Gremio, and Hortensio. Lucentio and Tranio stand by.]

Baptista
Gentlemen, importune me no farther,
For how I firmly am resolved you know;
That is, not to bestow my youngest daughter
Before I have a husband for the elder.
If either of you both love Katherine,
Because I know you well and love you well,
Leave shall you have to court her at your pleasure.

Gremio *[Aside]*
To cart her rather. She's too rough for me.
There, there, Hortensio. Will you any wife?

Katherine
I pray you, sir, is it your will
To make a stale of me amongst these mates?

Hortensio
'Mates', maid? How mean you that? No mates for you,
Unless you were of gentler, milder mould.

Katherine
I'faith, sir, you shall never need to fear:
I wis it is not half way to her heart;
But if it were, doubt not her care should be
To comb your noddle with a three-legg'd stool
And paint your face and use you like a fool.

Hortensia
From all such devils, good Lord deliver us!

Gremio
And me too, good Lord!

Tranio *[Aside]*
Hush, master! here's some good pastime toward:
That wench is stark mad or wonderful froward.

Lucentio *[Aside]*
But in the other's silence do I see
Maid's mild behavior and sobriety.
Peace, Tranio!

Tranio *[Aside]*
Well said, master. Mum! And gaze your fill.

Baptista
Gentlemen, that I may soon make good
What I have said, Bianca, get you in.
And let it not displease thee, good Bianca,
For I will love thee ne'er the less, my girl.

Katherine
A pretty peat! It is best
Put finger in the eye, an she knew why.

Bianca
Sister, content you in my discontent.
Sir, to your pleasure humbly I subscribe.
My books and instruments shall be my company,

On them to took and practise by myself.

Lucentio *[Aside]*
Hark, Tranio! Thou may'st hear Minerva speak.

Hortensio
Signor Baptista, will you be so strange?
Sorry am I that our good will effects
Bianca's grief.

Gremio
Why will you mew her up,
Signor Baptista, for this fiend of hell,
And make her bear the penance of her tongue?

Baptista
Gentlemen, content ye; I am resolved.
Go in, Bianca.

[Exit BIANCA]

And for I know she taketh most delight
In music, instruments, and poetry,
Schoolmasters will I keep within my house
Fit to instruct her youth. If you, Hortensio,
Or Signor Gremio, you know any such,
Prefer them hither; for to cunning men
I will be very kind, and liberal
To mine own children in good bringing up.
And so farewell. Katherine, you may stay,
For I have more to commune with Bianca.

[Exit]

Katherine
Why, and I trust I may go too, may I not? What,
shall I be appointed hours; as though, belike I
knew not what to take and what to leave? Ha!

[Exit]

Gremio
You may go to the devil's dam. Your gifts are so good here's none will hold you. Their love is not so great, Hortensio, but we may blow our nails together, and fast it fairly out. Our cake's dough on both sides. Farewell. Yet for the love I bear my sweet Bianca, if I can by any means light on a fit man to teach her that wherein she delights, I will wish him to her father.

Hortensio
So will I, Signor Gremio. But a word, I pray. Though the nature of our quarrel yet never brooked parle, know now, upon advice, it toucheth us both, that we may yet again have access to our fair mistress and be happy rivals in Bianca's love, to labour and effect one thing specially.

Gremio
What's that, I pray?

Hortensio
Marry, sir, to get a husband for her sister.

Gremio
A husband? A devil!

Hortensio
I say, a husband.

Gremio
I say, a devil. Thinkest thou, Hortensio, though her father be very rich, any man is so very a fool to be married to hell?

Hortensio
Tush, Gremio. Though it pass your patience and mine to endure her loud alarums, why, man, there be good fellows in the world, an a man could light on them, would take her with all faults, and money enough.

Gremio
I cannot tell, but I had as lief take her dowry with this condition: to be whipped at the high cross every morning.

Hortensio
Faith, as you say, there's small choice in rotten apples. But come, since this bar in law makes us friends, it shall be so far forth friendly maintained till by helping Baptista's eldest daughter to a husband we set his youngest free for a husband, and then have to't a fresh. Sweet Bianca! Happy man be his dole! He that runs fastest gets the ring. How say you, Signor Gremio?

Gremio
I am agreed, and would I had given him the best horse in Padua to begin his wooing that would thoroughly woo her, wed her, and bed her, and rid the house of her! Come on.

[Exeunt GREMIO and HORTENSIO]

Tranio
I pray, sir, tell me: is it possible
That love should of a sudden take such hold?

Lucentio
O Tranio, till I found it to be true
I never thought it possible or likely.
But see, while idly I stood looking on
I found the effect of love in idleness,
And now in plainness do confess to thee,
That art to me as secret and as dear
As Anna to the queen of Carthage was,
Tranio, I burn, I pine, I perish, Tranio,
If I achieve not this young modest girl.
Counsel me, Tranio, for I know thou canst.
Assist me, Tranio, for I know thou wilt.

Tranio
Master, it is no time to chide you now.
Affection is not rated from the heart.
If love have touch'd you, nought remains but so,
'Redime te captum quam queas minimo.'

Lucentio
Gramercies, lad. Go forward, this contents.
The rest will comfort, for thy counsel's sound.

Tranio
Master, you look'd so longly on the maid
Perhaps you mark'd not what's the pith of all.

Lucentio
O yes, I saw sweet beauty in her face,
Such as the daughter of Agenor had,
That made great Jove to humble him to her hand
When with his knees he kiss'd the Cretan strand.

Tranio
Saw you no more? Mark'd you not how her sister
Began to scold and raise up such a storm
That mortal ears might hardly endure the din?

Lucentio
  Tranio, I saw her coral lips to move,
  And with her breath she did perfume the air.
  Sacred and sweet was all I saw in her.

Tranio *[Aside]*
  Nay, then 'tis time to stir him from his trance.
  I pray, awake, sir. If you love the maid,
  Bend thoughts and wits to achieve her. Thus it stands:
  Her elder sister is so curst and shrewd
  That till the father rid his hands of her,
  Master, your love must live a maid at home,
  And therefore has he closely mew'd her up
  Because she will not be annoy'd with suitors.

Lucentio
  Ah, Tranio, what a cruel father's he!
  But art thou not advised he took some care
  To get her cunning schoolmasters to instruct her?

Tranio
  Ay, marry am I, sir, and now 'tis plotted.

Lucentio
  I have it, Tranio.

Tranio
  Master, for my hand,
  Both our inventions meet and jump in one.

Lucentio
  Tell me thine first.

Tranio
  You will be schoolmaster
  And undertake the teaching of the maid.
  That's your device.

Lucentio
  It is. May it be done?

Tranio
  Not possible; for who shall bear your part,
  And be in Padua here Vincentio's son,
  Keep house, and ply his book, welcome his friends,
  Visit his countrymen, and banquet them?

Lucentio
  Basta, content thee, for I have it full.
  We have not yet been seen in any house,
  Nor can we be distinguish'd by our faces
  For man or master. Then it follows thus:
  Thou shalt be master, Tranio, in my stead,
  Keep house, and port, and servants as I should.
  I will some other be, some Florentine,
  Some Neapolitan, or meaner man of Pisa.
  'Tis hatch'd, and shall be so. Tranio, at once
  Uncase thee. Take my colour'd hat and cloak.
  When Biondello comes he waits on thee,
  But I will charm him first to keep his tongue.

Tranio
  So had you need.
  In brief, sir, sith it your pleasure is,
  And I am tied to be obedient;
  For so your father charged me at our parting,
  'Be serviceable to my son,' quoth he,
  Although I think 'twas in another sense;
  I am content to be Lucentio
  Because so well I love Lucentio.

Lucentio
  Tranio, be so, because Lucentio loves,
  And let me be a slave to achieve that maid
  Whose sudden sight hath thrall'd my wounded eye.
  Here comes the rogue. Sirrah, where have you been?

[Enter BIONDELLO]

Biondello
  Where have I been? Nay, how now, where are *you*?
  Master, has my fellow Tranio stolen your clothes, or
  you stolen his, or both? Pray, what's the news?

Lucentio
  Sirrah, come hither. 'Tis no time to jest,
  And therefore frame your manners to the time.
  Your fellow Tranio here, to save my life
  Puts my apparel and my countenance on,
  And I for my escape have put on his,
  For in a quarrel since I came ashore
  I kill'd a man, and fear I was descried.
  Wait you on him, I charge you, as becomes,
  While I make way from hence to save my life.
  You understand me?

Biondello
  I, sir? Ne'er a whit.

Lucentio
  And not a jot of Tranio in your mouth.
  Tranio is changed into Lucentio.

Biondello
  The better for him. Would I were so too!

Tranio
  So could I, faith, boy, to have the next wish after,
  That Lucentio indeed had Baptista's youngest daughter.
  But sirrah, not for my sake but your master's I advise
  You use your manners discreetly in all kind of companies.
  When I am alone, why then I am Tranio,
  But in all places else your master, Lucentio.

Lucentio
  Tranio, let's go. One thing more rests that
  thyself execute, to make one among these wooers. If
  thou ask me why, sufficeth my reasons are both good
  and weighty.

[Exeunt]
[The presenters above speak]

First Servant
  My lord, you nod. You do not mind the play.

Sly
  Yes, by Saint Anne, do I. A good matter, surely.
  Comes there any more of it?

Page
  My lord, 'tis but begun.

Sly
  'Tis a very excellent piece of work, madam lady.
  Would 'twere done!

[They sit and mark]

ACT I
SCENE II

Padua. A public place.

[Enter PETRUCCIO and his man GRUMIO]

Petruccio
  Verona, for a while I take my leave
  To see my friends in Padua; but of all
  My best-beloved and approved friend

Hortensio, and I trow this is his house.
Here, sirrah Grumio, knock, I say.

Grumio
Knock, sir? Whom should I knock? Is there man has
rebused your worship?

Petruccio
Villain, I say, knock me here soundly.

Grumio
Knock you here, sir? Why, sir, what am I, sir, that
I should knock you here, sir?

Petruccio
Villain, I say, knock me at this gate,
And rap me well or I'll knock your knave's pate.

Grumio
My master is grown quarrelsome. I should knock
you first,
And then I know after who comes by the worst.

Petruccio
Will it not be?
Faith, sirrah, an you'll not knock, I'll ring it.
I'll try how you can sol-fa, and sing it.

[He wrings him by the ears]

Grumio *[Kneeling]*
Help, masters, help! My master is mad.

Petruccio
Now knock when I bid you, sirrah villain!

[Enter HORTENSIO]

Hortensio
How now, what's the matter? My old friend Grumio
and my good friend Petruccio? How do you all at
Verona?

Petruccio
Signor Hortensio, come you to part the fray?
'Con tutto il cuore, ben trovato,' may I say.

Hortensio
'Alla nostra casa ben venuto, molto honorato signor
mio Petruccio.' Rise, Grumio, rise. We will compound
this quarrel.

Grumio *[Rises]*
Nay, 'tis no matter, sir, what he 'leges in Latin.
If this be not a lawful case for me to leave his
service, look you, sir: he bid me knock him and rap
him soundly, sir. Well, was it fit for a servant to
use his master so, being perhaps, for aught I see,
two-and-thirty, a pip out? Whom would to God I had
well knock'd at first, then had not Grumio come by the
worst.

Petruccio
A senseless villain! Good Hortensio,
I bade the rascal knock upon your gate,
And could not get him for my heart to do it.

Grumio
Knock at the gate? O heavens, spake you not these
words plain? 'Sirrah, knock me here, rap me here,
knock me well, and knock me soundly'? And come you
now with knocking at the gate?

Petruccio
Sirrah, be gone, or talk not, I advise you.

Hortensio
Petruccio, patience. I am Grumio's pledge.
Why, this' a heavy chance 'twixt him and you,
Your ancient, trusty, pleasant servant Grumio.
And tell me now, sweet friend, what happy gale
Blows you to Padua here from old Verona?

Petruccio
Such wind as scatters young men through the world,
To seek their fortunes farther than at home,
Where small experience grows. But in a few,
Signor Hortensio, thus it stands with me:
Antonio, my father, is deceased,
And I have thrust myself into this maze
Haply to wive and thrive as best I may.
Crowns in my purse I have, and goods at home,
And so am come abroad to see the world.

Hortensio
Petruccio, shall I then come roundly to thee
And wish thee to a shrewd, ill-favour'd wife?
Thou'ldst thank me but a little for my counsel,
And yet I'll promise thee she shall be rich,
And very rich. But thou'rt too much my friend,
And I'll not wish thee to her.

Petruccio
Signor Hortensio, 'twixt such friends as we
Few words suffice; and therefore, if thou know
One rich enough to be Petruccio's wife,
As wealth is burden of my wooing dance,
Be she as foul as was Florentius' love,
As old as Sibyl, and as curst and shrewd
As Socrates' Xanthippe or a worse,
She moves me not, or not removes at least
Affection's edge in me, were she as rough
As are the swelling Adriatic seas.
I come to wive it wealthily in Padua;
If wealthily, then happily in Padua.

Grumio
Nay, look you, sir, he tells you flatly what his
mind is. Why, give him gold enough and marry him to
a puppet or an aglet-baby, or an old trot with ne'er
a tooth in her head, though she have as many diseases
as two-and-fifty horses. Why, nothing comes amiss
so money comes withal.

Hortensio
Petruccio, since we are stepp'd thus far in,
I will continue that I broach'd in jest.
I can, Petruccio, help thee to a wife
With wealth enough, and young and beauteous,
Brought up as best becomes a gentlewoman.
Her only fault, and that is faults enough,
Is that she is intolerable curst,
And shrewd and froward so beyond all measure
That, were my state far worser than it is,
I would not wed her for a mine of gold.

Petruccio
Hortensio, peace! Thou know'st not gold's effect.
Tell me her father's name and 'tis enough,
For I will board her though she chide as loud
As thunder when the clouds in autumn crack.

Hortensio
Her father is Baptista Minola,
An affable and courteous gentleman.

Her name is Katherine Minola,
Renown'd in Padua for her scolding tongue.

Petruccio
I know her father, though I know not her,
And he knew my deceased father well.
I will not sleep, Hortensio, till I see her,
And therefore let me be thus bold with you
To give you over at this first encounter,
Unless you will accompany me thither.

Grumio
I pray you, sir, let him go while the humour lasts.
O' my word, an she knew him as well as I do she
would think scolding would do little good upon him.
She may perhaps call him half a score knaves or so.
Why, that's nothing; an he begin once he'll rail in
his rope-tricks. I'll tell you what, sir, an she
stand him but a little, he will throw a figure in
her face and so disfigure her with it that she
shall have no more eyes to see withal than a cat.
You know him not, sir.

Hortensio
Tarry, Petruccio, I must go with thee,
For in Baptista's keep my treasure is.
He hath the jewel of my life in hold,
His youngest daughter, beautiful Binaca,
And her withholds from me and other more,
Suitors to her and rivals in my love,
Supposing it a thing impossible,
For those defects I have before rehearsed,
That ever Katherine will be woo'd.
Therefore this order hath Baptista ta'en:
That none shall have access unto Bianca
Till Katherine the curst have got a husband.

Grumio
Katherine the curst!
A title for a maid of all titles the worst.

Hortensio
Now shall my friend Petruccio do me grace,
And offer me disguised in sober robes
To old Baptista as a schoolmaster
Well seen in music, to instruct Bianca,
That so I may by this device at least
Have leave and leisure to make love to her,
And unsuspected court her by herself.

Grumio
Here's no knavery! See, to beguile the old folks,
how the young folks lay their heads together!

[Enter GREMIO, and LUCENTIO disguised]

Master, master, look about you. Who goes there, ha?

Hortensio
Peace, Grumio! It is the rival of my love.
Petruccio, stand by a while.

Grumio
A proper stripling, and an amorous!

Gremio *[Aside]*
O, very well; I have perused the note.
Hark you, sir, I'll have them very fairly bound:
All books of love, see that at any hand;
And see you read no other lectures to her.
You understand me. Over and beside
Signor Baptista's liberality,
I'll mend it with a largess. Take your paper, too,
And let me have them very well perfumed,
For she is sweeter than perfume itself
To whom they go to. What will you read to her?

Lucentio
Whate'er I read to her, I'll plead for you
As for my patron, stand you so assured,
As firmly as yourself were still in place:
Yea, and perhaps with more successful words
Than you, unless you were a scholar, sir.

Gremio
O this learning, what a thing it is!

Grumio *[Aside]*
O this woodcock, what an ass it is!

Petruccio
Peace, sirrah!

Hortensio
Grumio, mum! God save you, Signor Gremio.

Gremio
And you are well met, Signor Hortensio.
Trow you whither I am going? To Baptista Minola.
I promised to inquire carefully
About a schoolmaster for the fair Bianca,
And by good fortune I have lighted well
On this young man, for learning and behavior
Fit for her turn, well read in poetry
And other books, good ones, I warrant ye.

Hortensio
'Tis well, and I have met a gentleman
Hath promised me to help me to another,
A fine musician, to instruct our mistress.
So shall I no whit be behind in duty
To fair Bianca, so beloved of me.

Gremio
Beloved of me, and that my deeds shall prove.

Grumio *[Aside]*
And that his bags shall prove.

Hortensio
Gremio, 'tis now no time to vent our love.
Listen to me, and if you speak me fair,
I'll tell you news indifferent good for either.
Here is a gentleman whom by chance I met,
Upon agreement from us to his liking,
Will undertake to woo curst Katherine,
Yea, and to marry her, if her dowry please.

Gremio
So said, so done, is well.
Hortensio, have you told him all her faults?

Petruccio
I know she is an irksome brawling scold.
If that be all, masters, I hear no harm.

Gremio
No, say'st me so, friend? What countryman?

Petruccio
Born in Verona, old Antonio's son.
My father dead, my fortune lives for me,
And I do hope good days and long to see.

Gremio
O sir, such a life, with such a wife were strange!
But if you have a stomach, to't, i' God's name.
You shall have me assisting you in all.

But will you woo this wild-cat?

Petruccio
Will I live!

Grumio
Will he woo her? Ay, or I'll hang her.

Petruccio
Why came I hither but to that intent?
Think you a little din can daunt mine ears?
Have I not in my time heard lions roar?
Have I not heard the sea, puff'd up with winds,
Rage like an angry boar chafed with sweat?
Have I not heard great ordnance in the field,
And heaven's artillery thunder in the skies?
Have I not in a pitched battle heard
Loud 'larums, neighing steeds, and trumpets' clang?
And do you tell me of a woman's tongue,
That gives not half so great a blow to hear
As will a chestnut in a farmer's fire?
Tush, tush! Fear boys with bugs.

Grumio
For he fears none.

Gremio
Hortensio, hark.
This gentleman is happily arrived,
My mind presumes, for his own good and ours.

Hortensio
I promised we would be contributors
And bear his charging of wooing, whatsoe'er.

Gremio
And so we will, provided that he win her.

Grumio
I would I were as sure of a good dinner.

[Enter TRANIO brave, and BIONDELLO]

Tranio
Gentlemen, God save you. If I may be bold,
Tell me, I beseech you, which is the readiest way
To the house of Signor Baptista Minola?

Biondello
He that has the two fair daughters: is't he you mean?

Tranio
Even he, Biondello.

Gremio
Hark you, sir, you mean not her to—

Tranio
Perhaps him and her, sir. What have you to do?

Petruccio
Not her that chides, sir, at any hand, I pray.

Tranio
I love no chiders, sir. Biondello, let's away.

Lucentio *[Aside]*
Well begun, Tranio.

Hortensio
Sir, a word ere you go.
Are you a suitor to the maid you talk of, yea or no?

Tranio
And if I be, sir, is it any offence?

Gremio
No, if without more words you will get you hence.

Tranio
Why, sir, I pray, are not the streets as free
For me as for you?

Gremio
But so is not she.

Tranio
For what reason, I beseech you?

Gremio
For this reason, if you'll know,
That she's the choice love of Signor Gremio.

Hortensio
That she's the chosen of Signor Hortensio.

Tranio
Softly, my masters! If you be gentlemen
Do me this right, hear me with patience.
Baptista is a noble gentleman
To whom my father is not all unknown,
And were his daughter fairer than she is
She may more suitors have, and me for one.
Fair Leda's daughter had a thousand wooers;
Then well one more may fair Bianca have,
And so she shall. Lucentio shall make one,
Though Paris came in hope to speed alone.

Gremio
What, this gentleman will out-talk us all!

Lucentio
Sir, give him head, I know he'll prove a jade.

Petruccio
Hortensio, to what end are all these words?

Hortensio
Sir, let me be so bold as ask you,
Did you yet ever see Baptista's daughter?

Tranio
No, sir, but hear I do that he hath two,
The one as famous for a scolding tongue
As is the other for beauteous modesty.

Petruccio
Sir, sir, the first's for me, Let her go by.

Gremio
Yea, leave that labour to great Hercules,
And let it be more than Alcides' twelve.

Petruccio
Sir, understand you this of me in sooth:
The youngest daughter whom you hearken for
Her father keeps from all access of suitors,
And will not promise her to any man
Until the elder sister first be wed.
The younger then is free and not before.

Tranio
If it be so, sir, that you are the man
Must stead us all, and me amongst the rest,
And if you break the ice and do this feat,
Achieve the elder, set the younger free
For our access, whose hap shall be to have her
Will not so graceless be to be ingrate.

Hortensio
Sir, you say well, and well you do conceive;
And since you do profess to be a suitor,
You must, as we do, gratify this gentleman,
To whom we all rest generally beholding.

Tranio
  Sir, I shall not be slack. In sign whereof,
  Please ye we may contrive this afternoon,
  And quaff carouses to our mistress' health,
  And do as adversaries do in law,
  Strive mightily, but eat and drink as friends.

Grumio and Biondello together
  O excellent motion! Fellows, let's be gone.

Hortensio
  The motion's good indeed, and be it so.
  Petruccio, I shall be your *ben venuto*.

[Exeunt]

Answer *true* or *false* for each of the following statements.

3.52 _____ *The Taming of the Shrew* is a tragedy that is a play within a play.

3.53 _____ A comedy ends in restoration.

3.54 _____ After returning from hunting, a lord plays a practical joke on Christopher Sly.

3.55 _____ Sly is dressed up in his lord's clothes and told that he has been insane for many years.

3.56 _____ Baptista will not allow Katherine to be courted until Bianca is married.

3.57 _____ Lucentio exchanges identities with Tranio to become Bianca's tutor.

3.58 _____ Petruccio comes to Padua to get married.

3.59 _____ Bianca's three suitors refuse to help Petruccio court Katherine.

ACT II

SCENE I

Padua. Before HORTENSIO'S house.

[Enter KATHERINE and BIANCA]

Bianca
  Good sister, wrong me not, nor wrong yourself
  To make a bondmaid and a slave of me.
  That I disdain, but for these other goods,
  Unbind my hands, I'll pull them off myself,
  Yea, all my raiment to my petticoat;
  Or what you will command me will I do,
  So well I know my duty to my elders.

Katherine
  Of all thy suitors, here I charge thee, tell
  Whom thou lovest best. See thou dissemble not.

Bianca
  Believe me, sister, of all the men alive
  I never yet beheld that special face
  Which I could fancy more than any other.

Katherine
  Minion, thou liest. Is't not Hortensio?

Bianca
  If you affect him, sister, here I swear
  I'll plead for you myself, but you shall have him.

Katherine
  O then, belike, you fancy riches more:
  You will have Gremio to keep you fair.

Bianca
  Is it for him you do envy me so?
  Nay, then, you jest, and now I well perceive
  You have but jested with me all this while.
  I prithee, sister Kate, untie my hands.

Katherine
  If that be jest, then all the rest was so.

[Strikes her]
[Enter BAPTISTA]

Baptista
  Why, how now, dame! Whence grows this insolence?
  Bianca, stand aside. Poor girl! she weeps.
  Go ply thy needle; meddle not with her.
  For shame, thou hilding of a devilish spirit,
  Why dost thou wrong her that did ne'er wrong thee?
  When did she cross thee with a bitter word?

Katherine
  Her silence flouts me, and I'll be revenged.

[Flies after BIANCA]

Baptista
  What, in my sight? Bianca, get thee in.

[Exit BIANCA]

Katherine
  What, will you not suffer me? Nay, now I see
  She is your treasure, she must have a husband;
  I must dance bare-foot on her wedding day,
  And for your love to her lead apes in hell.
  Talk not to me: I will go sit and weep
  Till I can find occasion of revenge.

[Exit]

Baptista
  Was ever gentleman thus grieved as I?
  But who comes here?

[Enter GREMIO, LUCENTIO in the habit of a mean man; PETRUCCIO, with HORTENSIO as a musician; and TRANIO, with BIONDELLO bearing a lute and books]

Gremio
  Good morrow, neighbour Baptista.

Baptista
Good morrow, neighbour Gremio.
God save you, gentlemen!

Petruccio
And you, good sir! Pray, have you not a daughter
Call'd Katherine, fair and virtuous?

Baptista
I have a daughter, sir, called Katherine.

Gremio
You are too blunt: go to it orderly.

Petruccio
You wrong me, Signor Gremio: give me leave.
I am a gentleman of Verona, sir,
That, hearing of her beauty and her wit,
Her affability and bashful modesty,
Her wondrous qualities and mild behavior,
Am bold to show myself a forward guest
Within your house to make mine eye the witness
Of that report which I so oft have heard.
And, for an entrance to my entertainment,
I do present you with a man of mine,

[Presenting HORTENSIO]

Cunning in music and the mathematics,
To instruct her fully in those sciences,
Whereof I know she is not ignorant.
Accept of him, or else you do me wrong:
His name is Licio, born in Mantua.

Baptista
You're welcome, sir, and he, for your good sake.
But for my daughter Katherine, this I know:
She is not for your turn, the more my grief.

Petruccio
I see you do not mean to part with her,
Or else you like not of my company.

Baptista
Mistake me not; I speak but as I find.
Whence are you, sir? What may I call your name?

Petruccio
Petruccio is my name; Antonio's son,
A man well known throughout all Italy.

Baptista
I know him well. You are welcome for his sake.

Gremio
Saving your tale, Petruccio, I pray
Let us that are poor petitioners speak too.
Baccare! You are marvellous forward.

Petruccio
O, pardon me, Signor Gremio; I would fain be doing.

Gremio
I doubt it not, sir. But you will curse your wooing.
Neighbour, this is a gift very grateful, I am
sure of it. To express the like kindness, myself,
that have been more kindly beholding to you than any,
freely give unto you this young scholar,

[Presenting LUCENTIO]

that hath been long studying at Rheims; as cunning in
Greek, Latin, and other languages, as the other in
music and mathematics. His name is Cambio. Pray,
accept his service.

Baptista
A thousand thanks, Signor Gremio.
Welcome, good Cambio.

[To TRANIO]

But, gentle sir, methinks you walk like a stranger.
May I be so bold to know the cause of your
coming?

Tranio
Pardon me, sir, the boldness is mine own,
That, being a stranger in this city here,
Do make myself a suitor to your daughter,
Unto Bianca, fair and virtuous.
Nor is your firm resolve unknown to me,
In the preferment of the eldest sister.
This liberty is all that I request:
That upon knowledge of my parentage
I may have welcome 'mongst the rest that woo,
And free access and favour as the rest.
And, toward the education of your daughters,
I here bestow a simple instrument,
And this small packet of Greek and Latin books.
If you accept them, then their worth is great.

Baptista
Lucentio is your name—of whence, I pray?

Tranio
Of Pisa, sir; son to Vincentio.

Baptista
A mighty man of Pisa, By report
I know him well. You are very welcome, sir,
Take you the lute, and you the set of books;
You shall go see your pupils presently.
Holla, within!

[Enter a Servant]

Sirrah, lead these gentlemen
To my daughters; and tell them both
These are their tutors. Bid them use them well.

[Exit Servant, with LUCENTIO and HORTENSIO, BIONDELLO following]

We will go walk a little in the orchard,
And then to dinner. You are passing welcome,
And so I pray you all to think yourselves.

Petruccio
Signor Baptista, my business asketh haste,
And every day I cannot come to woo.
You knew my father well, and in him me,
Left solely heir to all his lands and goods,
Which I have better'd rather than decreased:
Then tell me, if I get your daughter's love,
What dowry shall I have with her to wife?

Baptista
After my death the one half of my lands,
And in possession twenty thousand crowns.

Petruccio
And, for that dowry, I'll assure her of
Her widowhood, be it that she survive me,
In all my lands and leases whatsoever:
Let specialties be therefore drawn between us,
That covenants may be kept on either hand.

Baptista
Ay, when the special thing is well obtain'd—
That is, her love; for that is all in all.

Petruccio
Why, that is nothing: for I tell you, father,
I am as peremptory as she proud-minded;
And where two raging fires meet together
They do consume the thing that feeds their fury:
Though little fire grows great with little wind,
Yet extreme gusts will blow out fire and all.
So I to her, and so she yields to me;
For I am rough and woo not like a babe.

Baptista
Well mayst thou woo, and happy be thy speed!
But be thou arm'd for some unhappy words.

Petruccio
Ay, to the proof; as mountains are for winds,
That shake not, though they blow perpetually.

[Re-enter HORTENSIO, with his head broke]

Baptista
How now, my friend! Why dost thou look so pale?

Hortensio
For fear, I promise you, if I look pale.

Baptista
What, will my daughter prove a good musician?

Hortensio
I think she'll sooner prove a soldier
Iron may hold with her, but never lutes.

Baptista
Why, then thou canst not break her to the lute?

Hortensio
Why, no; for she hath broke the lute to me.
I did but tell her she mistook her frets,
And bow'd her hand to teach her fingering;
When, with a most impatient devilish spirit,
'Frets, call you these?' quoth she; 'I'll fume
with them:'
And, with that word, she struck me on the head,
And through the instrument my pate made way;
And there I stood amazed for a while,
As on a pillory, looking through the lute;
While she did call me rascal fiddler
And twangling Jack; with twenty such vile terms,
As had she studied to misuse me so.

Petruccio
Now, by the world, it is a lusty wench!
I love her ten times more than e'er I did:
O, how I long to have some chat with her!

Baptista
Well, go with me, and be not so discomfited.
Proceed in practise with my younger daughter;
She's apt to learn and thankful for good turns.
Signor Petruccio, will you go with us,
Or shall I send my daughter Kate to you?

Petruccio
I pray you do.

[Exeunt all but PETRUCCIO]

I will attend her here,
And woo her with some spirit when she comes.
Say that she rail; why then I'll tell her plain
She sings as sweetly as a nightingale.
Say that she frown, I'll say she looks as clear
As morning roses newly wash'd with dew.
Say she be mute and will not speak a word;
Then I'll commend her volubility,
And say she uttereth piercing eloquence:
If she do bid me pack, I'll give her thanks,
As though she bid me stay by her a week:
If she deny to wed, I'll crave the day
When I shall ask the banns and when be
married.
But here she comes; and now, Petruccio, speak.

[Enter KATHERINE]

Good morrow, Kate; for that's your name, I hear.

Katherine
Well have you heard, but something hard of hearing:
They call me Katherine that do talk of me.

Petruccio
You lie, in faith; for you are call'd plain Kate,
And bonny Kate and sometimes Kate the curst;
But Kate, the prettiest Kate in Christendom
Kate of Kate Hall, my super-dainty Kate,
For dainties are all cates, and therefore—"Kate"—
Take this of me, Kate of my consolation;
Hearing thy mildness praised in every town,
Thy virtues spoke of, and thy beauty sounded—
Yet not so deeply as to thee belongs—
Myself am moved to woo thee for my wife.

Katherine
Moved? In good time. Let him that moved you hither
Remove you hence. I knew you at the first
You were a moveable.

Petruccio
Why, what's a moveable?

Katherine
A join'd-stool.

Petruccio
Thou hast hit it. Come, sit on me.

Katherine
Asses are made to bear, and so are you.

Petruccio
Women are made to bear, and so are you.

Katherine
No such jade as you, if me you mean.

Petruccio
Alas! good Kate, I will not burden thee;
For knowing thee to be but young and light.

Katherine
Too light for such a swain as you to catch;
And yet as heavy as my weight should be.

Petruccio
Should be? Should buzz!

Katherine
Well ta'en, and like a buzzard.

Petruccio
O slow-wing'd turtle! Shall a buzzard take thee?

Katherine
Ay, for a turtle, as he takes a buzzard.

Petruccio
Come, come, you wasp; i' faith, you are too angry.

Katherine
If I be waspish, best beware my sting.

Petruccio
My remedy is then to pluck it out.

Katherine
Ay, if the fool could find it where it lies.

Petruccio
Who knows not where a wasp does
wear his sting? In his tail.

Katherine
In his tongue.

Petruccio
Whose tongue?

Katherine
Yours, if you talk of tales, and so farewell.

Petruccio
What, with my tongue in your tail? Nay, come again,
Good Kate; I am a gentleman.

Katherine
That I'll try.

[She strikes him]

Petruccio
I swear I'll cuff you if you strike again.

Katherine
So may you lose your arms.
If you strike me, you are no gentleman,
And if no gentleman, why then, no arms.

Petruccio
A herald, Kate? O, put me in thy books!

Katherine
What is your crest—a coxcomb?

Petruccio
A combless cock, so Kate will be my hen.

Katherine
No cock of mine; you crow too like a craven.

Petruccio
Nay, come, Kate, come; you must not look so sour.

Katherine
It is my fashion when I see a crab.

Petruccio
Why, here's no crab; and therefore look not sour.

Katherine
There is, there is.

Petruccio
Then show it me.

Katherine
Had I a glass, I would.

Petruccio
What, you mean my face?

Katherine
Well aim'd of such a young one.

Petruccio
Now, by Saint George, I am too young for you.

Katherine
Yet you are wither'd.

Petruccio
'Tis with cares.

Katherine
I care not.

Petruccio
Nay, hear you, Kate: in sooth you scape not so.

Katherine
I chafe you if I tarry. Let me go.

Petruccio
No, not a whit: I find you passing gentle.
'Twas told me you were rough and coy and sullen,
And now I find report a very liar;
For thou are pleasant, gamesome, passing courteous,
But slow in speech, yet sweet as spring-time flowers:
Thou canst not frown, thou canst not look askance,
Nor bite the lip, as angry wenches will,
Nor hast thou pleasure to be cross in talk,
But thou with mildness entertain'st thy wooers,
With gentle conference, soft and affable.
Why does the world report that Kate doth limp?
O slanderous world! Kate like the hazel-twig
Is straight and slender and as brown in hue
As hazel nuts and sweeter than the kernels.
O, let me see thee walk: thou dost not halt.

Katherine
Go, fool, and whom thou keep'st command.

Petruccio
Did ever Dian so become a grove
As Kate this chamber with her princely gait?
O, be thou Dian, and let her be Kate;
And then let Kate be chaste and Dian sportful!

Katherine
Where did you study all this goodly speech?

Petruccio
It is extempore, from my mother-wit.

Katherine
A witty mother! Witless else her son.

Petruccio
Am I not wise?

Katherine
Yes; keep you warm.

Petruccio
Marry, so I mean, sweet Katherine, in thy bed:
And therefore, setting all this chat aside,
Thus in plain terms: your father hath consented
That you shall be my wife; your dowry 'greed on;
And will you, nill you, I will marry you.
Now, Kate, I am a husband for your turn;
For, by this light, whereby I see thy beauty—
Thy beauty, that doth make me like thee well—
Thou must be married to no man but me;

[Re-enter BAPTISTA, GREMIO, and TRANIO]

For I am he am born to tame you, Kate,
And bring you from a wild Kate to a Kate
Conformable as other household Kates.
Here comes your father. Never make denial.
I must and will have Katherine to my wife.

Baptista
Now, Signor Petruccio, how speed you with my daughter?

Petruccio
How but well, sir, how but well?
It were impossible I should speed amiss.

Baptista
    Why, how now, daughter Katherine! In your dumps?

Katherine
    Call you me daughter? Now I promise you
    You have show'd a tender fatherly regard,
    To wish me wed to one half-lunatic;
    A madcap ruffian and a swearing Jack,
    That thinks with oaths to face the matter out.

Petruccio
    Father, 'tis thus: yourself and all the world,
    That talk'd of her, have talk'd amiss of her.
    If she be curst, it is for policy,
    For she's not froward, but modest as the dove.
    She is not hot, but temperate as the morn.
    For patience she will prove a second Grissel,
    And Roman Lucrece for her chastity.
    And to conclude, we have 'greed so well together,
    That upon Sunday is the wedding-day.

Katherine
    I'll see thee hang'd on Sunday first.

Gremio
    Hark, Petruccio; she says she'll see thee
    hang'd first.

Tranio
    Is this your speeding? Nay, then, good night our part!

Petruccio
    Be patient, gentlemen; I choose her for myself.
    If she and I be pleased, what's that to you?
    'Tis bargain'd 'twixt us twain, being alone,
    That she shall still be curst in company.
    I tell you, 'tis incredible to believe
    How much she loves me. O, the kindest Kate!
    She hung about my neck; and kiss on kiss
    She vied so fast, protesting oath on oath,
    That in a twink she won me to her love.
    O, you are novices! 'Tis a world to see
    How tame, when men and women are alone,
    A meacock wretch can make the curstest shrew.
    Give me thy hand, Kate: I will unto Venice,
    To buy apparel 'gainst the wedding-day.
    Provide the feast, father, and bid the guests;
    I will be sure my Katherine shall be fine.

Baptista
    I know not what to say, but give me your hands;
    God send you joy, Petruccio! 'Tis a match.

Gremio and Tranio together
    Amen, say we. We will be witnesses.

Petruccio
    Father, and wife, and gentlemen, adieu.
    I will to Venice; Sunday comes apace.
    We will have rings and things and fine array;
    And kiss me, Kate. We will be married o'Sunday.

[Exeunt PETRUCCIO and KATHERINE, severally]

Gremio
    Was ever match clapp'd up so suddenly?

Baptista
    Faith, gentlemen, now I play a merchant's part,
    And venture madly on a desperate mart.

Tranio
    'Twas a commodity lay fretting by you:
    'Twill bring you gain, or perish on the seas.

Baptista
    The gain I seek is quiet in the match.

Gremio
    No doubt but he hath got a quiet catch.
    But now, Baptista, to your younger daughter:
    Now is the day we long have looked for.
    I am your neighbour, and was suitor first.

Tranio
    And I am one that love Bianca more
    Than words can witness, or your thoughts can guess.

Gremio
    Youngling, thou canst not love so dear as I.

Tranio
    Graybeard, thy love doth freeze.

Gremio
    But thine doth fry.
    Skipper, stand back: 'tis age that nourisheth.

Tranio
    But youth in ladies' eyes that flourisheth.

Baptista
    Content you, gentlemen: I will compound this strife.
    'Tis deeds must win the prize; and he of both
    That can assure my daughter greatest dower
    Shall have my Bianca's love.
    Say, Signor Gremio, what can you assure her?

Gremio
    First, as you know, my house within the city
    Is richly furnished with plate and gold;
    Basins and ewers to lave her dainty hands;
    My hangings all of Tyrian tapestry;
    In ivory coffers I have stuff'd my crowns;
    In cypress chests my arras counterpoints,
    Costly apparel, tents, and canopies,
    Fine linen, Turkey cushions boss'd with pearl,
    Valance of Venice gold in needlework,
    Pewter and brass and all things that belong
    To house or housekeeping. Then at my farm
    I have a hundred milch-kine to the pail,
    Sixscore fat oxen standing in my stalls,
    And all things answerable to this portion.
    Myself am struck in years, I must confess;
    And if I die to-morrow, this is hers,
    If whilst I live she will be only mine.

Tranio
    That 'only' came well in. Sir, list to me:
    I am my father's heir and only son.
    If I may have your daughter to my wife,
    I'll leave her houses three or four as good,
    Within rich Pisa walls, as any one
    Old Signor Gremio has in Padua;
    Besides two thousand ducats by the year
    Of fruitful land, all which shall be her jointure.
    What, have I pinch'd you, Signor Gremio?

Gremio
    Two thousand ducats by the year of land!
    My land amounts not to so much in all:
    That she shall have; besides an argosy
    That now is lying in Marseilles road.
    What, have I choked you with an argosy?

Tranio
    Gremio, 'tis known my father hath no less
    Than three great argosies; besides two galliases,

And twelve tight galleys. These I will assure her,
And twice as much, whate'er thou offer'st next.

Gremio
Nay, I have offer'd all, I have no more;
And she can have no more than all I have:
If you like me, she shall have me and mine.

Tranio
Why, then the maid is mine from all the world,
By your firm promise: Gremio is out-vied.

Baptista
I must confess your offer is the best;
And, let your father make her the assurance,
She is your own; else, you must pardon me,
if you should die before him, where's her dower?

Tranio
That's but a cavil: he is old, I young.

Gremio
And may not young men die as well as old?

Baptista
Well, gentlemen,
I am thus resolved: on Sunday next you know
My daughter Katherine is to be married:
Now, on the Sunday following shall Bianca
Be bride to you, if you make this assurance;
If not, to Signor Gremio.
And so I take my leave, and thank you both.

Gremio
Adieu, good neighbour.

[Exit BAPTISTA]

Sirrah, young gamester, your father were a fool
To give thee all, and in his waning age
Set foot under thy table. Tut, a toy!
An old Italian fox is not so kind, my boy.

[Exit]

Tranio
A vengeance on your crafty wither'd hide!
Yet I have faced it with a card of ten.
'Tis in my head to do my master good:
I see no reason but supposed Lucentio
Must get a father, call'd 'supposed Vincentio;'
And that's a wonder: fathers commonly
Do get their children; but in this case of wooing,
A child shall get a sire, if I fail not of my cunning.

[Exit]

Answer *true* or *false* for each of the following statements.

3.60 _____ Katherine ties Petruccio up and demands to know who Bianca's suitors are.

3.61 _____ Bianca tells her father, Baptista, that Katherine is his favorite.

3.62 _____ Eager to wed his daughter, Baptista tells Petruccio that Katherine is the kindest woman he will every meet.

3.63 _____ Baptista unknowingly allows Lucentio and Hortensio to tutor Bianca.

3.64 _____ Katherine hits Hortensio in the head with a lute.

3.65 _____ Petruccio tells Baptista that he will beat Katherine into submission.

3.66 _____ Baptista is unconcerned about the financial arrangements surrounding the marriage.

3.67 _____ Petruccio insists on renaming Katherine and calls her "Kate."

3.68 _____ Katherine and Petruccio fight over the meanings of various words.

3.69 _____ Petruccio is permitted to marry Bianca on the following Sunday.

3.70 _____ Baptista will allow Bianca to marry the smartest tutor on the Sunday after Katherine's wedding.

ACT III
SCENE I

Padua. A room in BAPTISTA'S house.
[Enter LUCENTIO, HORTENSIO, and BIANCA]

Lucentio
Fiddler, forbear. You grow too forward, sir.
Have you so soon forgot the entertainment
Her sister Katherine welcomed you withal?

Hortensio
But, wrangling pedant, this is
The patroness of heavenly harmony:
Then give me leave to have prerogative;
And when in music we have spent an hour,
Your lecture shall have leisure for as much.

Lucentio
Preposterous ass, that never read so far
To know the cause why music was ordain'd!
Was it not to refresh the mind of man
After his studies or his usual pain?
Then give me leave to read philosophy,
And while I pause, serve in your harmony.

Hortensio
Sirrah, I will not bear these braves of thine.

Bianca
Why, gentlemen, you do me double wrong,
To strive for that which resteth in my choice.
I am no breeching scholar in the schools;
I'll not be tied to hours nor 'pointed times,
But learn my lessons as I please myself.
And, to cut off all strife, here sit we down:
Take you your instrument, play you the whiles;
His lecture will be done ere you have tuned.

Hortensio
You'll leave his lecture when I am in tune?

Lucentio
That will be never: tune your instrument.

Bianca
Where left we last?

Lucentio
Here, madam:
'Hic ibat Simois; hic est Sigeia tellus;
Hic steterat Priami regia celsa senis.'

Bianca
Construe them.

Lucentio
'Hic ibat,' as I told you before, 'Simois,' I am
Lucentio, 'hic est,' son unto Vincentio of Pisa,
'Sigeia tellus,' disguised thus to get your love;
'Hic steterat,' and that Lucentio that comes
a-wooing, 'Priami,' is my man Tranio, 'regia,'
bearing my port, 'celsa senis,' that we might
beguile the old pantaloon.

Hortensio
Madam, my instrument's in tune.

Bianca
Let's hear. O fie! the treble jars.

Lucentio
Spit in the hole, man, and tune again.

Bianca
Now let me see if I can construe it: 'Hic ibat
Simois,' I know you not, 'hic est Sigeia tellus,' I
trust you not; 'Hic steterat Priami,' take heed
he hear us not, 'regia,' presume not, 'celsa senis,'
despair not.

Hortensio
Madam, 'tis now in tune.

Lucentio
All but the bass.

Hortensio
The bass is right; 'tis the base knave that jars.

[Aside]

How fiery and forward our pedant is!
Now, for my life, the knave doth court my love:
Pedascule, I'll watch you better yet.

Bianca
In time I may believe, yet I mistrust.

Lucentio
Mistrust it not: for, sure, Aeacides
Was Ajax, call'd so from his grandfather.

Bianca
I must believe my master; else, I promise you,
I should be arguing still upon that doubt:
But let it rest. Now, Licio, to you:
Good master, take it not unkindly, pray,
That I have been thus pleasant with you both.

Hortensio
You may go walk, and give me leave a while:
My lessons make no music in three parts.

Lucentio
Are you so formal, sir? Well, I must wait,

[Aside]

And watch withal; for, but I be deceived,
Our fine musician groweth amorous.

Hortensio
Madam, before you touch the instrument,
To learn the order of my fingering,
I must begin with rudiments of art,
To teach you gamut in a briefer sort,
More pleasant, pithy, and effectual
Than hath been taught by any of my trade:
And there it is in writing, fairly drawn.

Bianca
Why, I am past my gamut long ago.

Hortensio
Yet read the gamut of Hortensio.

Bianca [Reads]
"Gamut' I am, the ground of all accord,
'A—re'—to Plead Hortensio's passion;
'B—mi'—Bianca, take him for thy lord,
'C—fa ut'—that loves with all affection:
'D—sol re'—one clef, two notes have I:
'E—la mi'—show pity, or I die.'
Call you this gamut? Tut, I like it not:
Old fashions please me best; I am not so nice
To change true rules for old inventions.

[Enter a Servant]

Servant
  Mistress, your father prays you leave your books
  And help to dress your sister's chamber up:
  You know to-morrow is the wedding-day.

Bianca
  Farewell, sweet masters both; I must be gone.

[Exeunt BIANCA and Servant]

Lucentio
  Faith, mistress, then I have no cause to stay.

[Exit]

Hortensio
  But I have cause to pry into this pedant:
  Methinks he looks as though he were in love:
  Yet if thy thoughts, Bianca, be so humble
  To cast thy wandering eyes on every stale,
  Seize thee that list. If once I find thee ranging,
  Hortensio will be quit with thee by changing.

[Exit]

ACT III
SCENE II

  Padua. A room in BAPTISTA'S house.

[Enter BAPTISTA, GREMIO, TRANIO, KATHERINE, BIANCA, LUCENTIO, and others, attendants]

Baptista *[To TRANIO]*
  Signor Lucentio, this is the 'pointed day.
  That Katherine and Petruccio should be married,
  And yet we hear not of our son-in-law.
  What will be said? what mockery will it be,
  To want the bridegroom when the priest attends
  To speak the ceremonial rites of marriage?
  What says Lucentio to this shame of ours?

Katherine
  No shame but mine: I must, forsooth, be forced
  To give my hand opposed against my heart
  Unto a mad-brain rudesby full of spleen,
  Who woo'd in haste and means to wed at leisure.
  I told you, I, he was a frantic fool,
  Hiding his bitter jests in blunt behavior:
  And, to be noted for a merry man,
  He'll woo a thousand, 'point the day of marriage,
  Make friends, invite them, and proclaim the banns,
  Yet never means to wed where he hath woo'd.
  Now must the world point at poor Katherine
  And say, 'Lo, there is mad Petruccio's wife,
  If it would please him come and marry her!'

Tranio
  Patience, good Katherine, and Baptista, too.
  Upon my life, Petruccio means but well.
  Whatever fortune stays him from his word,
  Though he be blunt, I know him passing wise;
  Though he be merry, yet withal he's honest.

Katherine
  Would Katherine had never seen him, though!

[Exit weeping, followed by BIANCA and others]

Baptista
  Go, girl; I cannot blame thee now to weep;
  For such an injury would vex a very saint,
  Much more a shrew of thy impatient humour.

[Enter BIONDELLO]

Biondello
  Master, master! News—old news, and such news as you never heard of!

Baptista
  Is it new and old too? How may that be?

Biondello
  Why, is it not news to hear of Petruccio's coming?

Baptista
  Is he come?

Biondello
  Why, no, sir.

Baptista
  What then?

Biondello
  He is coming.

Baptista
  When will he be here?

Biondello
  When he stands where I am and sees you there.

Tranio
  But say, what to thine old news?

Biondello
  Why, Petruccio is coming in a new hat and an old jerkin, a pair of old breeches thrice turned, a pair of boots that have been candle-cases, one buckled, another laced, an old rusty sword ta'en out of the town-armory, with a broken hilt, and chapeless; with two broken points: his horse hipped with an old mothy saddle and stirrups of no kindred; besides, possessed with the glanders and like to mose in the chine; troubled with the lampass, infected with the fashions, full of wingdalls, sped with spavins, rayed with yellows, past cure of the fives, stark spoiled with the staggers, begnawn with the bots, swayed in the back and shoulder-shotten; near-legged before and with, a half-chequed bit and a head-stall of sheeps leather which, being restrained to keep him from stumbling, hath been often burst and now repaired with knots; one girth six times pieced and a woman's crupper of velure, which hath two letters for her name fairly set down in studs, and here and there pieced with packthread.

Baptista
  Who comes with him?

Biondello
  O, sir, his lackey, for all the world caparisoned like the horse; with a linen stock on one leg and a kersey boot-hose on the other, gartered with a red and blue list; an old hat and 'the humour of forty fancies' pricked in't for a feather: a monster, a very monster in apparel, and not like a Christian footboy or a gentleman's lackey.

Tranio
  'Tis some odd humour pricks him to this fashion;
  Yet oftentimes he goes but mean-apparell'd.

Baptista
  I am glad he's come, howsoe'er he comes.

Biondello
  Why, sir, he comes not.

Baptista
Didst thou not say he comes?

Biondello
Who? That Petruccio came?

Baptista
Ay, that Petruccio came.

Biondello
No, sir, I say his horse comes, with him on his back.

Baptista
Why, that's all one.

Biondello
Nay, by Saint Jamy,
I hold you a penny,
A horse and a man
Is more than one,
And yet not many.

[Enter PETRUCCIO and GRUMIO]

Petruccio
Come, where be these gallants? Who's at home?

Baptista
You are welcome, sir.

Petruccio
And yet I come not well.

Baptista
And yet you halt not.

Tranio
Not so well apparell'd as I wish you were.

Petruccio
Were it better, I should rush in thus.
But where is Kate? Where is my lovely bride?
How does my father? Gentles, methinks you frown:
And wherefore gaze this goodly company,
As if they saw some wondrous monument,
Some comet or unusual prodigy?

Baptista
Why, sir, you know this is your wedding-day:
First were we sad, fearing you would not come;
Now sadder, that you come so unprovided.
Fie, doff this habit, shame to your estate,
An eye-sore to our solemn festival!

Tranio
And tells us, what occasion of import
Hath all so long detain'd you from your wife,
And sent you hither so unlike yourself?

Petruccio
Tedious it were to tell, and harsh to hear:
Sufficeth I am come to keep my word,
Though in some part enforced to digress,
Which, at more leisure, I will so excuse
As you shall well be satisfied withal.
But where is Kate? I stay too long from her.
The morning wears, 'tis time we were at church.

Tranio
See not your bride in these unreverent robes.
Go to my chamber; put on clothes of mine.

Petruccio
Not I, believe me. Thus I'll visit her.

Baptista
But thus, I trust, you will not marry her.

Petruccio
Good sooth, even thus. Therefore ha' done with words.
To me she's married, not unto my clothes:
Could I repair what she will wear in me,
As I can change these poor accoutrements,
'Twere well for Kate and better for myself.
But what a fool am I to chat with you
When I should bid good morrow to my bride,
And seal the title with a lovely kiss!

[Exeunt PETRUCCIO and GRUMIO]

Tranio
He hath some meaning in his mad attire.
We will persuade him, be it possible,
To put on better ere he go to church.

Baptista
I'll after him, and see the event of this.

[Exeunt BAPTISTA, GREMIO, and attendants]

Tranio
But, sir, to love concerneth us to add
Her father's liking, which to bring to pass,
As I before imparted to your worship,
I am to get a man—whate'er he be,
It skills not much, we'll fit him to our turn—
And he shall be Vincentio of Pisa,
And make assurance here in Padua
Of greater sums than I have promised.
So shall you quietly enjoy your hope,
And marry sweet Bianca with consent.

Lucentio
Were it not that my fellow-school-master
Doth watch Bianca's steps so narrowly,
'Twere good, methinks, to steal our marriage,
Which once perform'd, let all the world say no,
I'll keep mine own, despite of all the world.

Tranio
That by degrees we mean to look into,
And watch our vantage in this business.
We'll over-reach the greybeard Gremio,
The narrow-prying father Minola,
The quaint musician, amorous Licio;
All for my master's sake, Lucentio.

[Re-enter GREMIO]

Signor Gremio, came you from the church?

Gremio
As willingly as e'er I came from school.

Tranio
And is the bride and bridegroom coming home?

Gremio
A bridegroom, say you? 'Tis a groom indeed—
A grumbling groom, and that the girl shall find.

Tranio
Curster than she? Why, 'tis impossible.

Gremio
Why he's a devil, a devil, a very fiend.

Tranio
Why, she's a devil, a devil, the devil's dam.

Gremio
Tut, she's a lamb, a dove, a fool to him!
I'll tell you, Sir Lucentio: when the priest
Should ask, if Katherine should be his wife,

'Ay, by Gogs-wouns,' quoth he, and swore so loud,
That, all-amazed, the priest let fall the book;
And, as he stoop'd again to take it up,
The mad-brain'd bridegroom took him such a cuff
That down fell priest and book and book and priest:
'Now take them up,' quoth he, 'if any list.'

Tranio
What said the vicar when he rose again?

Gremio
Trembled and shook; for why, he stamp'd and swore,
As if the vicar meant to cozen him.
But after many ceremonies done,
He calls for wine: 'A health!' quoth he, as if
He had been aboard, carousing to his mates
After a storm; quaff'd off the muscadel
And threw the sops all in the sexton's face,
Having no other reason
But that his beard grew thin and hungerly
And seem'd to ask him sops as he was drinking.
This done, he took the bride about the neck
And kiss'd her lips with such a clamorous smack
That at the parting all the church did echo:
And I seeing this came thence for very shame;
And after me, I know, the rout is coming.
Such a mad marriage never was before:
Hark, hark! I hear the minstrels play.

[Music]

[Re-enter PETRUCCIO, KATHERINE, BIANCA, BAPTISTA, HORTENSIO, GRUMIO, and Train]

Petruccio
Gentlemen and friends, I thank you for your pains:
I know you think to dine with me to-day,
And have prepared great store of wedding cheer;
But so it is, my haste doth call me hence,
And therefore here I mean to take my leave.

Baptista
Is't possible you will away to-night?

Petruccio
I must away to-day, before night come:
Make it no wonder. If you knew my business,
You would entreat me rather go than stay.
And, honest company, I thank you all,
That have beheld me give away myself
To this most patient, sweet, and virtuous wife:
Dine with my father, drink a health to me,
For I must hence; and farewell to you all.

Tranio
Let us entreat you stay till after dinner.

Petruccio
It may not be.

Gremio
Let me entreat you.

Petruccio
It cannot be.

Katherine
Let me entreat you.

Petruccio
I am content.

Katherine
Are you content to stay?

Petruccio
I am content you shall entreat me stay;
But yet not stay, entreat me how you can.

Katherine
Now, if you love me, stay.

Petruccio
Grumio, my horse.

Grumio
Ay, sir, they be ready: the oats have eaten the horses.

Katherine
Nay, then,
Do what thou canst, I will not go to-day;
No, nor to-morrow, not till I please myself.
The door is open, sir; there lies your way;
You may be jogging whiles your boots are green;
For me, I'll not be gone till I please myself:
'Tis like you'll prove a jolly, surly groom,
That take it on you at the first so roundly.

Petruccio
O Kate, content thee; prithee, be not angry.

Katherine
I will be angry: what hast thou to do?
Father, be quiet; he shall stay my leisure.

Gremio
Ay, marry, sir. Now it begins to work.

Katherine
Gentlemen, forward to the bridal dinner:
I see a woman may be made a fool
If she had not a spirit to resist.

Petruccio
They shall go forward, Kate, at thy command.
Obey the bride, you that attend on her;
Go to the feast, revel and domineer,
Carouse full measure to her maidenhead,
Be mad and merry, or go hang yourselves:
But for my bonny Kate, she must with me.
Nay, look not big, nor stamp, nor stare, nor fret;
I will be master of what is mine own:
She is my goods, my chattels; she is my house,
My household stuff, my field, my barn,
My horse, my ox, my ass, my anything;
And here she stands, touch her whoever dare.
I'll bring mine action on the proudest he
That stops my way in Padua. Grumio,
Draw forth thy weapon, we are beset with thieves.
Rescue thy mistress, if thou be a man.
Fear not, sweet wench, they shall not touch
thee, Kate:
I'll buckler thee against a million.

[Exeunt PETRUCCIO, KATHERINE, and GRUMIO]

Baptista
Nay, let them go, a couple of quiet ones.

Gremio
Went they not quickly, I should die with laughing.

Tranio
Of all mad matches never was the like.

Lucentio
Mistress, what's your opinion of your sister?

Bianca
That, being mad herself, she's madly mated.

Gremio
I warrant him, Petruccio is Kated.

Baptista
Neighbours and friends, though bride and bridegroom wants
For to supply the places at the table,
You know there wants no junkets at the feast.
Lucentio, you shall supply the bridegroom's place:
And let Bianca take her sister's room.

Tranio
Shall sweet Bianca practise how to bride it?

Baptista
She shall, Lucentio. Come, gentlemen, let's go.

[Exeunt]

♣ **Answer *true* or *false* for each of the following statements.**

3.71 _____ Lucentio tells Bianca his true identity while he is giving her a Latin lesson.

3.72 _____ Petruccio arrives at the wedding late and dressed in strange clothing.

3.73 _____ Petruccio behaves wildly during the wedding.

3.74 _____ During the reception, Kate draws a sword and announces to all that Petruccio is her property.

3.75 _____ When Petruccio and Kate leave early, Baptista tells Bianca to take her sister's place.

ACT IV
SCENE I

Padua. BAPTISTA'S house.

[Enter GRUMIO]

Grumio
Fie, fie on all tired jades, on all mad masters, and all foul ways! Was ever man so beaten? Was ever man so rayed? Was ever man so weary? I am sent before to make a fire, and they are coming after to warm them. Now, were not I a little pot and soon hot, my very lips might freeze to my teeth, my tongue to the roof of my mouth, my heart in my belly, ere I should come by a fire to thaw me: but I, with blowing the fire, shall warm myself; for, considering the weather, a taller man than I will take cold. Holla, ho! Curtis.

[Enter CURTIS]

Curtis
Who is that calls so coldly?

Grumio
A piece of ice: if thou doubt it, thou mayst slide from my shoulder to my heel with no greater a run but my head and my neck. A fire, good Curtis!

Curtis
Is my master and his wife coming, Grumio?

Grumio
O, ay, Curtis, ay: and therefore fire, fire; cast on no water.

Curtis
Is she so hot a shrew as she's reported?

Grumio
She was, good Curtis, before this frost: but, thou knowest, winter tames man, woman, and beast; for it hath tamed my old master and my new mistress and myself, fellow Curtis.

Curtis
Away, you three-inch fool! I am no beast.

Grumio
Am I but three inches? Why, thy horn is a foot; and so long am I at the least. But wilt thou make a fire, or shall I complain on thee to our mistress, whose hand—she being now at hand—thou shalt soon feel, to thy cold comfort, for being slow in thy hot office?

Curtis
I prithee, good Grumio, tell me, how goes the world?

Grumio
A cold world, Curtis, in every office but thine; and therefore fire: do thy duty, and have thy duty; for my master and mistress are almost frozen to death.

Curtis
There's fire ready; and therefore, good Grumio, the news.

Grumio
Why, 'Jack, boy! ho! boy!' and as much news as will thaw.

Curtis
Come, you are so full of cony-catching!

Grumio
Why, therefore fire, for I have caught extreme cold. Where's the cook? Is supper ready, the house trimmed, rushes strewed, cobwebs swept; the serving-men in their new fustian, their white stockings, and every officer his wedding-garment on? Be the Jacks fair within, the Jills fair without, the carpets laid, and every thing in order?

Curtis
All ready; and therefore, I pray thee, news.

Grumio
First, know my horse is tired, my master and mistress fallen out.

Curtis
How?

Grumio
Out of their saddles into the dirt; and thereby hangs a tale.

Curtis
Let's ha't, good Grumio.

Grumio
Lend thine ear.

Curtis
Here.

Grumio
There.

[Strikes him]

Curtis
This is to feel a tale, not to hear a tale.

Grumio
And therefore 'tis called a sensible tale, and this cuff was but to knock at your ear and beseech listening. Now I begin: *Imprimis,* we came down a foul hill, my master riding behind my mistress.

Curtis
Both of one horse?

Grumio
What's that to thee?

Curtis
Why, a horse.

Grumio
Tell thou the tale: but hadst thou not crossed me, thou shouldst have heard how her horse fell and she under her horse; thou shouldst have heard in how miry a place, how she was bemoiled, how he left her with the horse upon her, how he beat me because her horse stumbled, how she waded through the dirt to pluck him off me, how he swore, how she prayed, that never prayed before, how I cried, how the horses ran away, how her bridle was burst, how I lost my crupper, with many things of worthy memory, which now shall die in oblivion and thou return unexperienced to thy grave.

Curtis
By this reckoning he is more shrew than she.

Grumio
Ay; and that thou and the proudest of you all shall find when he comes home. But what talk I of this? Call forth Nathaniel, Joseph, Nicholas, Philip, Walter, Sugarsop, and the rest. Let their heads be sleekly combed, their blue coats brushed, and their garters of an indifferent knit. Let them curtsy with their left legs and not presume to touch a hair of my master's horse-tail till they kiss their hands. Are they all ready?

Curtis
They are.

Grumio
Call them forth.

Curtis *[Calling]*
Do you hear, ho? You must meet my master to countenance my mistress.

Grumio
Why, she hath a face of her own.

Curtis
Who knows not that?

Grumio
Thou, it seems, that calls for company to countenance her.

Curtis
I call them forth to credit her.

Grumio
Why, she comes to borrow nothing of them.

[Enter four or five Serving-men]

Nathaniel
Welcome home, Grumio!

Philip
How now, Grumio?

Joseph
What, Grumio?

Nicholas
Fellow Grumio!

Nathaniel
How now, old lad?

Grumio
Welcome, you;—how now, you;— what, you;—fellow, you;—and thus much for greeting. Now, my spruce companions, is all ready, and all things neat?

Nathaniel
All things is ready. How near is our master?

Grumio
E'en at hand, alighted by this; and therefore be not—Cock's passion, silence! I hear my master.

[Enter PETRUCCIO and KATHERINE]

Petruccio
Where be these knaves? What, no man at door
To hold my stirrup nor to take my horse?
Where is Nathaniel, Gregory, Philip?

All Serving-men
Here, here, sir; here, sir.

Petruccio
Here, sir! Here, sir! Here, sir! Here, sir!
You logger-headed and unpolish'd grooms!
What! No attendance? No regard? No duty?
Where is the foolish knave I sent before?

Grumio
Here, sir; as foolish as I was before.

Petruccio
You peasant swain! You whoreson, malt-horse drudge!
Did I not bid thee meet me in the park,
And bring along these rascal knaves with thee?

Grumio
Nathaniel's coat, sir, was not fully made,
And Gabriel's pumps were all unpink'd i' the heel;
There was no link to colour Peter's hat,
And Walter's dagger was not come from sheathing:
There were none fine but Adam, Ralph, and Gregory;
The rest were ragged, old, and beggarly.
Yet, as they are, here are they come to meet you.

Petruccio
Go, rascals, go, and fetch my supper in.

[Exeunt Servants]
[Singing]

Where is the life that late I led?

Where are those—Sit down, Kate, and welcome.
Soud, soud, soud, soud!

[Re-enter Servants with supper]

Why, when, I say? Nay, good sweet Kate, be merry.
Off with my boots, you rogues, you villains! When?

[Sings]

It was the friar of orders grey,
As he forth walked on his way.
Out, you rogue! you pluck my foot awry.
Take that, and mend the plucking off the other.

[Strikes him]

Be merry, Kate. Some water, here. What, ho!
Where's my spaniel Troilus? Sirrah, get you hence,
And bid my cousin Ferdinand come hither—
One, Kate, that you must kiss, and be acquainted with.
Where are my slippers? Shall I have some water?

[Enter one with water]

Come, Kate, and wash, and welcome heartily.
You whoreson villain! Will you let it fall?

[Strikes him]

Katherine
Patience, I pray you; 'twas a fault unwilling.

Petruccio
A whoreson, beetle-headed, flap-ear'd knave!
Come, Kate, sit down. I know you have a stomach.
Will you give thanks, sweet Kate; or else shall I?
What's this? Mutton?

First Servant
Ay.

Petruccio
Who brought it?

Peter
I.

Petruccio
'Tis burnt; and so is all the meat.
What dogs are these? Where is the rascal cook?
How durst you, villains, bring it from the dresser,
And serve it thus to me that love it not?
There take it to you, trenchers, cups, and all;

[Throws the meat, & c. about the stage]

You heedless jolt-heads and unmanner'd slaves!
What, do you grumble? I'll be with you straight.

[Chases the servants away]

Katherine
I pray you, husband, be not so disquiet.
The meat was well, if you were so contented.

Petruccio
I tell thee, Kate, 'twas burnt and dried away;
And I expressly am forbid to touch it,
For it engenders choler, planteth anger;
And better 'twere that both of us did fast,
Since, of ourselves, ourselves are choleric,
Than feed it with such over-roasted flesh.
Be patient; to-morrow 't shall be mended,
And, for this night, we'll fast for company:
Come, I will bring thee to thy bridal chamber.

[Exeunt]
[Re-enter Servants severally]

Nathaniel
Peter, didst ever see the like?

Peter
He kills her in her own humour.

[Re-enter CURTIS]

Grumio
Where is he?

Curtis
In her chamber, making a sermon of continency to her;
And rails, and swears, and rates, that she, poor soul,
Knows not which way to stand, to look, to speak,
And sits as one new-risen from a dream.
Away, away, for he is coming hither!

[Exeunt]
[Re-enter PETRUCCIO]

Petruccio
Thus have I politicly begun my reign,
And 'tis my hope to end successfully.
My falcon now is sharp and passing empty;
And till she stoop she must not be full-gorged,
For then she never looks upon her lure.
Another way I have to man my haggard,
To make her come and know her keeper's call—
That is, to watch her, as we watch these kites
That bate and beat and will not be obedient.
She ate no meat to-day, nor none shall eat.
Last night she slept not, nor to-night she shall not;
As with the meat, some undeserved fault
I'll find about the making of the bed;
And here I'll fling the pillow, there the bolster,
This way the coverlet, another way the sheets:
Ay, and amid this hurly I intend
That all is done in reverend care of her;
And in conclusion she shall watch all night:
And if she chance to nod I'll rail and brawl
And with the clamour keep her still awake.
This is a way to kill a wife with kindness;
And thus I'll curb her mad and headstrong humour.
He that knows better how to tame a shrew,
Now let him speak: 'tis charity to show.

[Exit]

ACT IV
SCENE II

Padua. BAPTISTA'S house.

[Enter TRANIO and HORTENSIO]

Tranio
Is't possible, friend Licio, that Mistress Bianca
Doth fancy any other but Lucentio?
I tell you, sir, she bears me fair in hand.

Hortensio
Sir, to satisfy you in what I have said,
Stand by and mark the manner of his teaching.

[Enter BIANCA and LUCENTIO]

Lucentio
Now, mistress, profit you in what you read?

Bianca
What, master, read you? first resolve me that.

Lucentio
I read that I profess, *The Art to Love*.

Bianca
 And may you prove, sir, master of your art!

Lucentio
 While you, sweet dear, prove mistress of my heart!

Hortensio
 Quick proceeders, marry! Now, tell me, I pray,
 You that durst swear at your mistress Bianca
 Loved none in the world so well as Lucentio.

Tranio
 O despiteful love! unconstant womankind!
 I tell thee, Licio, this is wonderful.

Hortensio
 Mistake no more: I am not Licio,
 Nor a musician, as I seem to be;
 But one that scorn to live in this disguise,
 For such a one as leaves a gentleman,
 And makes a god of such a cullion:
 Know, sir, that I am call'd Hortensio.

Tranio
 Signor Hortensio, I have often heard
 Of your entire affection to Bianca;
 And since mine eyes are witness of her lightness,
 I will with you, if you be so contented,
 Forswear Bianca and her love for ever.

Hortensio
 See, how they kiss and court! Signor Lucentio,
 Here is my hand, and here I firmly vow
 Never to woo her no more, but do forswear her,
 As one unworthy all the former favours
 That I have fondly flatter'd her withal.

Tranio
 And here I take the like unfeigned oath
 Never to marry with her though she would entreat:
 Fie on her! see, how beastly she doth court him!

Hortensio
 Would all the world but he had quite forsworn!
 For me, that I may surely keep mine oath
 I will be married to a wealthy widow
 Ere three days pass, which hath as long loved me
 As I have loved this proud disdainful haggard.
 And so farewell, Signor Lucentio.
 Kindness in women, not their beauteous looks,
 Shall win my love: and so I take my leave,
 In resolution as I swore before.

[Exit]

Tranio
 Mistress Bianca, bless you with such grace
 As 'longeth to a lover's blessed case!
 Nay, I have ta'en you napping, gentle love,
 And have forsworn you with Hortensio.

Bianca
 Tranio, you jest: but have you both forsworn me?

Tranio
 Mistress, we have.

Lucentio
 Then we are rid of Licio.

Tranio
 I' faith, he'll have a lusty widow now,
 That shall be wooed and wedded in a day.

Bianca
 God give him joy!

Tranio
 Ay, and he'll tame her.

Bianca
 He says so, Tranio.

Tranio
 Faith, he is gone unto the taming-school.

Bianca
 The taming-school! What, is there such a place?

Tranio
 Ay, mistress, and Petruccio is the master;
 That teacheth tricks eleven-and-twenty long,
 To tame a shrew and charm her chattering tongue.

[Enter BIONDELLO]

Biondello
 O master, master, I have watch'd so long
 That I am dog-weary, but at last I spied
 An ancient angel coming down the hill,
 Will serve the turn.

Tranio
 What is he, Biondello?

Biondello
 Master, a mercantant or a pedant,
 I know not what; but format in apparel,
 In gait and countenance surely like a father.

Lucentio
 And what of him, Tranio?

Tranio
 If he be credulous and trust my tale,
 I'll make him glad to seem Vincentio
 And give assurance to Baptista Minola
 As if he were the right Vincentio
 Take in your love, and then let me alone.

[Exeunt LUCENTIO and BIANCA]
[Enter a Pedant]

Pedant
 God save you, sir!

Tranio
 And you, sir! You are welcome.
 Travel you far on, or are you at the farthest?

Pedant
 Sir, at the farthest for a week or two:
 But then up farther, and as far as Rome,
 And so to Tripoli, if God lend me life.

Tranio
 What countryman, I pray?

Pedant
 Of Mantua.

Tranio
 Of Mantua, sir? Marry, God forbid!
 And come to Padua, careless of your life?

Pedant
 My life, sir? how, I pray? For that goes hard.

Tranio
 'Tis death for any one in Mantua
 To come to Padua. Know you not the cause?
 Your ships are stay'd at Venice, and the duke,
 For private quarrel 'twixt your duke and him,

Hath publish'd and proclaim'd it openly.
'Tis, marvel, but that you are but newly come,
You might have heard it else proclaim'd about.

Pedant
Alas! sir, it is worse for me than so;
For I have bills for money by exchange
From Florence and must here deliver them.

Tranio
Well, Sir, to do you courtesy,
This will I do, andt this I will advise you:
First, tell me, have you ever been at Pisa?

Pedant
Ay, sir, in Pisa have I often been,
Pisa renowned for grave citizens.

Tranio
Among them know you one Vincentio?

Pedant
I know him not, but I have heard of him,
A merchant of incomparable wealth.

Tranio
He is my father, sir, and, sooth to say,
In countenance somewhat doth resemble you.

Biondello *[Aside]*
As much as an apple doth an oyster,
and all one.

Tranio
To save your life in this extremity,
This favour will I do you for his sake;
And think it not the worst of an your fortunes
That you are like to Sir Vincentio.
His name and credit shall you undertake,
And in my house you shall be friendly lodged.
Look that you take upon you as you should.
You understand me, sir? So shall you stay
Till you have done your business in the city.
If this be courtesy, sir, accept of it.

Pedant
O sir, I do, and will repute you ever
The patron of my life and liberty.

Tranio
Then go with me to make the matter good.
This, by the way, I let you understand—
My father is here look'd for every day
To pass assurance of a dower in marriage
'Twixt me and one Baptista's daughter here.
In all these circumstances I'll instruct you.
Go with me to clothe you as becomes you.

[Exeunt]

ACT IV
SCENE III

Padua. BAPTISTA'S house.

[Enter KATHERINE and GRUMIO]

Grumio
No, no, forsooth; I dare not for my life.

Katherine
The more my wrong, the more his spite appears.
What, did he marry me to famish me?
Beggars that come unto my father's door
Upon entreaty have a present aims;
If not, elsewhere they meet with charity.
But I, who never knew how to entreat,
Nor never needed that I should entreat,
Am starved for meat, giddy for lack of sleep,
With oath kept waking and with brawling fed:
And that which spites me more than all these wants,
He does it under name of perfect love;
As who should say, if I should sleep or eat,
'Twere deadly sickness or else present death.
I prithee go and get me some repast;
I care not what, so it be wholesome food.

Grumio
What say you to a neat's foot?

Katherine
'Tis passing good: I prithee let me have it.

Grumio
I fear it is too choleric a meat.
How say you to a fat tripe finely broil'd?

Katherine
I like it well. Good Grumio, fetch it me.

Grumio
I cannot tell; I fear 'tis choleric.
What say you to a piece of beef and mustard?

Katherine
A dish that I do love to feed upon.

Grumio
Ay, but the mustard is too hot a little.

Katherine
Why then, the beef, and let the mustard rest.

Grumio
Nay, then I will not: you shall have the mustard,
Or else you get no beef of Grumio.

Katherine
Then both, or one, or anything thou wilt.

Grumio
Why then, the mustard without the beef.

Katherine
Go, get thee gone, thou false, deluding slave,

[Beats him]

That feed'st me with the very name of meat:
Sorrow on thee and all the pack of you,
That triumph thus upon my misery!
Go, get thee gone, I say.

[Enter PETRUCCIO and HORTENSIO with meat]

Petruccio
How fares my Kate? What, sweeting, all amort?

Hortensio
Mistress, what cheer?

Katherine
Faith, as cold as can be.

Petruccio
Pluck up thy spirits; look cheerfully upon me.
Here, love, thou see'st how diligent I am
To dress thy meat myself and bring it thee.
I am sure, sweet Kate, this kindness merits thanks.
What, not a word? Nay, then thou lovest it not,
And all my pains is sorted to no proof.
Here, take away this dish.

Katherine
I pray you, let it stand.

Petruccio
The poorest service is repaid with thanks;
And so shall mine, before you touch the meat.

Katherine
I thank you, sir.

Hortensio
Signor Petruccio, fie! You are to blame.
Come, mistress Kate, I'll bear you company.

Petruccio *[Aside]*
Eat it up all, Hortensio, if thou lovest me.
Much good do it unto thy gentle heart!
Kate, eat apace: and now, my honey love,
Will we return unto thy father's house
And revel it as bravely as the best,
With silken coats and caps and golden rings,
With ruffs and cuffs and farthingales and things;
With scarfs and fans and double change of bravery,
With amber bracelets, beads and all this knavery.
What, hast thou dined? The tailor stays thy leisure,
To deck thy body with his ruffling treasure.

[Enter Tailor]

Come, tailor, let us see these ornaments;
Lay forth the gown.
[Enter Haberdasher]
What news with you, sir?

Haberdasher
Here is the cap your worship did bespeak.

Petruccio
Why, this was moulded on a porringer—
A velvet dish. Fie, fie! 'Tis lewd and filthy.
Why, 'tis a cockle or a walnut-shell,
A knack, a toy, a trick, a baby's cap.
Away with it! Come, let me have a bigger.

Katherine
I'll have no bigger: this doth fit the time,
And gentlewomen wear such caps as these.

Petruccio
When you are gentle, you shall have one too,
And not till then.

Hortensio *[Aside]*
That will not be in haste.

Katherine
Why, sir, I trust I may have leave to speak,
And speak I will. I am no child, no babe.
Your betters have endured me say my mind,
And if you cannot, best you stop your ears.
My tongue will tell the anger of my heart,
Or else my heart concealing it will break,
And rather than it shall, I will be free
Even to the uttermost, as I please, in words.

Petruccio
Why, thou say'st true; it is a paltry cap,
A custard-coffin, a bauble, a silken pie.
I love thee well in that thou likest it not.

Katherine
Love me or love me not, I like the cap;
And it I will have, or I will have none.

[Exit Haberdasher]

Petruccio
Thy gown? Why, ay. Come, tailor, let us see't.
O mercy, God! What masquing stuff is here?
What's this? A sleeve? 'Tis like a demi-cannon.
What, up and down carved like an apple-tart?
Here's snip and nip and cut and slish and slash,
Like to a censer in a barber's shop:
Why, what, i' devil's name, tailor, call'st thou this?

Hortensio *[Aside]*
I see she's like to have neither cap nor gown.

Tailor
You bid me make it orderly and well,
According to the fashion and the time.

Petruccio
Marry, and did; but if you be remember'd,
I did not bid you mar it to the time.
Go, hop me over every kennel home,
For you shall hop without my custom, sir:
I'll none of it. Hence, make your best of it.

Katherine
I never saw a better-fashion'd gown,
More quaint, more pleasing, nor more commendable.
Belike you mean to make a puppet of me.

Petruccio
Why, true; he means to make a puppet of thee.

Tailor
She says your worship means to make
a puppet of her.

Petruccio
O monstrous arrogance! Thou liest, thou thread,
thou thimble,
Thou yard, three-quarters, half-yard, quarter, nail!
Thou flea, thou nit, thou winter-cricket thou!
Braved in mine own house with a skein of thread?
Away, thou rag, thou quantity, thou remnant;
Or I shall so be-mete thee with thy yard
As thou shalt think on prating whilst thou livest!
I tell thee, I, that thou hast marr'd her gown.

Tailor
Your worship is deceived; the gown is made
Just as my master had direction:
Grumio gave order how it should be done.

Grumio
I gave him no order; I gave him the stuff.

Tailor
But how did you desire it should be made?

Grumio
Marry, sir, with needle and thread.

Tailor
But did you not request to have it cut?

Grumio
Thou hast faced many things.

Tailor
I have.

Grumio
Face not me. Thou hast braved many men; brave not me. I will neither be faced nor braved. I say unto thee, I bid thy master cut out the gown; but I did not bid him cut it to pieces. *Ergo*, thou liest.

Tailor
Why, here is the note of the fashion to testify.

Petruccio
Read it.

Grumio
The note lies in's throat if he say I said so.

Tailor *[Reads]*
'Imprimis, a loose-bodied gown.'

Grumio
Master, if ever I said loose-bodied gown, sew me in the skirts of it, and beat me to death with a bottom of brown thread. I said a gown.

Petruccio
Proceed.

Tailor *[Reads]*
With a small compassed cape:'

Grumio
I confess the cape.

Tailor *[Reads]*
'With a trunk sleeve.'

Grumio
I confess two sleeves.

Tailor *[Reads]*
'The sleeves curiously cut.'

Petruccio
Ay, there's the villany.

Grumio
Error i' the bill, sir; error i' the bill. I commanded the sleeves should be cut out and sewed up again; and that I'll prove upon thee, though thy little finger be armed in a thimble.

Tailor
This is true that I say: an I had thee in place where, thou shouldst know it.

Grumio
I am for thee straight: take thou the bill, give me thy mete-yard, and spare not me.

Hortensio
God-a-mercy, Grumio! Then he shall have no odds.

Petruccio
Well, sir, in brief, the gown is not for me.

Grumio
You are i' the right, sir. 'Tis for my mistress.

Petruccio
Go, take it up unto thy master's use.

Grumio
Villain, not for thy life. Take up my mistress' gown for thy master's use!

Petruccio
Why, sir, what's your conceit in that?

Grumio
O, sir, the conceit is deeper than you think for: "Take up my mistress' gown to his master's use!" O, fie, fie, fie!

Petruccio *[Aside]*
Hortensio, say thou wilt see the tailor paid. Go take it hence; be gone, and say no more.

Hortensio
Tailor, I'll pay thee for thy gown tomorrow: Take no unkindness of his hasty words:

Away! I say. Commend me to thy master.

[Exit Tailor]

Petruccio
Well, come, my Kate; we will unto your father's
Even in these honest mean habiliments:
Our purses shall be proud, our garments poor;
For 'tis the mind that makes the body rich;
And as the sun breaks through the darkest clouds,
So honour peereth in the meanest habit.
What is the jay more precious than the lark,
Because his feathers are more beautiful?
Or is the adder better than the eel,
Because his painted skin contents the eye?
O, no, good Kate; neither art thou the worse
For this poor furniture and mean array.
if thou account'st it shame, lay it on me,
And therefore frolic, we will hence forthwith,
To feast and sport us at thy father's house.
Go, call my men, and let us straight to him;
And bring our horses unto Long Lane end.
There will we mount, and thither walk on foot
Let's see; I think 'tis now some seven o'clock,
And well we may come there by dinner-time.

Katherine
I dare assure you, sir, 'tis almost two;
And 'twill be supper-time ere you come there.

Petruccio
It shall be seven ere I go to horse:
Look, what I speak, or do, or think to do,
You are still crossing it. Sirs, let't alone:
I will not go to-day; and ere I do,
It shall be what o'clock I say it is.

Hortensio *[Aside]*
Why, so this gallant will command the sun.

[Exeunt]

ACT IV
SCENE IV

Padua. BAPTISTA'S house.

[Enter TRANIO, and the Pedant dressed like VINCENTIO]

Tranio
Sir, this is the house: please it you that I call?

Pedant
Ay, what else? And but I be deceived,
Signor Baptista may remember me
Near twenty years ago in Genoa—

Tranio
Where we were lodgers at the Pegasus—
'Tis well; and hold your own, in any case
With such austerity as 'longeth to a father.

Pedant
I warrant you.

[Enter BIONDELLO]

But, sir, here comes your boy;
'Twere good he were school'd.

Tranio
Fear you not him. Sirrah Biondello,
Now do your duty throughly, I advise you.
Imagine 'twere the right Vincentio.

Biondello
Tut, fear not me.

Tranio
But hast thou done thy errand to Baptista?

Biondello
I told him that your father was at Venice,
And that you look'd for him this day in Padua.

Tranio *[Giving money]*
Thou'rt a tall fellow: hold thee that to drink.
Here comes Baptista: set your countenance, sir.

[Enter BAPTISTA and LUCENTIO]

Signor Baptista, you are happily met.

[To the Pedant]

Sir, this is the gentleman I told you of.
I pray you stand good father to me now.
Give me Bianca for my patrimony.

Pedant
Soft, son!
Sir, by your leave, having come to Padua
To gather in some debts, my son Lucentio
Made me acquainted with a weighty cause
Of love between your daughter and himself,
And, for the good report I hear of you,
And for the love he beareth to your daughter,
And she to him, to stay him not too long
I am content in a good father's care
To have him match'd, and if you please to like
No worse than I, upon some agreement
Me shall you find ready and willing
With one consent to have her so bestow'd,
For curious I cannot be with you,
Signor Baptista, of whom I hear so well.

Baptista
Sir, pardon me in what I have to say.
Your plainness and your shortness please me well.
Right true it is your son Lucentio here
Doth love my daughter, and she loveth him,
Or both dissemble deeply their affections.
And therefore if you say no more than this,
That like a father you will deal with him
And pass my daughter a sufficient dower,
The match is made, and all is done.
Your son shall have my daughter with consent.

Tranio
I thank you, sir. Where then do you know best
We be affied, and such assurance ta'en
As shall with either part's agreement stand?

Baptista
Not in my house, Lucentio, for you know
Pitchers have ears, and I have many servants.
Besides, old Gremio is hearkening still,
And happily we might be interrupted.

Tranio
Then at my lodging, an it like you.
There doth my father lie, and there this night
We'll pass the business privately and well.
Send for your daughter by your servant here.
My boy shall fetch the scrivener presently.
The worst is this, that at so slender warning
You are like to have a thin and slender pittance.

Baptista
It likes me well. Biondello, hie you home,
And bid Bianca make her ready straight;
And, if you will, tell what hath happened—
Lucentio's father is arrived in Padua,
And how she's like to be Lucentio's wife.

[Exit LUCENTIO]

Biondello
I pray the gods she may with all my heart!

Tranio
Dally not with the gods, but get thee gone.

[Exit BIONDELLO]

Signor Baptista, shall I lead the way?
Welcome! One mess is like to be your cheer.
Come, sir; we will better it in Pisa.

Baptista
I follow you.

ACT IV
SCENE V

[Exeunt TRANIO, Pedant, and BAPTISTA]
[Re-enter BIONDELLO and LUCENTIO]

Biondello
Cambio!

Lucentio
What sayest thou, Biondello?

Biondello
You saw my master wink and laugh upon you?

Lucentio
Biondello, what of that?

Biondello
Faith, nothing; but has left me here behind to expound the meaning or moral of his signs and tokens.

Lucentio
I pray thee, moralize them.

Biondello
Then thus: Baptista is safe, talking with the deceiving father of a deceitful son.

Lucentio
And what of him?

Biondello
His daughter is to be brought by you to the supper.

Lucentio
And then?

Biondello
The old priest of Saint Luke's church is at your command at all hours.

Lucentio
And what of all this?

Biondello
I cannot tell; except they are busied about a counterfeit assurance. Take you assurance of her *'cum privilegio ad imprimendum solum:'* to the church; take the priest, clerk, and some sufficient honest witnesses. If this be not that you look for, I have no more to say, but bid Bianca farewell for ever and a day.

Lucentio
Hearest thou, Biondello?

Biondello
I cannot tarry: I knew a wench married in an afternoon as she went to the garden for parsley to stuff a rabbit; and so may you, sir, and so adieu, sir. My master hath appointed me to go to Saint Luke's to bid the priest be ready t' attend against you come with your appendix.

[Exit]

Lucentio
I may, and will, if she be so contented.
She will be pleased, then wherefore should I doubt?
Hap what hap may, I'll roundly go about her.
It shall go hard if Cambio go without her.

[Exit]

ACT IV
SCENE VI

Padua. BAPTISTA'S house.

[Enter PETRUCCIO, KATHERINE, HORTENSIO, and Servants]

Petruccio
Come on, i' God's name. Once more toward our father's.
Good Lord, how bright and goodly shines the moon!

Katherine
The moon? The sun. It is not moonlight now.

Petruccio
I say it is the moon that shines so bright.

Katherine
I know it is the sun that shines so bright.

Petruccio
Now, by my mother's son, and that's myself,
It shall be moon, or star, or what I list
Or ere I journey to your father's house.
Go on, and fetch our horses back again.
Evermore cross'd and cross'd, nothing but cross'd!

Hortensio
Say as he says, or we shall never go.

Katherine
Forward, I pray, since we have come so far,
And be it moon, or sun, or what you please,
An if you please to call it a rush-candle,
Henceforth I vow it shall be so for me.

Petruccio
I say it is the moon.

Katherine
I know it is the moon.

Petruccio
Nay, then you lie: it is the blessed sun.

Katherine
Then God be bless'd, it is the blessed sun,
But sun it is not when you say it is not,
And the moon changes even as your mind.
What you will have it named, even that it is;
And so it shall be still for Katherine.

Hortensio
Petruccio, go thy ways; the field is won.

Petruccio
Well, forward, forward! Thus the bowl should run,
And not unluckily against the bias.
But soft, company is coming here!

[Enter VINCENTIO]
[To VINCENTIO]

Good morrow, gentle mistress, where away?
Tell me, sweet Kate, and tell me truly too,
Hast thou beheld a fresher gentlewoman?
Such war of white and red within her cheeks?
What stars do spangle heaven with such beauty
As those two eyes become that heavenly face?
Fair lovely maid, once more good day to thee.
Sweet Kate, embrace her for her beauty's sake.

Hortensio
A' will make the man mad to make the woman of him.

Katherine
Young budding virgin, fair and fresh and sweet,
Whither away, or where is thy abode?
Happy the parents of so fair a child;
Happier the man whom favourable stars
Allot thee for his lovely bed-fellow!

Petruccio
Why, how now, Kate! I hope thou art not mad.
This is a man, old, wrinkled, faded, wither'd,
And not a maiden as thou say'st he is.

Katherine
Pardon, old father, my mistaking eyes
That have been so bedazzled with the sun
That everything I look on seemeth green.
Now I perceive thou art a reverend father.
Pardon, I pray thee, for my mad mistaking.

Petruccio
Do, good old grandsire, and withal make known
Which way thou travellest: if along with us,
We shall be joyful of thy company.

Vincentio
Fair sir, and you my merry mistress,
That with your strange encounter much amazed me,
My name is call'd Vincentio; my dwelling Pisa;
And bound I am to Padua, there to visit
A son of mine, which long I have not seen.

Petruccio
What is his name?

Vincentio
Lucentio, gentle sir.

Petruccio
Happily met, the happier for thy son.
And now by law, as well as reverend age,
I may entitle thee my loving father.
The sister to my wife, this gentlewoman,
Thy son by this hath married. Wonder not,
Nor be grieved. She is of good esteem,
Her dowery wealthy, and of worthy birth;
Beside, so qualified as may beseem
The spouse of any noble gentleman.
Let me embrace with old Vincentio,
And wander we to see thy honest son,
Who will of thy arrival be full joyous.

[PETRUCCIO embraces VINCENTIO]

Vincentio
But is it true? Or is it else your pleasure
Like pleasant travellers to break a jest
Upon the company you overtake?

Hortensio
I do assure thee, father, so it is.

Petruccio
Come, go along, and see the truth hereof;
For our first merriment hath made thee jealous.

[Exeunt all but HORTENSIO]

Hortensio
Well, Petruccio, this has put me in heart.
Have to my widow! And if she be froward,
Then hast thou taught Hortensio to be untoward.

[Exit]

◆ **Answer *true* or *false* for each of the following statements.**

3.76 _____ During the trip to Petruccio's house, Kate's horse trips and throws her into the mud.

3.77 _____ Petruccio graciously helps his new wife out of the mud and cleans her off.

3.78 _____ Petruccio is pleased to see all of his servants lined up to meet his new wife.

3.79 _____ Displeased, Kate throws the meat that is served and strikes a servant for spilling some water.

3.80 _____ Petruccio says that taming Kate is like training a falcon.

3.81 _____ Petruccio does not allow Kate to eat or sleep on their wedding night.

3.82 _____ Hortensio and Tranio watch Lucentio and Bianca together.

3.83 _____ Petruccio forces Kate to thank him for the food he has prepared for her.

3.84 _____ Petruccio shows Kate a new gown and allows her to wear it.

3.85 _____ Baptista agrees to meet Lucentio's father (the Pedant in disguise) to settle Bianca's dowry.

3.86 _____ Kate refuses to continue on the trip to her father's until Petruccio agrees that the sun is the moon or that the moon is the sun simply because she said it so.

3.87 _____ Vincentio is on his way to visit his son in Padua when Kate and Petruccio meet him on the road.

3.88 _____ Kate disagrees with Petruccio when he calls Vincentio a girl.

ACT V
SCENE I

Padua. Before BAPTISTA'S house.

[GREMIO discovered. Enter behind BIONDELLO, LUCENTIO, and BIANCA]

Biondello
Softly and swiftly, sir, for the priest is ready.

Lucentio
I fly, Biondello; but they may chance to need thee at home; therefore leave us.

Biondello
Nay, faith, I'll see the church o' your back and then come back to my master's as soon as I can.

[Exeunt LUCENTIO, BIANCA, and BIONDELLO]

Gremio
I marvel Cambio comes not all this while.

[Enter PETRUCCIO, KATHERINE, VINCENTIO, GRUMIO, with Attendants]

Petruccio
Sir, here's the door. This is Lucentio's house.
My father's bears more toward the market-place;
Thither must I, and here I leave you, sir.

Vincentio
You shall not choose but drink before you go.
I think I shall command your welcome here,
And, by all likelihood, some cheer is toward.

[Knocks]

Gremio
They're busy within; you were best knock louder.

[Pedant looks out of the window]

Pedant
What's he that knocks as he would beat down the gate?

Vincentio
Is Signor Lucentio within, sir?

Pedant
He's within, sir, but not to be spoken withal.

Vincentio
What if a man bring him a hundred pound or two to make merry withal?

Pedant
Keep your hundred pounds to yourself. He shall need none so long as I live.

Petruccio
Nay, I told you your son was well beloved in Padua. Do you hear, sir, to leave frivolous circumstances, I pray you, tell Signor Lucentio that his father is come from Pisa and is here at the door to speak with him.

Pedant
Thou liest. His father is come from Padua and here looking out at the window.

Vincentio
Art thou his father?

Pedant
Ay, sir, so his mother says, if I may believe her.

Petruccio *[To VINCENTIO]*
Why, how now, gentleman? Why, this is flat knavery, to take upon you another man's name.

Pedant
Lay hands on the villain. I believe a means to cozen somebody in this city under my countenance.

[Re-enter BIONDELLO]

Biondello *[Aside]*
I have seen them in the church together, God send 'em good shipping! But who is here? Mine old master, Vincentio! Now we are undone and brought to nothing.

Vincentio *[Seeing BIONDELLO]*
Come hither, crack-hemp.

Biondello
Hope I may choose, sir.

Vincentio
Come hither, you rogue. What, have you forgot me?

Biondello
Forgot you? No, sir, I could not forget you, for I never saw you before in all my life.

Vincentio
What, you notorious villain, didst thou never see thy master's father, Vincentio?

Biondello
What, my old worshipful old master? Yes, marry, sir, see where he looks out of the window.

Vincentio
Is't so indeed?

[Beats BIONDELLO]

Biondello
Help, help, help! Here's a madman will murder me.

[Exit]

Pedant
Help, son! Help, Signor Baptista!

[Exit from above]

Petruccio
Prithee, Kate, let's stand aside and see the end of this controversy.

[They retire]
[Re-enter Pedant below; TRANIO as LUCENTIO, BAPTISTA, and Servants]

Tranio
Sir, what are you that offer to beat my servant?

Vincentio
What am I, sir? Nay, what are you, sir? O immortal gods! O fine villain! A silken doublet! A velvet hose! A scarlet cloak! And a copintank hat! O, I am undone! I am undone! While I play the good husband at home, my son and my servant spend all at the university.

Tranio
How now! What's the matter?

Baptista
What, is the man lunatic?

Tranio
Sir, you seem a sober ancient gentleman by your habit, but your words show you a madman. Why, sir, what 'cerns it you if I wear pearl and gold? I thank my good father, I am able to maintain it.

Vincentio
Thy father! O villain! He is a sailmaker in Bergamo.

Baptista
You mistake, sir, you mistake, sir. Pray, what do you think is his name?

Vincentio
His name? As if I knew not his name—I have brought him up ever since he was three years old, and his name is Tranio.

Pedant
Away, away, mad ass! His name is Lucentio and he is mine only son, and heir to the lands of me, Signor Vincentio.

Vincentio
Lucentio? O, he hath murdered his master! Lay hold on him, I charge you, in the duke's name. O, my son, my son! Tell me, thou villain, where is my son Lucentio?

Tranio
Call forth an officer.

[Enter one with an Officer]

Carry this mad knave to the gaol. Father Baptista, I charge you see that he be forthcoming.

Vincentio
Carry me to the gaol?

Gremio
Stay, officer, he shall not go to prison.

Baptista
Talk not, Signor Gremio. I say he shall go to prison.

Gremio
Take heed, Signor Baptista, lest you be cony-catched in this business. I dare swear this is the right Vincentio.

Pedant
Swear, if thou darest.

Gremio
Nay, I dare not swear it.

Tranio
Then thou wert best say that I am not Lucentio.

Gremio
Yes, I know thee to be Signor Lucentio.

Baptista
Away with the dotard! To the gaol with him!

Vincentio
Thus strangers may be hailed and abused. O monstrous villain!

[Re-enter BIONDELLO, with LUCENTIO and BIANCA]

Biondello
O! We are spoiled and—yonder he is. Deny him, forswear him, or else we are all undone.

Lucentio [Kneeling]
Pardon, sweet father.

Vincentio
Lives my sweet son?

[Exeunt BIONDELLO, TRANIO, and Pedant, as fast as may be]

Bianca
Pardon, dear father.

Baptista
How hast thou offended?
Where is Lucentio?

Lucentio
Here's Lucentio,
Right son to the right Vincentio,
That have by marriage made thy daughter mine,
While counterfeit supposes bleared thine eyne.

Gremio
Here's packing with a witness, to deceive us all!

Vincentio
Where is that damned villain Tranio,
That faced and braved me in this matter so?

Baptista
Why, tell me, is not this my Cambio?

Bianca
Cambio is changed into Lucentio.

Lucentio
Love wrought these miracles. Bianca's love
Made me exchange my state with Tranio,
While he did bear my countenance in the town,
And happily I have arrived at the last
Unto the wished haven of my bliss.
What Tranio did, myself enforced him to.
Then pardon him, sweet father, for my sake.

Vincentio
I'll slit the villain's nose that would have sent me to the gaol.

Baptista
But do you hear, sir? Have you married my daughter without asking my good will?

Vincentio
Fear not, Baptista. We will content you. Go to, but I will in to be revenged for this villany.

[Exit]

Baptista
And I, to sound the depth of this knavery.

[Exit]

Lucentio
Look not pale, Bianca. Thy father will not frown.

[Exeunt LUCENTIO and BIANCA]

Gremio
My cake is dough, but I'll in among the rest,
Out of hope of all, but my share of the feast.

[Exit]

Katherine
Husband, let's follow to see the end of this ado.

Petruccio
First kiss me, Kate, and we will.

Katherine
What, in the midst of the street?

Petruccio
What, art thou ashamed of me?

Katherine
No, sir, God forbid; but ashamed to kiss.

Petruccio
Why, then, let's home again. Come, sirrah, let's away.

Katherine
Nay, I will give thee a kiss. Now pray thee, love, stay.

[They kiss]

Petruccio
Is not this well? Come, my sweet Kate.
Better once than never, for never too late.

[Exeunt]

ACT V
SCENE II

Padua. Before BAPTISTA'S house.

[Enter BAPTISTA, VINCENTIO, GREMIO, the Pedant, LUCENTIO, BIANCA, PETRUCCIO, KATHERINE, HORTENSIO, and Widow, TRANIO, BIONDELLO, and GRUMIO the Serving-men with Tranio bringing in a banquet]

Lucentio
At last, though long, our jarring notes agree,
And time it is when raging war is done
To smile at scapes and perils overblown.
My fair Bianca, bid my father welcome,
While I with self-same kindness welcome thine.
Brother Petruccio, sister Katherine,
And thou, Hortensio, with thy loving widow,
Feast with the best, and welcome to my house.
My banquet is to close our stomachs up
After our great good cheer. Pray you, sit down,
For now we sit to chat as well as eat.

Petruccio
Nothing but sit and sit, and eat and eat!

Baptista
Padua affords this kindness, son Petruccio.

Petruccio
Padua affords nothing but what is kind.

Hortensio
For both our sakes, I would that word were true.

Petruccio
Now, for my life, Hortensio fears his widow.

Widow
Then never trust me, if I be afeard.

Petruccio
You are very sensible, and yet you miss my sense:
I mean, Hortensio is afeard of you.

Widow
He that is giddy thinks the world turns round.

Petruccio
Roundly replied.

Katherine
Mistress, how mean you that?

Widow
Thus I conceive by him.

Petruccio
Conceives by me! How likes Hortensio that?

Hortensio
My widow says thus she conceives her tale.

Petruccio
Very well mended. Kiss him for that, good widow.

Katherine
'He that is giddy thinks the world turns round'—
I pray you, tell me what you meant by that.

Widow
Your husband, being troubled with a shrew,
Measures my husband's sorrow by his woe.
And now you know my meaning.

Katherine
A very mean meaning.

Widow
Right, I mean you.

Katherine
And I am mean indeed, respecting you.

Petruccio
To her, Kate!

Hortensio
To her, widow!

Petruccio
A hundred marks my Kate does put her down.

Hortensio
That's my office.

Petruccio
Spoke like an officer! Ha' to thee, lad!

[Drinks to HORTENSIO]

Baptista
How likes Gremio these quick-witted folks?

Gremio
Believe me, sir, they butt together well.

Bianca
Head and butt? An hasty-witted body
Would say your head and butt were head and horn.

Vincentio
Ay, mistress bride, hath that awaken'd you?

Bianca
Ay, but not frighted me; therefore I'll sleep again.

Petruccio
Nay, that you shall not. Since you have begun,
Have at you for a better jest or two!

Bianca
Am I your bird? I mean to shift my bush,
And then pursue me as you draw your bow.
You are welcome all.

[Exeunt BIANCA, KATHERINE, and Widow]

Petruccio
She hath prevented me here, Signor Tranio.
This bird you aim'd at, though you hit her not.
Therefore a health to all that shot and miss'd.

Tranio
O, sir, Lucentio slipp'd me like his greyhound,
Which runs himself and catches for his master.

Petruccio
A good swift simile, but something currish.

Tranio
'Tis well, sir, that you hunted for yourself.
'Tis thought your deer does hold you at a bay.

Baptista
O, O, Petruccio! Tranio hits you now.

Lucentio
I thank thee for that gird, good Tranio.

Hortensio
Confess, confess, hath he not hit you here?

Petruccio
A' has a little gall'd me, I confess;
And, as the jest did glance away from me,
'Tis ten to one it maim'd you two outright.

Baptista
Now, in good sadness, son Petruccio,
I think thou hast the veriest shrew of all.

Petruccio
Well, I say no. And therefore, Sir Assurance,
Let's each one send unto his wife;
And he whose wife is most obedient
To come at first when he doth send for her
Shall win the wager which we will propose.

Hortensio
Content. What is the wager?

Lucentio
Twenty crowns.

Petruccio
Twenty crowns!
I'll venture so much of my hawk or hound,
But twenty times so much upon my wife.

Lucentio
A hundred then.

Hortensio
Content.

Petruccio
A match! 'Tis done.

Hortensio
Who shall begin?

Lucentio
That will I.
Go, Biondello, bid your mistress come to me.

Biondello
I go.

[Exit].

Baptista
Son, I'll be your half, Bianca comes.

Lucentio
I'll have no halves; I'll bear it all myself.

[Re-enter BIONDELLO]

How now! What news?

Biondello
Sir, my mistress sends you word
That she is busy and she cannot come.

Petruccio
How? She is busy and she cannot come?
Is that an answer?

Gremio
Ay, and a kind one too.
Pray God, sir, your wife send you not a worse.

Petruccio
I hope better.

Hortensio
Sirrah Biondello, go and entreat my wife
To come to me forthwith.

[Exit BIONDELLO]

Petruccio
O ho, 'entreat' her—
Nay, then she must needs come.

Hortensio
I am afraid, sir,
Do what you can, yours will not be entreated.

[Re-enter BIONDELLO]

Now, where's my wife?

Biondello
She says you have some goodly jest in hand.
She will not come. She bids you come to her.

Petruccio
Worse and worse! She will not come! O vile,
Intolerable, not to be endured!
Sirrah Grumio, go to your mistress.
Say, I command her to come to me.

[Exit GRUMIO]

Hortensio
I know her answer.

Petruccio
What?

Hortensio
She will not.

Petruccio
The fouler fortune mine, and there an end.

Baptista
Now, by my halidom, here comes Katherine!

[Re-enter KATHERINE]

Katherine
What is your will, sir, that you send for me?

Petruccio
Where is your sister and Hortensio's wife?

Katherine
They sit conferring by the parlor fire.

Petruccio
Go, fetch them hither. If they deny to come,
Swinge me them soundly forth unto their husbands.
Away, I say, and bring them hither straight.

[Exit KATHERINE]

Lucentio
Here is a wonder, if you talk of a wonder.

Hortensio
And so it is. I wonder what it bodes.

Petruccio
Marry, peace it bodes, and love and quiet life;
And awful rule and right supremacy;
And, to be short, what not that's sweet and happy?

Baptista
Now, fair befall thee, good Petruccio!
The wager thou hast won; and I will add
Unto their losses twenty thousand crowns,
Another dowry to another daughter,
For she is changed as she had never been.

Petruccio
Nay, I will win my wager better yet
And show more sign of her obedience,
Her new-built virtue and obedience.
See where she comes and brings your froward wives
As prisoners to her womanly persuasion.

[Re-enter KATHERINE, with BIANCA and Widow]

Katherine, that cap of yours becomes you not.
Off with that bauble, throw it under-foot.

Widow
Lord, let me never have a cause to sigh,
Till I be brought to such a silly pass!

Bianca
Fie! What a foolish duty call you this?

Lucentio
I would your duty were as foolish too.
The wisdom of your duty, fair Bianca,
Hath cost me an hundred crowns since supper-time.

Bianca
The more fool you for laying on my duty.

Petruccio
Katherine, I charge thee, tell these headstrong women
What duty they do owe their lords and husbands.

Widow
Come, come, you're mocking. We will have no telling.

Petruccio
Come on, I say, and first begin with her.

Widow
She shall not.

Petruccio
I say she shall: and first begin with her.

Katherine
Fie, fie! Unknit that threatening unkind brow,
And dart not scornful glances from those eyes,
To wound thy lord, thy king, thy governor.
It blots thy beauty as frosts do bite the meads,
Confounds thy fame as whirlwinds shake fair buds,
And in no sense is meet or amiable.
A woman moved is like a fountain troubled,
Muddy, ill-seeming, thick, bereft of beauty;
And while it is so, none so dry or thirsty
Will deign to sip or touch one drop of it.

Thy husband is thy lord, thy life, thy keeper,
Thy head, thy sovereign; one that cares for thee,
And for thy maintenance commits his body
To painful labour both by sea and land,
To watch the night in storms, the day in cold,
Whilst thou liest warm at home, secure and safe;
And craves no other tribute at thy hands
But love, fair looks and true obedience;
Too little payment for so great a debt.
Such duty as the subject owes the prince
Even such a woman oweth to her husband;
And when she is froward, peevish, sullen, sour,
And not obedient to his honest will,
What is she but a foul contending rebel
And graceless traitor to her loving lord?
I am ashamed that women are so simple
To offer war where they should kneel for peace;
Or seek for rule, supremacy, and sway,
When they are bound to serve, love, and obey.
Why are our bodies soft and weak and smooth,
Unapt to toil and trouble in the world,
But that our soft conditions and our hearts
Should well agree with our external parts?
Come, come, you froward and unable worms!
My mind hath been as big as one of yours,
My heart as great, my reason haply more,
To bandy word for word and frown for frown;
But now I see our lances are but straws,
Our strength as weak, our weakness past compare,
That seeming to be most which we indeed least are.
Then vail your stomachs, for it is no boot,
And place your hands below your husband's foot,
In token of which duty, if he please,
My hand is ready; may it do him ease.

Petruccio
Why, there's a wench! Come on, and kiss me, Kate.

[They kiss]

Lucentio
Well, go thy ways, old lad, for thou shalt ha't.

Vincentio
'Tis a good hearing when children are toward.

Lucentio
But a harsh hearing when women are froward.

Petruccio
Come, Kate, we'll to bed.
We three are married, but you two are sped.

[To LUCENTIO]

'Twas I won the wager, though you hit the white;
And, being a winner, God give you good night!

[Exeunt PETRUCCIO and KATHERINE]

Hortensio
Now, go thy ways; thou hast tamed a curst shrew.

Lucentio
'Tis a wonder, by your leave, she will be tamed so.

[Exeunt]

➤ **Answer *true* or *false* for each of the following statements.**

3.89 _____ Biondella and Hortensio led Vincentio to Lucentio's house.

3.90 _____ Biondella beats Vincentio when he refuses to acknowledge that he knows him.

3.91 _____ Vincentio becomes convinced that his son has been murdered.

3.92 _____ After Lucentio returns from the church with Bianca, Vincentio insists that they get a divorce.

3.93 _____ Kate agrees right away to kiss Petruccio in the street.

3.94 _____ Lucentio bets that he has the most obedient wife.

3.95 _____ Petruccio shows his obedience to Kate by fetching Hortensio and Bianca.

3.96 _____ Hortensio calls Kate's obedience a "wonder."

3.97 _____ Petruccio asks Kate to tell the "headstrong" women what duty they owe to their husbands and lords.

3.98 _____ Kate tells the other women that a husband is the "head" of the wife and the "one that cares for" her.

The English Bible. The English Reformation was a revolution of heart and mind based on the teachings of a single book, the Bible. Leaders of the movement believed that "the knowledge of the Scriptures belonged unto all men." "The lively word of God, that every Christian person is bound to embrace, believe and follow" is contained within its pages. A translation that all men could read was, without doubt, needed.

During the Medieval Ages, the church based its doctrine and traditions on the Latin Vulgate, a translation of the bible by Jerome in the fifth century. Jerome based his translation on older Latin versions and the original Greek and Hebrew texts. However, within his Latin Vulgate are many mistakes. Attempting to make the Scriptures as accessible to the common man as possible (*vulgate* means common language), Jerome simplified the message, often replacing Catholic tradition for the literal meaning of a word. For example, Jerome replaced the phrase "to do penance" for *repent* in Matthew 4:17: "From that time Jesus began to preach and to say, 'repent for the kingdom of heaven is at hand.'" The error, of course, is not small. Priests reading the Latin Vulgate led the people to believe something contrary to the rest of Scripture. Penance is one of the seven sacraments of the Roman Catholic Church by which an individual performs certain religious acts that express sorrow and repentance for his or her sin.

Perceiving the errors of Roman Catholic tradition, John Wycliff (1330–1384) risked his life that the common man might have the Bible in his own language. His efforts were largely met with opposition. To read a translation of the Bible in English was punishable by death. In 1523 another man rose in Wycliff's place. William Tyndale, a student of Greek and Hebrew, was converted through the reading of the Scripture in its original languages. Determined that "even the boy that driveth the plough" should know more of the Scriptures than the pope, Tyndale began translating the original texts into English. After suffering much

Three Philosophers-1505

tribulation in England and in Europe, Tyndale finished his translation of the New Testament in 1526. The English copies were then smuggled into England and circulated widely. Because Tyndale worked without the sanction of the church, Henry VIII and his bishops considered his work to be full of heresy. Just before he completed the translation of the Old Testament, Tyndale was burned at the stake as a heretic. His dying words were, "O Lord, open the King of England's eyes."

God answered Tyndale's prayer. In 1537 Miles Coverdale was authorized to complete a revision of Tyndale's work. (Coverdale had published his own translation in 1535 in Zurich.) In 1540 the Great Bible was published under official sanction. By the command of Henry VIII, the Great Bible was to be used by the churches to "expressly provoke, stir and exhort every person to read the same." The Great Bible was used throughout Edward VI's reign but was later replaced by the Geneva translation.

The Geneva Bible was a product of the Puritan exiles during the tumultuous reign of Mary. It was published in 1560 and was the most accurate translation to date, although it also contained some errors. The Puritans took special care to translate the Word as literally as possible to avoid the errors of "popery." To make the Geneva as accessible as possible, its editors incorporated many changes. It was the first Bible to use marginal notes and divide the passages by numbered verses. It also traded the traditional black letter, or Gothic type, for the more readable Roman type. The Geneva Bible is typically viewed as the Puritan's Bible and was used by Cromwell and the churches in Scotland, but it also enjoyed lasting popularity among the general public. As noted by one writer, it was the Bible of Shakespeare, Sir Philip Sidney, and the Pilgrims.

Anglicans who protested the Puritan-based commentary of the Geneva Bible set out to produce another English translation. Revising the Great Bible, they produced the Bishops' Bible of 1568. Because the Geneva Bible contained comments that were undeniably Puritan, Queen Elizabeth named the Bishops' Bible the official Bible of the Anglican Church. However, the Geneva Bible remained the choice version among many English Protestants in their homes, noted one historian.

In response to the so called "false translations" of the Protestants, the Roman Catholic Church responded with the Douay-Rheims version. The English translation was based not upon the original Greek and Hebrew texts but upon the error-ridden Latin Vulgate. The completed edition was published in 1609–10.

Not long after King James I ascended the throne of England, a decree was issued that a new translation of the Bible would be made for the use of the Anglican Church. The king appointed forty-seven scholars to complete the work. The numbers were evenly divided between Anglicans and Puritans. The Authorized Version, published in 1611, was no new translation. It was a compilation of previous translations, the Geneva Bible being its largest contributor. However, unlike any of its predecessors, the King James Version has been considered "the noblest monument of English prose." Its editors avoided the most literal or direct translation, inserting words or phrases that would be most clearly understood by the people. Their aim was to produce a whole Bible, "as consonant as can be to the original Hebrew and Greek" but in a way that could be readily understood by the unlearned and accepted by Anglicans and Puritans. Its language is both beautiful and conservative. It is, as one critic has noted, the sum of English translations.

Underline the correct answer in each of the following statements.

3.99 The English (Renaissance, Enlightenment, Reformation) was a revolution of heart and mind based on the teachings of a single book, the Bible.

3.100 During the Medieval Ages, the church based its doctrine and traditions on the (Latin Vulgate, Geneva Bible, original Greek texts).

3.101 In the Latin Vulgate, Jerome replaced the word (*forgive, salvation, repent*) with the phrase "to do penance."

3.102 William Tyndale was converted by reading the Scriptures in (Latin, Greek and Hebrew, English).

3.103 (Wycliff's, Erasmus's, Tyndale's) English New Testament was first published in 1526.

3.104 Tyndale was burned at the stake for (treason, translating the Bible, marrying Princess Elizabeth).

3.105 In 1540 the Great Bible was published under official sanction of the (Roman Catholic, English, French) church.

3.106 The Great Bible was a completion of (Wycliff's, Jerome's, Tyndale's) translation of the Old and New Testament.

3.107 First published in 1560, The (Geneva Bible, Great Bible, Latin Vulgate) was produced by the Puritan exiles during Queen Mary's reign.

3.108 The (Great Bible, Geneva Bible, King James Version) was the first translation to include marginal notes and divide the passages by numbered verses.

3.109 The version most readily available to Shakespeare was the (Great Bible, Geneva Bible, King James Version).

3.110 (King James, Queen Mary, Queen Elizabeth) named the Bishops' Bible the official Bible of the Anglican Church.

3.111 The Catholic Douay-Rheims version was based upon the (Latin Vulgate, Eramus's Greek text, Tyndale's translation).

3.112 Published in 1611, the (Latin Vulgate, Authorized Version, Douay-Rheims Version) is a compilation of pervious English translations.

3.113 The largest contributor to the King James Version was the (Great Bible, Geneva Bible, Latin Vulgate).

3.114 The editors of the (King James Version, Geneva Bible, Great Bible) avoided the most literal or direct translation, inserting words or phrases that would be most clearly understood by the (scholars, priests, people).

3.115 The (King James Version, Geneva Bible, Great Bible) has been considered "the noblest monument of English prose."

What to Look For:

Considering the central part that the Bible played in the English Reformation, examine the following various English translations. As you read, compare and contrast the clarity of meaning and the style of the different Bibles. Also, think about the sources of the various translations.

Isaiah 53: 3–6

From *The Coverdale Bible*

He shall be the most simple and despised of all, which yet hath good experienced of sorrows and infirmities. We shall reckon him so simple and so vile that we shall hide our faces from him.

Howbeit (of a truth) he only taketh away our infirmity, and beareth our pain: Yet we shall judge him, as though he were plagued and cast down of God:

Whereas he (notwithstanding) shall be wounded for our offenses, and smitten for our wickedness. For the pain of our punishment shall be laid upon him, and with his stripes shall we be healed.

As for us, we go all astray (like sheep), everyone turneth his own way. But through him, the Lord pardoneth all our sins.

1535

From *The Great Bible*

He is despised and abhorred of men. He is such a man as is full of sorrow and as hath good experience of infirmities. We have reckoned him so vile that we hid our faces from him. Yea, he was despised and therefore we regarded him not.

Howbeit he only hath taken on him our infirmities and borne our pains. Yet we did judge him, as though he were plagued and cast down of God and punished.

Whereas he (notwithstanding) was wounded for our offenses and smitten for our wickedness. For the chastisement of our peace was laid upon him and with his stripes we are healed.

As for us, we have gone all astray, like sheep; every one hath turned his own way. But the Lord hath heaped together upon him the iniquity of us all.

1539–1540

From *The Geneva Bible*

He is despised and rejected of men. He is a man full of sorrows and hath experience of infirmities. We hid as it were our faces from him. He was despised and we esteemed him not.

Surely he hath borne our infirmities and carried our sorrows; yet we did judge him as plagued, and smitten of God, and humbled.

But he was wounded for our transgressions; he was broken for our iniquities; the chastisement of our peace was upon him, and with his stripes we are healed. All we like sheep have gone astray. We have turned every one to his own way, and the Lord hath laid upon him the iniquity of us all.

1560

From *The Douay-Rheims Bible*

Despised, and most abject of men, a man of sorrows, and knowing infirmity. And his look as it were hid and despised, whereupon neither have we esteemed him.

He surely hath borne our infirmities, and our sorrows he hath carried.

And we have thought him as it were a leper, and stricken of God and humbled. But he was wounded for our iniquities; he was broken for our sins. The discipline of our peace upon him, and with the wail of his stripe we are healed.

All we have strayed as sheep; everyone hath declined into his own way, and our Lord hath put upon him the iniquity of all us.

1609

From *The King James Bible*

He is despised and rejected of men; a man of sorrows, and acquainted with grief. And we hid as it were our faces from him. He was despised, and we esteemed him not.

Surely he hath borne our griefs and carried our sorrows; yet we did esteem him stricken, smitten of God, and afflicted.

But he was wounded for our transgressions; he was bruised for our iniquities. The chastisement of our peace was upon him, and with his stripes we are healed.

All we like sheep have gone astray; we have turned every one to his own way; and the Lord hath laid on him the iniquity of us all.

1611

Excerpts quoted, from <u>Norton Anthology of English Literature</u>, vol. 1, ed. M. H. Abrams (New York: W. W. Norton & Company, 1986), pp.1004-1005

 Fill in each of the following blanks with the correct answer.

3.116 Unlike the other Protestant translations, the Coverdale Bible phrases "the chastisement of our peace" as "the pain of our _____."

3.117 The Great Bible uses the word "_____" to modify "he" to indicate exactly who takes on our infirmities and bares our pains.

3.118 The Geneva Bible states that "we did judge him as _____, and smitten of God, and _____."

3.119 The Douay-Rheims Bible replaces the term *plagued,* as in the Great Bible and the Geneva, with the phrase "as it were a _____."

3.120 The last sentence of the King James text matches the last two sentences of the _____ Bible.

Before you take this last Self Test, you might want to do one or more of the following self checks.

1. _____ Read the objectives. Determine if you can do them.
2. _____ Restudy the material related to any objectives that you cannot do.
3. _____ Use the **SQ3R** study procedure to review the material.
   a. **S**can the sections.
   b. **Q**uestion yourself again (review the questions that you wrote initially).
   c. **R**ead to answer your questions.
   d. **R**ecite the answers to yourself.
   e. **R**eview areas that you didn't understand.
4. _____ Review all vocabulary, activities, and Self Tests, writing the correct answer for each answer you got wrong.

SELF TEST 3

Underline the correct answer in each of the following statements (each answer, 2 points).

3.01 The Protestant Reformers in England believed that (the church, Scripture, the king) alone was the guide to faith and life.

3.02 The (Renaissance, Reformation, Middle Ages) was a man-centered movement.

3.03 The ideals of the Renaissance and the Reformation shaped (Elizabethan, Classical, Modern) literature.

3.04 During his time, Sir Philip Sidney was considered the near-perfect (writer, courtier, soldier).

3.05 Sidney completed the first (epic, play, sonnet sequence) in England known as *Astrophil and Stella.*

3.06 Sir Walter Raleigh was a soldier and a seaman as well as a philosopher, a historian, and a (prince, merchant, poet).

3.07 Raleigh was one of (King James's, Queen Mary's, Queen Elizabeth's) most trusted advisors.

3.08 (King James, Queen Mary, Queen Elizabeth) imprisoned Raleigh on charges of treason and eventually had him beheaded.

3.09 William Shakespeare was born in (Stratford-on-Avon, London, Edinburgh).

3.010 Shakespeare was married to (Anne Burton, Anne Hathaway, Queen Elizabeth).

3.011 Shakespeare's first published work was a (narrative poem, play, sonnet sequence) titled *Venus and Adonis.*

3.012 *The Complete Edition of Shakespeare's Works,* also known as the (First Folio, First Quarto, First Book), was first published in (1603, 1599, 1623).

3.013 During the third period (1600–1608) of his career, Shakespeare wrote a rapid succession of (tragedies, comedies, history chronicles), which include *Hamlet, King Lear,* and *Othello.*

3.014 The English (Renaissance, Enlightenment, Reformation) was a revolution of heart and mind based on the teachings of a single book, the Bible.

3.015 Tyndale was burned at the stake for (treason, translating the Bible, marrying Princess Elizabeth).

3.016 In 1540 the Great Bible was published under official sanction of the (Roman Catholic, English, French) church.

3.017 First published in 1560, The (Geneva Bible, Great Bible, Latin Vulgate) was the first translation to include marginal notes and divide the passages by numbered verses.

3.018 The Catholic Douay-Rheims version was based upon the (Latin Vulgate, Eramus's Greek text, Tyndale's translation).

3.019 The editors of the (King James Version, Geneva Bible, Great Bible) avoided the most literal or direct translation, inserting words or phrases that would be most clearly understood by the (scholars, priests, people).

Answer *true* or *false* for each of the following statements (each answer, 1 point).

3.020 _____ The Utopians of Sir Thomas More's book value gold and silver highly.

3.021 _____ Before being burned at the stake, Thomas Cranmer denounced his recantation and called the pope Christ's enemy.

3.022 _____ Sir Thomas Wyatt's poem "My Galley" is a translation of a sonnet by Petrarch.

3.023 _____ The "murdering boy" in Sonnet 20 of Sidney's sonnet sequence *Astrophil and Stella* is Cupid.

3.024 _____ In *Defense of Posey*, Sidney asserts that the purpose of writing fiction and poetry is to teach and delight.

3.025 _____ In *The Faerie Queene*, the Red Cross Knight represents the unbeliever.

3.026 _____ The lovely lady is representative of truth and true religion.

3.027 _____ The lovely lady instructs the knight to add faith to his force so that he might be able to escape the power of Error.

3.028 _____ In Sir Walter Raleigh's response to Marlowe, the shepherd bids his beloved to be his love based on the pleasures of nature.

3.029 _____ In the fourth stanza of "The Nymph's Answer to the Shepherd," the poet says that the flowers and tokens of romance are soon forgotten.

3.030 _____ According to the last stanza of "The Nymph's Answer to the Shepherd," the speaker has not been moved by the beauties of nature to be the shepherd's love.

3.031 _____ In his *History of the World*, Raleigh comments that man has divine understanding so that he may serve himself.

3.032 _____ Raleigh stated in his *History of the World* that the animals have the intellect of angels and the sensual nature of man.

3.033 _____ According to Raleigh, because man was created from the dust of the earth, he is considered a macrocosm, or large world.

3.034 _____ *The Taming of the Shrew* is a tragedy that is a play within a play.

3.035 _____ In *The Taming of the Shrew*, Christopher Sly is dressed up in his lord's clothes and told that he has been insane for many years.

3.036 _____ Baptista will not allow Katherine to be courted until Bianca is married.

3.037 _____ Petruccio insists on renaming Katherine and calls her "Kate."

3.038 _____ Katherine and Petruccio fight over the meanings of various words.

3.039 _____ Petruccio arrives at the wedding late, dressed in strange clothing, and behaves wildly during and after the wedding.

3.040 _____ Angered with Petruccio, Kate throws the meat that is served and strikes a servant for spilling some water.

3.041 _____ Petruccio says that taming Kate is like training a falcon.

3.042 _____ Kate refuses to continue on the trip to her father's until Petruccio agrees that the sun is the moon or that the moon is the sun, simply because she said it is so.

3.043 _____ After Lucentio returns from the church with Bianca, Vincentio insists that they get a divorce.

3.044 _____ At the end of the play, Kate tells the other women that a husband is the "head" of the wife and the "one that cares for" her.

Fill in each of the blanks using items from the following word list (each answer, 2 points).

learning	Scripture	conceit
roses	humbled	historical
divine	rare	archaic
England	*Utopia*	leper
Geneva	plagued	ever-fixed
music		

3.045 John Foxe wrote *Acts and Monuments* as a _____ testament to the fact that evangelicalism has been persecuted throughout the centuries because it embodies the true biblical faith.

3.046 Sir Thomas More's masterpiece, _____, is a fantastical vision of a New World free of societal ills.

3.047 Roger Ascham believed that the study of certain Latin and Greek classics in subjection to the authority of _____ was a means to "truth in religion, honesty of living, and right order in _____."

3.048 Sir Thomas Wyatt introduced the Italian sonnet into _____.

3.049 A _____ is an elaborate comparison made by the poet within the sonnet.

3.050 *The Faerie Queene* is an epic that uses _____ language and medieval symbols of _____.

3.051 The Countess was known the "_____ poet."

3.052 According to line 5 of Shakespeare's Sonnet 116, true love is an "_____ mark."

3.053 According to line 6 of Shakespeare's Sonnet 130, the poet's mistress does not have _____ in her cheeks.

3.054 The speaker states in Shakespeare's Sonnet 130 that _____ is far more pleasing than the sound of his mistress's voice.

3.055 Despite her "imperfections," the poet thinks that his mistress is "_____."

3.056 The Geneva Bible states that "we did judge him as _____, and smitten of God, and _____."

3.057 The Rheims-Douay Bible replaces the term *plagued,* as in the Great Bible and the Geneva, with the phrase "as it were a _____."

3.058 In the selected readings from Isaiah, the last sentence of the King James text matches the last two sentences of the _____ Bible.

For Thought and Discussion:

Explain to a Parent/Teacher William Shakespeare's play *The Taming of the Shrew*. Be sure to describe the relationship between Petruccio and Katherine. In light of Ephesians 5:22-33, discuss who Petruccio and Katherine resemble. In what ways does Petruccio "sanctify and cleanse" Katherine?

82 / 103

Score _____

Adult Check _____
            Initial   Date

Before taking the LIFEPAC Test, you might want to do one or more of the following self checks.

1. _____ Read the objectives. Check to see if you can do them.
2. _____ Restudy the material related to any objectives that you cannot do.
3. _____ Use the **SQ3R** study procedure to review the material.
4. _____ Review activities, Self Tests, and LIFEPAC vocabulary words.
5. _____ Restudy areas of weakness that were indicated by the last Self Test.